William Markby

Elements of Law

Considered with reference to Principles of general jurisprudence

William Markby

Elements of Law
Considered with reference to Principles of general jurisprudence

ISBN/EAN: 9783337312718

Printed in Europe, USA, Canada, Australia, Japan

Cover: Foto ©Suzi / pixelio.de

More available books at **www.hansebooks.com**

Clarendon Press Series.

ELEMENTS OF LAW.

MARKBY.

London

MACMILLAN AND CO.

PUBLISHERS TO THE UNIVERSITY OF

Oxford.

Clarendon Press Series

ELEMENTS OF LAW

CONSIDERED WITH REFERENCE TO

PRINCIPLES OF GENERAL JURISPRUDENCE

BY

WILLIAM MARKBY, M.A.

JUDGE OF THE HIGH COURT OF JUDICATURE AT CALCUTTA

Oxford

AT THE CLARENDON PRESS

1871

PREFACE.

I have explained, in a place where it is likely to receive more attention than in a preface, the object of this book, and the use which I intend to be made of it. I have now only to add a word or two as to its form, and its arrangement.

Its form is that of Lectures : and in fact a good deal of what the book at present contains formed part of a series of Lectures delivered to a small class of Hindoo and Mahommedan law students in Calcutta, in the year 1870. It would have cost me no additional trouble to divest the book of that form, but I have preserved it, for this reason :—it enables me to speak in the first person, and thus to show more clearly than I could otherwise do, how far I have depended on the labours of others, and how far I must take the whole responsibility of what I have said upon myself.

The arrangement is obviously defective ; and this, in a work which professes to be a contribution (however small) to the scientific study of law, is a serious admission. But I do not think it possible to enter here into an explanation of the cause of this defect. I have indicated it very partially, in one particular, in a note at the commencement of Chapter V. What I maintain is, that when a work is written on English Law, which is complete in point of arrangement, the long series of labours which are now just commencing will have been brought very nearly to a conclusion.

London. *October*, 1871.

CONTENTS.

INTRODUCTION.

In order that this work may accomplish, to any extent, its very limited object, it is absolutely necessary that it should be understood from what point of view of the study of law it is written, and what is the particular use which it is intended to serve.

For this purpose it is necessary to bear in mind that, until very lately, the only study of law known in England was that preparation for the actual practice of the profession which was procured by attendance in the chambers of a barrister or pleader. The Universities had almost entirely ceased to teach law ; and there was nowhere in England any faculty, or body of learned persons, who made it their business to give instruction in law after a systematic method. Nor were there any persons desirous of learning law after that fashion. Forensic skill, skill in the art of drawing up legal documents, and skilfulness in the advice given to clients, were all that was taught, or learnt, by a process of imitation very similar to that in which an apprentice learns a handicraft, or a schoolboy learns a game.

This method of training produced its natural results. The last rays of learning seemed to be dying away from English Law with the old race of conveyancers and pleaders; the only lawyers of eminence who were undisturbed by the bustling activity of the courts. The Chancery lawyers as a rule have retained a higher standard of culture than those of the Common Law Bar ; and at both Bars there always were, and still are, to be found many men of eminent attainments in all departments of knowledge. But the law itself is, at present, little influenced by these attainments, and no one would venture to assert that they lie in the direct path of a successful professional career.

This is not the place to consider the effect of this
decay of legal learning, and exclusively 'professional'
training, either upon the profession itself, or upon the
law, or upon the judges who administer the law. Nor
is it the place to consider the causes which have led men
to seek for a higher standard of legal knowledge, and thus
to a revival of the demand for a systematic education
in law, apart from professional training.

All I have now to take notice of is that, as a natural
consequence of this demand, the Universities of Oxford, of
Cambridge, and of London are taking active steps to re-
constitute the study of law as part of their course.

But it is only with the earliest, and, what I may call,
the preliminary portion of a lawyer's education that a
University has to deal. Towards imparting *directly*
that professional skill of which I have spoken above,
no University or Faculty of Law can do anything
whatever. That must be done elsewhere and at a
later stage. I am indeed one of those who are persuaded
that the skill in question will be at least more easily
acquired, if not carried even to a higher point than it
has at present reached, after such a preparation and
grounding as a University is able to give. But the only
preparation and grounding which a University is either
able, or, I suppose, would be desirous to give, is in law
considered as a science ; or at least, if that is not yet
possible, in law considered as a collection of principles
capable of being systematically arranged, and resting,
not on bare authority, but on sound logical deduction ;
all departures from which, in the existing system, must
be marked and explained. In other words, law must be
studied in a University, not merely as it has resulted from
the exigencies of society, but in its general relations to the
several parts of the same system, and to other systems.

But it is not sufficient simply to take a resolution to

teach law in this way. Experience shows that to establish
a study on this footing we must have books and teachers
specially suited for the purpose. At present, of the first
we have scarcely any. I do not wish to say a word in
disparagement of the books which are now usually read
by students; I only wish to observe, that with two or
three notable exceptions, which cover, however, but little
ground, they belong to that period of the study of English
Law which is now passing away, and that they are only
suited to assist in the acquisition of professional skill;
this being the object which master and student have
hitherto kept steadily and exclusively in view.

The first two or three generations of those who take to
the study of law after the new fashion will undoubtedly
find this a considerable difficulty in their way. It must
be many years before the scattered rules of English Law
are gathered up and discussed in a systematic and orderly
treatise; and for some time to come students of law will
find themselves obliged to work a good deal with the old
tools. Nor does it follow, because these tools are not
quite perfect, that they are to be discarded as useless.
The actual state of the English Law on a variety of subjects is laid down with clearness, brevity, and precision
in several elementary works; and though it is very easy to
exaggerate the use of acquiring a knowledge of the existing rules of law; though this knowledge, standing alone, is
only part of the skill of which I have spoken above, and
will always be far better acquired in a barrister's chambers
than in the lecture room of a professor; though this
knowledge is emphatically *not* that which it is the chief
object of the preliminary training which I have now under
consideration,—yet the existing law is (if I may use the
expression) the raw material upon which the student has
to begin to work. Being told that the law contains such
and such a rule, it will be his business to examine it, to

ascertain whence it sprung, its exact import, and the measure of its application. Having done so, he must assign to it its proper place in the system; and must mark out its relations with the other parts of the system to which it belongs. This will require a comparison with analogous institutions in other countries, in order to see how far it is a deduction from those principles of law which are generally deemed universal, and how far it is peculiar to ourselves. For this purpose some acquaintance with the Roman Law will be at least desirable, if not absolutely necessary; because the principles of that law, and its technical expressions, have largely influenced our own law, as well as that of every other country in Europe[1].

It is for students of law who occupy the position indicated in the above observations that this book is intended, and I repeat that it is absolutely necessary that those who use it should bear this in mind. I have presumed that they are in the course of making acquaintance with the more elementary rules of English Law; that they are desirous to understand those rules, and to know something of their origin and relation; not merely to use them as weapons of attack or defence. This difficult, but by no means uninviting inquiry is the one in which I have made some attempt to assist them.

[1] This is the great difficulty of Indian law students. They can hardly be expected to make themselves generally acquainted with the Roman Law. But I do not think that it is at all impossible for them, even with a very slight knowledge of Latin, to obtain a useful insight into some of its leading principles. Being most desirous to render some assistance to this class of students. I have simplified, as much as possible, the references to the Roman Law.

ELEMENTS OF LAW.

CHAPTER I.

GENERAL CONCEPTION OF LAW.

1. LAW is a term which is used in a variety of different meanings, but widely as these differ, there runs throughout them all the common idea of a regular succession of events, governed by a rule, which originates in some power, condition, or agency, upon which the succession depends. *General conception of Law.*

2. The conception of that law which we are about to consider—the law of the lawyer—is contained within and forms part of the conception of a Political Society. Fully to develope the ideas comprehended under the term political society would require a very long discussion. Nor is this full developement necessary for our present purpose. *Part of the conception of a political society.*

3. For this purpose it is sufficient to observe some of its most striking features; and one that mainly distinguishes a political society from other associations of men is, that in a political society one member, or a certain definite body of members, possesses the absolute power of issuing commands to the rest, to which commands the rest are generally obedient. *Characteristic of a political society.*

4. It is desirable to observe that this, though a characteristic of a political society, does not belong to

it exclusively, so as to serve as a definition of it. Though
not, however, a distinguishing characteristic of a political society, it is a marked and conspicuous one ; just
as the habit of walking erect is a marked and conspicuous characteristic of the human race. But, in the
same way as animals other than man have been known
to walk erect, so societies other than political ones are
known, of which the members are in the habit of obedience to a ruler, who is acknowledged to have the
right to issue and to enforce his commands. The association called a 'family' has existed in many countries,
and possibly still does exist in some, in such a form
that, just as in a political society, the members of it
are in the habit of complete obedience to its head, who
has the absolute right to enforce, and actually does
enforce, that obedience.

What
commands
issued in a
political
society are
laws pro-
perly so
called.

5.　It is the body of commands issued by the rulers
of a political society to its members, which lawyers
call by the name 'Law.' It is only necessary to modify
this conception of the term, as used by lawyers, by ex-
cepting two small and very insignificant classes of the
commands so issued. Very rarely notifications in the
form of commands are issued by the rulers of a political
society, which are nevertheless not enforced : as, for
instance, rules of rank and precedence in society, orders
to wear mourning when a great person dies, and so
forth. These are no part of law in our sense of the
term. So also the rulers of a political society sometimes, but very rarely, address a command to a particular individual or individuals by name. Such occa-
sional and specific commands are not properly comprised
under the term law, which, as we have said, involves
the idea of a general rule, applicable to all cases which
come under a common class.

Most of the orders issued by the Sovereign through the ordinary legal tribunals are not strictly laws, being commands addressed to individuals by name. But though these commands are not laws, the tribunals which issue them are called legal tribunals, the action of such tribunals is comprised under the general term law, and persons engaged in the business there transacted are called lawyers. And these terms are correct. For though the commands ultimately issued by these tribunals are addressed to individuals by name, they are not original commands, but the pre-arranged consequences of other commands, which are general, and which are therefore law.

6. A special order of forfeiture of property, as a punishment for open rebellion, is an instance of a command which is not a law, though issued by the rulers of a political society : so is such an Act of Parliament as the 29 Vict. c. 20, for indemnifying Mr. Forsyth against certain penalties ; or such an Act of the Legislative Council of India as Act xiv. of 1860, which relates to the titular King of Oudh.

7. We thus arrive at a conception of the term law, which may be summed up as follows. That it is the general body of rules, which are addressed by the rulers of a political society to the members of that society, and which are generally obeyed. *Summary of conception of law.*

8. The aggregate of powers which is possessed by the rulers of a political society is called Sovereignty. The single ruler, where there is one, is called the Sovereign ; the body of rulers, where there are several, is called the Sovereign Body, or the Government, or the Supreme Government. The rest of the members of a political society, in contradistinction to the rulers of it, are called Subjects. *Sovereignty.*

9. The Queen of England is sometimes called the Sovereign, but this is only out of courtesy. The ruling power of Great Britain and her dependencies is the sovereign body, consisting of the Queen and the Houses of Parliament. This use of the word 'Sovereign' as a title of honour, not expressing exactly any political condition, is now very common in Europe.

Popular ideas of conflict between different kinds of law.

10. That this is the true conception of law is now pretty well established; though it is only very recently, and after much discussion, that all the obscurity in which the conception was involved has been swept away. The subject has been exhausted by the late Mr. John Austin in his Lectures on the 'Province of Jurisprudence;' and what I have stated above are his conclusions[1]. These conclusions have been since generally accepted by English jurists, and many of them rest upon arguments drawn from Austin's celebrated predecessors, Hobbes and Jeremy Bentham. They in no way depend on the theory of utility, discussed and advocated by Austin, in his second, third and fourth Lectures; as the interposition of that discussion in an inquiry to which, strictly speaking, it does not belong, has led many persons erroneously to suppose.

11. But persons who do not either doubt or deny Austin's conclusions, very often lose sight of them. For, unfortunately, common language is not yet so framed as to mark out clearly the distinctions which he has insisted upon. So that we find in almost every page of history angry disputes, which have arisen out of the supposed conflicting authority of the laws set by human sovereigns, the laws set by God, the laws of morality, and the laws of nature. Every modern political controversy contains some appeal from the law as it exists, to what are called the

[1] See the first, fifth and sixth Lectures.

inherent rights and liberties of man ; that is, rights
and liberties derived from a higher authority than the
Sovereign.

12. Such a conflict of laws proceeding from different No such
authorities, if it existed, would undoubtedly contradict possible.
those ideas of a political society and absolute sovereignty
from which we have derived our definition of law; and
perceiving this contradiction, various writers have attempted to qualify their definition of law, so as to include
in it, not only the law set by the sovereign body to its
subjects, but some one or more of the other laws just now
mentioned. And as the subject has been generally discussed on religious and political grounds, we find placed
above the laws which proceed from the Sovereign, sometimes the laws of God, sometimes the laws of nature, sometimes the dictates of morality, just as such an appeal best
suits the particular ideas which it is desired to inculcate.

13. It was the object of Austin in his lectures on the Relation
between
'Province of Jurisprudence' to shew, that, to whatever sub- Law and
Ethics.
jects other than the commands of the sovereign authority
we may apply the term law, they are not that law with
which the lawyer has to deal. The lawyer, as such, has
only to deal with the express or tacit commands of the
sovereign authority; which law, because it is imposed by
a definite authority upon definite persons, Austin calls
Positive Law, and he shews very clearly the distinction
between positive law and the divine law, or moral law,
or law of nature, or whatever term may be used to
express the ideas of what ought to be, as distinguished
from what is.

14. Both the legislator and the lawyer will no doubt
constantly find themselves engaged in ethical discussions,
but this Austin shews not to arise from any confusion
between the boundaries of Law and Ethics. The functions

of the *legislator* are in reality not legal but moral. With him the primary inquiry is, what ought to be, and he only inquires what is, in order to suit his provisions to the law already in force, and to make himself intelligible. With the *lawyer*, on the other hand, what is, is always the primary inquiry, and there his inquiry stops, unless the case be one, in which the commands of the sovereign authority are indefinite or obscure; in which case, in a manner which will be hereafter more fully explained, the lawyer resorts to a consideration of what ought to be, as a standard to which he assumes that the sovereign authority would always seek to conform.

15. It appears then that this is really a question of terms. When I speak of law, I mean that law, which is set by a sovereign authority to a political society; by a political society I mean a nation, which is in the habit of obedience to that sovereign authority. If the nation refuse obedience, or obey some other authority than this, it either ceases to be a political society, or the sovereign authority is changed.

No political or religious theory involved in our conception of law.

16. No theory of religion, or of morals, or of politics, is involved in these views of law. They are alike true for Hindoos, Mahommedans, and Christians; for the subject of a monarchy and the citizen of a republic. They merely mark out the field of labour for the lawyer; they leave clear the field of politics and religion for the statesman and the priest. It is only when one or the other seeks to outstep the proper boundaries of his office, that he will find himself in conflict with these principles.

Sovereignty not capable of limitation by law.

17. It is of course little more than a truism, to assert from this point of view, that, as Bentham[1] and Austin[2]

[1] Fragment on Government, s. 26; vol. i. p. 288 of Bowring's edition.

[2] Lect. vi. pp. 271 and 285 (third ed.).

have shewn, and Blackstone[1] has been forced to admit, the sovereign authority is supreme, and, from a purely legal point of view, absolute. No doubt we commonly speak of some governments as free, and of others as despotic; and it would be idle to deny that those terms have important meanings; but they do not mean that the powers vested in the one are, in the aggregate, less than the powers vested in the other. As Bentham has pointed out, the distinction between a government which is despotic, and one which is free, turns upon circumstances of an entirely different kind: 'on the manner in which the whole mass of power, which taken together is supreme, is in a free state distributed among the several ranks of persons that are sharers in it; on the source from whence their titles to it are successively derived; on the frequent and easy changes of condition between governors and governed; whereby the interests of one class are more or less indistinguishably blended with those of the other; on the responsibility of the governors; on the right which the subject has of having the reasons publicly assigned and canvassed of every act of power that is exerted over him.' But to speak of the authority of the supreme body being limited, or of their acts as being illegal, is, in Bentham's opinion, a simple abuse of terms.

18. There is only one limitation of supreme authority which Bentham thinks possible, namely, 'by express convention.' I am inclined to doubt, whether the real effect of such a convention would be anything more than a redistribution of power. Bentham has elsewhere[2] shewn the fallacy of irrevocable laws, and there must be, therefore, some body which has the power to revoke, or, in exceptional cases, to set aside even the most fundamental

Limitation by express convention.

---

[1] See infra, sect. 34, note.   [2] Vol. ii. p. 401.

principles; and in that body the supreme authority will reside. For instance, it was no doubt intended to limit the authority of the President and Congress of the United States, by the fifth article[1] of the Constitution. But it is Austin's opinion, that the effect of that article is to place the ultimate sovereignty in the States' governments, taken as forming one aggregate body, and to render the general government, consisting of the President and Congress, as well as the States' governments, taken severally, subordinate thereto[2].

19. There would still be this peculiarity in the United States' Constitution, that the ultimate sovereign power was generally dormant, and was only called into active existence on rare and special occasions. I do not say that this is inconsistent with supreme sovereignty, or with our conception of a political society; but it is a peculiarity. And the exact nature of the American Constitution may possibly, in relation to certain questions of international law, become a topic of further discussion.

20. It is this peculiarity in the American Constitution,

---

[1] This article provides that Congress, whenever two-thirds of both Houses shall deem it necessary, shall propose amendments to the Constitution, or, on the application of the legislatures of two-thirds of the several states, shall call a convention for proposing amendments, which, in either case, shall be valid to all intents and purposes, as part of the Constitution, when ratified by the legislatures of three-fourths of the several states, or by conventions in three-fourths thereof, as the one or the other mode of ratification may be proposed by Congress. See also Art X. of Amendments to the Constitution.

[2] Lect. vi. p. 268 (third ed.). So too Mr. Mountague Bernard says: 'Behind both general and local authorities there is a power, intricate in respect of its machinery, and extremely difficult to set in motion, requiring the concurrence of three-fourths of the States acting by their legislatures or in conventions, which can amend the Constitution itself. This power is unlimited, or very nearly so.'—Neutrality of Great Britain during the American War, p. 43.

which gives the Supreme Court of the United States its apparently anomalous character. Of course, whatever may be the effect of the Articles of the Constitution upon the question, whether the sovereign powers of the President and Congress are delegated or supreme, those provisions would fall far short of the object they were intended to secure, if there were not some ready means of declaring when they had been violated, and that all acts in violation of them were void. This function has accordingly been exercised by the Supreme Court; and if Austin is right in considering the President and Congress as *not* supreme, this is only an ordinary function of a Court of Law. The acts of every authority, *short* of the supreme, are everywhere submitted to the test of judicial opinion as to their validity. It may, therefore, be perhaps doubted whether De Tocqueville is correct in calling this function of American judges an 'immense political power[1].' It is, if Austin is correct in his view of the American Constitution, not a political power at all, but precisely the same power as any court is called upon to exercise, when judging of the acts of a subordinate legislature. The High Courts in India, for instance, exercise a similar power, when judging of the acts of the Governor-General in Council. And it might be claimed as one of the advantages of Austin's view of the American Constitution, that it makes the position of the Supreme Court capable of a clear definition; and thus renders the transition from a strict judicial inquiry to considerations of a political character, when the validity of acts of the Government is called in question, though still far from improbable, at least less easy.

21. Moreover, if the power of the Supreme Court is correctly described as a political power at all, I doubt whether it has not been exaggerated. Should the Supreme

[1] Democracy in America, chap. vi.

Court and the President and Congress ever really measure their strength, it must be remembered that by the Constitution [1] the President nominates, and with the advice and consent of the Senate appoints the Judges of the Supreme Court, to hold their office during good behaviour [2]. This would probably be taken to mean, that they could be removed after conviction, upon impeachment for misconduct. They are thus appointed by, and are responsible to, the very persons to whom they would by the hypothesis be opposed; and who by the hypothesis are tyrannical [3]. Now it is not at all impossible that, so long as the Supreme Court preserves its high character for integrity and independence, it may serve many very useful purposes; but it seems to me to go too far to say, as De Tocqueville says, that ' the power vested in the American courts of justice of pronouncing a statute to be unconstitutional, forms one of the most powerful barriers which has been ever devised against the tyranny of political assemblies.' I think Bentham, in the passage I have just now quoted, has much more correctly stated the true securities against tyranny, whether of individuals or of political assemblies, so far as it is possible for this protection to be constitutionally secured. These securities Americans enjoy to the fullest extent, coupled with certain national sentiments of perhaps even greater importance.

Practical limitations on the absolute nature of sovereignty.

22. It is also necessary to observe, that what I have said as to the supremacy of the sovereign authority, which is the purely legal view of the relation between subjects

[1] Art. II. sect. 2. cl. 2.   [2] Art. III. sect. 1.

[3] I assume this, and also that the President, the Senate, and the House of Representatives are acting unanimously in their opposition to the Supreme Court. As a check on each other these separate bodies can act to any extent. And it is upon their tyrannical action that an *external* check of some kind is required.

and their rulers, does not in any way represent this relation in many of its most important aspects. Though for
legal purposes all sovereign authority is supreme, as a
matter of fact the most absolute government is not so
powerful as to be unrestrained. Though not restrained
by law, the supreme rulers of every country avow their
intention to govern, not for their own benefit, or for the
benefit of any particular class, but for the benefit of the
members of the society generally; and they cannot altogether neglect the duty which they have assumed. In
our own country we possess nearly all the institutions,
which have been above referred to as the characteristics
of a free government. A regular machinery exists for
introducing into the ruling body persons taken from all
classes of the community, and for changing them, if the
measures of those in power become distasteful. Liberty
of the press is everywhere conceded. The humblest
subjects, though they may have no defined power, have a
right to meet, and to state their grievances, provided they
do not disturb the public peace. And the Government
hardly ever refuses to listen to such remonstrances, though,
through ignorance and selfishness, they not unfrequently
turn out to be unfounded, or to represent but very feebly,
if at all, the real interests of the community at large.

23. We must also distinguish the independence of
the sovereign body itself, from the independence of the
members who happen to compose that body. The Queen,
the Members of the British Parliament, the Viceroys of
India and of Ireland, the President of the United States
of America, are all subject to the same general laws as
ourselves: only for reasons of convenience the process
against them in case of disobedience is somewhat different.

Persons exercising sovereign power are generally subject to law.

24. I have dwelt upon these practical qualifications of
the doctrine of the supremacy of the sovereign authority,

Importance of under- standing

distinction
between
law and
politics.

because it has been thought to arm the actual rulers of a
country with unlimited powers; to destroy the distinction
between free and despotic governments; and to absolve
the holders of power from all responsibility. It does
nothing of the kind. Even where no attempt has been
made, as in America, to bind the exercise of authority by
a special set of rules, or to submit it, as in France under
the Republic and the Second Empire, to the popular will[1],
powerful checks exist upon the exercise of arbitrary
authority, which are none the less effectual because they
do not belong to the province of law.

Delegation of
sovereignty.

25. Having then established that the sovereign body,
as such, is independent of law, and that the sovereign
body lays down, as positive law, the rules which are
to regulate the conduct of the political society which
it governs, the inquiry into the relation of rulers and
their subjects would, for legal purposes, seem to be complete. It would be a simple relation of governors and
governed.

26. But, in fact, this simple state of things is nowhere known to exist. Not only does the sovereign
body find it necessary to employ others to execute its
commands, by enforcing obedience whenever particular
individuals evince a disinclination to obey the law;
but in almost every country authority is delegated by
the sovereign body, to some person or body of persons
subordinate to itself, who are thereby empowered, not

[1] The Constitution of the Fourteenth of January 1851, does not,
like that of the Fourth of November 1848, contain the empty
declaration 'that the sovereignty resides in the whole mass of
French citizens taken together' (Art. I), but it attempts to give
effect to a similar notion by declaring the right of the Emperor
(then called President) to appeal to the people at large (Art. V): at
best a misty phrase, and open to every possible abuse.

merely to carry out the sovereign commands in particular cases, but to exercise the sovereign power itself, in a far more general manner; sometimes extending even to the making of rules, which are law in the strictest sense of the term.

27. When the sovereign body thus substitutes for its own will the will of another person, or body of persons, it is said to delegate its sovereignty[1].

28. There is scarcely any authority even to execute a specific command, which is conferred by the sovereign body in terms so precise, as not to leave something to the discretion of the person on whom it is conferred. On the other hand, there is scarcely any delegation of sovereignty which is so general and extensive, as to leave the exercise of it, at any time, completely uncontrolled. And it would be easy to construct out of the powers usually delegated to others by the sovereign body, a continuous series, advancing by insensible degrees, from the most precise order, where the discretion is scarcely perceptible, up to a viceregal authority, which is very nearly absolute. Any attempt, therefore, to divide these powers accurately into groups, by a division founded on the extent of the authority conferred, must necessarily fail.

Gradation of powers delegated by Sovereign.

29. It is, however, common to mark off and classify some of the more extensive and general of the delegated powers by describing them as 'sovereign' or 'legislative;' or (in order to distinguish these delegated powers from the powers of the supreme sovereign body itself) as 'subordinate sovereign' and 'subordinate legislative;' whilst the powers which are specific are described as 'judicial' or 'executive.' The term 'administrative,' so far as it has any definite meaning at all, seems to be used to describe powers, which lie somewhere between

[1] Austin, Lecture vi. vol. i. p. 250 (third edition).

the powers which are more general, and those which are more specific.

30. No harm results from the use of these terms, which are sometimes convenient, if it be borne in mind that they do not mark any precise distinction. They are just as useful as the terms 'great' and 'small,' 'long' and 'short,' but are not more precise.

Different modes of delegating sovereignty.

31. To confer the power of making laws is the most conspicuous mode of delegating sovereign authority, and it has been sometimes spoken of as if it were the only mode. But it is not so. The Viceroy of India, when he declares war, or makes a treaty, exercises the sovereign authority as directly and completely as when, in conjunction with his Council, he passes an Act. So the Lieutenant-Governor of Bengal, when he grants a pardon, exercises a peculiar prerogative of sovereignty. So every Judge, from a Justice of the Peace in England up to the Lord Chancellor, from a Moonsiff in India up to the Judges of a High Court, exercises a power which in its origin, and still theoretically, belongs exclusively to the Sovereign, and which was at one time considered the most conspicuous attribute of sovereign authority[1].

Origin of political societies.

32. It would be by no means out of place, by way of illustrating our conception of law and of a political society, if we were at this point to inquire, how it was that people first came to be governed by a sovereign authority; how it was that one man came to make laws for another; why this, which was the practice of the earlier associations of men, is still the characteristic of every political society; in short, to inquire into the origin and foundation of government. It is indeed the practice of most

---

[1] Vide infra, sect. 53.

writers on law to commence their works with some
statements on this head.

33. We find, however, that so far from there being Conflicting notions as to it.
any clear and precise views on this subject which a
student can be asked to accept, the views of one author
flatly contradict those of another; so that, if I were now
to attempt anything in this direction, it would be necessary to defend every assertion by long and wearisome
arguments.

34. Of course one must submit to this, if the inquiry Not neces- sary to dis- cuss it.
is a necessary part of the subject. But contrary to what
is generally supposed, a very slight consideration will
shew that it is not so. Authors whose views are in many
respects diametrically opposite, and who hardly agree
upon a single other point, Blackstone and Bentham, for
instance, still arrive at this result, that the sovereign
authority is supreme[1]. That is really all that the lawyer
requires for his conception of law; the rest he can work
out for himself.

35. We are at liberty therefore to pass over this topic,
and I shall do so, merely indicating how the controversy
stands. And I cannot do this better than by contrasting
the views of the two great leaders of English opinion on
this subject.

36. Blackstone[2], speaking perhaps of the present

---

[1] Blackstone says (Commentaries, vol. i. p. 48) of governments
that, 'however they began, or by what right soever they subsist,
there is and must be in all of them a supreme, irresistible, absolute,
uncontrolled authority, in which the *jura summi imperii*, or the
rights of sovereignty, reside.' Bentham's opinion I have already
quoted; supra, sect. 17.

[2] Commentaries, vol. i. p. 47. Blackstone here adopts the
views of Hobbes, but he uses language far less precise than the
original. See sect. 3 of the 'Elementa Philosophiæ,' in vol. ii. of
Molesworth's edition of the collected Latin Works. This derivation

Opposite views of Blackstone and Bentham.
foundation rather than of the origin of government, says that their foundations are laid in the wants and fears of individuals; that the necessity of protection is what keeps men in subjection, and that an agreement for protection on the one hand, and obedience on the other, is always understood and implied in every state.

37. Bentham, in the pamphlet called ' A Fragment on Government[1],' contests most strongly this notion of an implied contract between governors and governed, and no one can for a moment doubt that he has done so successfully. For his own part he would base government on its claim to secure the greatest happiness of all those whose interest is in question ; and probably many who would not accept all the principles of the utilitarian school will accept this as the true, as it undoubtedly is the avowed, basis of the claim to govern. As to the historical inquiry, Bentham probably never troubled himself at all about it, and Blackstone thought it was hopeless.

38. Subsequently Austin drew a clear line between such inquiries and the province of jurisprudence : but it is not a little remarkable that he should have somewhat marred the effect of his own work, by inserting in the midst of it a discussion, which, it appears to me, is by his own shewing extraneous to the matter he had in hand. By so doing he has overstepped his own boundaries, just at the point where he had been at the most pains to draw them. But be this as it may, Austin has established that the question—what is the origin and foundation of government ? is in truth not a legal question at all, and that the

of government from a fictitious agreement is the second of what Austin considers to be Hobbes' two ' capital errors.' See a note to the Sixth Lecture, where the value of Hobbes' speculations is in other respects maintained.

[1] Published in 1776 as a criticism on Blackstone.

true province of jurisprudence is to inquire what is law, and not how or why it is, or came to be so.

39. In the next place, Sir Henry Maine has shewn, in his work on 'Ancient Law,' that the historical inquiry how, as a matter of fact, political societies have grown up, is not, as Blackstone supposed, an altogether hopeless one. He has shewn that the rise and growth of law may be traced by a process, somewhat similar to that by which the geologist has traced the formation of the world, and the scholar is tracing the formation of language; and it is obvious that the inquiry into the origin of government must, henceforth, be a historical one, for it is only where history has been exhausted, that we are at liberty to speculate at all on such a subject as the origin of our existing institutions.

40. It must not be supposed, moreover, that these inquiries, though they fall, strictly speaking, outside the province of jurisprudence, are altogether foreign to the study of law: on the contrary, it is almost impossible to grasp clearly many of the conceptions with which the lawyer has to deal, without having traced their history. Many of the terms in which they are expressed are very ancient. The conceptions themselves are neither new nor old. They came long ago into existence, but have been brought under the influence of a long succession of antagonistic philosophies and conflicting creeds. By these they have been, very often at the time imperceptibly, but upon the whole greatly modified. So that, whilst the name has remained the same, the ideas comprised under it have greatly varied. And such researches as those of Sir Henry Maine, in which the connection is traced between modern legal ideas and the rudimentary institutions of early social life, have a value in assisting the

Inquiry into this subject useful to the lawyer.

student of law to grasp these ideas, quite apart from their
value to the philosopher and historian.

41. This is (to my mind) the true use of such
inquiries—to bring before us clearly the modern ideas
of jurisprudence, and to exhibit their relation to social
life. Some persons would also fain see in the early institutions which historical inquiry has brought to light, a
pattern for modern social reforms, and would apparently
claim for these, because they are ancient, just the same
sort of superiority that has been frequently claimed, on
no better grounds, for a supposed state of nature. It is
with no such views that I have directed attention to these
historical inquiries [1].

---

[1] Probably Mr. John Stuart Mill, in the use he makes of Sir
Henry Maine's historical inquiries as to the earlier notions of ownership of land, does not mean to do anything more, than to weaken
the sentiment of respect for existing institutions arising from their
supposed antiquity. I do not suppose he could have intended to
lend any countenance to the popular misconception, that only rights
of the highest order of antiquity can claim the benefit of prescription.
See the article on Maine's Village Communities in the Fortnightly
Review of May, 1871.

CHAPTER II.

Sources of Law.

42. There are several inquiries which have been prosecuted under this head, and some writers have thrown themselves and their readers into inextricable confusion, by pursuing more than one of these at the same time, without perceiving the distinction between them. What is meant by sources of law.

I am not now about to inquire whence it is that rules of conduct acquire the binding force of law—that I have already made to depend on the will of the sovereign authority.

Nor am I about to inquire how or why the sovereign authority came to have the power to make laws; that, as I have already shewn, is not, strictly speaking, a legal inquiry.

What I mean by the sources of law is simply the place where, if a man wants to get at the law, he must go to look for it[1].

43. The primary and most direct source, and, where it is to be found, the exclusive source of law, is the ex- The primary source is declared will of the supreme

[1] Even with these limitations there is still room for much indefiniteness in the term 'sources of law.' We generally mean by it, as will appear from the text (sect. 63), something more than mere *literature;* I do not pretend, however, that it would be possible to draw an exact distinction between *literatura* and *auctoritas.* Lawyers frequently fortify their conclusions by references to opinions which are not, in a forensic sense, *authoritative.*

pressly declared will of the sovereign authority. When
the sovereign authority declares its will in the form of
a law, it is said to legislate; and this function of sovereignty is called Legislation : the body which deliberates
on the form and substance of such laws before they are
promulgated is called the Legislature; and the laws so
made are called Acts of the Legislature.

**or sub-
ordinate
legislature.** 43 *a*. It has already been remarked that legislation,
like any other function of sovereignty, may be delegated
to a subordinate person or body of persons. In this
case the subordinate legislature is the mouthpiece of the
sovereign authority, and the declarations of the subordinate legislature derive their binding force from the
will of the sovereign authority, just as much as if they had
been framed and issued by the sovereign authority itself.

**Subordinate
legislation
in the
Colonies.** 44. All the colonies of England present examples of
this delegation of the legislative power, but nowhere have
they been multiplied to so great an extent as in India.
Thus in the province of Lower Bengal alone there are four
distinct bodies or persons, each possessing a very extensive
legislative authority. There is first the British Queen
and Parliament, the supreme authority; then the General
Legislative Council; next the Governor-General himself
with or without his Council; and lastly the Council of the
Lieutenant-Governor of Bengal. And the powers of some
Lieutenant-Governors and Commissioners, acting alone, are
in other parts of Bengal so large and ill-defined that, as
a matter of fact, they do exercise a power of issuing
ordinances, which can hardly be distinguished from an
exercise of legislative authority. This example of subordinate legislation illustrates not only the extent and
importance of the function, but also the evils which
may attend it. Where the power of legislation is so
loosely conferred on such a variety of persons, it is

certain there will be great confusion of laws, and there
is also great danger of the worst of all evils, namely, of
doubts being raised as to whether the legislative authority
of some of the subordinate bodies has not been exceeded.
For the supreme sovereign authority is always obliged to
allow the authority of its subordinates to be questioned, in
some form or other, by judicial authority, in order to keep
up a check on their usurpation of power; though sometimes it resorts to that highly unsatisfactory expedient
for getting out of the difficulty—an *ex post facto* ratification of acts which are admittedly illegal.

45. It may also be desirable here to notice that Methods of
sovereignty is delegated upon two distinct principles to delegation.
the dependencies of England. In India the Governor-
General and Legislative Council constitute together a
legislature whose functions are expressly limited in several
directions, and whose action is expressly made subject to
the control of the British Parliament, which it is obviously
contemplated will in no wise discontinue the habit of
occasionally making laws for India. On the other hand,
most of the colonies possess constitutions which confer
upon their respective legislative assemblies, together with
the Queen of England (usually represented by a Governor),
legislative authority of the most general kind, and which
obviously contemplate that all the functions of legislation
will be carried on within the colony itself. But colonies
possessing such constitutions are equally subject to the
same sovereign body, the Queen and the two Houses of
Parliament. The power of the British Parliament over
a colony, though dormant, is not extinguished by the
grant of such a constitution as I have described. There
is amply sufficient in the Acts of Parliament which grant
colonial constitutions to make the very acceptance of them
a mark of subordination. Nevertheless the form of these

constitutions is not without importance; they not only give a greater practical independence, but they are calculated to render the transition to complete independence easier to accomplish, should the colony think fit to ask, or the mother country desire to grant it [1].

Indirect delegations of legislative authority.

46. Legislative functions are also exercised, not only by bodies expressly constituted for that purpose, and under the name of legislation, but by bodies of persons who have the power to frame rules for the protection or convenience of the inhabitants of certain localities. Thus in large and populous towns we frequently find a body called by the name of a municipality, which has power to make bye-laws, as they are called, for regulating the conduct of the inhabitants, and even to impose taxes. So the Privy Council, and sometimes Boards of Revenue, and of Education, frame rules for special objects entrusted to them, which are some of them laws in the proper sense of the term. So too Courts of Law issue general rules of procedure in matters of litigation which are also law. In these cases the power thus exercised has been expressly conferred.

Subordinate legislatures cannot delegate.

47. The sovereign body can always delegate its function of legislation to any extent it pleases; it being wholly uncontrolled not only in the matter, but in the manner of legislation. In other words, the sovereign body not only exercises the legislative function, but is the author of it also.

But a subordinate legislature, not being the author of

---

[1] See the 15 and 16 Vict. chap. lxxii. (New Zealand), and the 30 and 31 Vict. chap. iii. (British North America). In all these Acts the supreme sovereignty of England is, in accordance with traditional usage, studiously referred to as if it were vested in the Queen alone. But of course no one can doubt that the Queen and the Colonial Parliament are subordinate to the Queen and the English Parliament.

its own functions, and having no control over the manner of legislation, can only delegate its functions so far as it has been authorised to do so. Such general legislative powers as are possessed by the Legislative Council in India would undoubtedly carry with them some powers of delegation; such, for instance, as are necessary to authorise a municipality to make bye-laws for the preservation of health. They have indeed been presumed to exist so far, as to warrant the Legislative Council in leaving it to individuals to say when, and where, and to what extent their acts shall come in force; and sometimes details, which one would ordinarily find in the act itself, are left to be supplied by a subordinate officer. Such a method of legislation requires very careful watching, lest the bounds of authority be exceeded.

48. When no act of the legislature, subordinate or supreme, can be found which lays down the course to be taken in any specific case which may arise, where will a man then go in order to discover the law? That, according to our definition, is the next source of law.

Second source of law—Judicial decisions.

There is no doubt at all what he would do. He would search and see what the expounders of the law have on similar occasions said about the matter. But then immediately arises the question—who are the expounders of the law?

49. This is a question which might not at all times and in all countries receive precisely the same answer; but there is no doubt about the answer in England, and in countries governed by her. The expounders of the law are primarily the judges of the Courts of Law. The books we should go to in order to find out the law would be the 'Reports,' as they are called—that is, the account of cases heard and decided up to the present time.

Binding authority of judicial decisions.

50. But it may be said, that this is after all doing no more than is done by every man of sense on an occasion of difficulty ; that it is natural on such an occasion to see what other men, whose opinions we respect, have done under similar circumstances; but that the conduct of our predecessors, although it may be useful as a guide and an example, is in no way binding upon us, and is not law.

51. This remark would be perfectly just, if the lawyer searched his reports only for the purpose which is here supposed. But any one who sits for an hour and listens to a legal argument in a Court of Law, or reads a dozen pages of any account of what there takes place, will see that this is a very inadequate conception of the use which the lawyer makes of the opinions of those who have gone before him. If it is found in the course of a legal discussion, that there is a long and uniform course of decisions on the point, or even a single decision of the highest Court of Appeal, the advocate will argue, and the judge will declare, that this is the law, with nearly as much confidence as if it was so written in an Act of the Legislature.

Origin of authority to make law by means of judicial decisions.

52. But then at once there starts up in the mind a fresh series of questions. Who made this law? The judges? If so, by what authority? And if without authority, how is it law?

True conception of the office of judge: a function of the Sovereign.

53. Now fully to answer these questions requires the consideration of a few cognate topics. In the first place let us consider what is the nature of the office of a judge. If we look at the history of all early societies we find that the principal duty of the Sovereign, in time of peace, is not the making of law, but the decision of law suits. It is the King himself who decides all disputes between his subjects; he is the judge before whom the issue is tried [1] ;

[1] See Grote's History of Greece, Part I. ch. xx.

and whilst in some of the oldest treatises on law we find
the judicial function of Kings carefully and prominently
considered, the legislative function is scarcely noticed.
This is notably the case in the treatise of Menu, where the
King is always spoken of as ' the dispenser of justice,' and
his duties as such are minutely laid down ; whereas I do
not recollect a single passage which enjoins him to make
wise and good laws. Nor does this in any way result
from the claim of Hindoos to have received a divine
revelation. We find the same thing in societies which lay
no such extensive claim, and indeed which hardly claim
at all to have received commands direct from God.

54. Even in England, where Austin thinks the judicial
function was more completely separated from the legislative than in any other country[1], we find strong indications
of the extent to which those functions were mixed in
early times. The present judicial authority of the House
of Lords is generally traced to its representation of the
Aula Regis, which was at the same time the supreme court
of justice and the supreme legislative assembly in the
kingdom. It required a special clause in Magna Carta
to enable the Court of Common Pleas to sit anywhere
except in the place where the King happened to reside.
By a fiction the Sovereign is always supposed, even at the
present day, to preside in person at every sitting of the
Court of Queen's Bench ; and it is as keeper of the King's
conscience that the Chancellor is often said to exercise his
authority.

55. The truth is, as Sir Henry Maine has shewn [2], that Idea of law
the idea of law itself is posterior in date to that of judicial that of
decision ; and it was the actual observation of a succession decision.
of similar decisions of the same kind, which gave rise to

[1] Lect. xxviii. p. 536 (third edition).
[2] Ancient Law, p. 5 (ed. 1861).

the idea of a rule or standard to which a case might be referred. As soon as this observation was made, every one would naturally recognise the advantage of stating in an abstract form the rule which might be inferred from a series of uniform decisions, and which, it might be reckoned with tolerable certainty, would be applied, whenever a similar dispute should arise. This was the first germ of law : and the first recognised laws were probably collections of the scattered rules which had thus come to be adopted.

Delegation of judicial office by Sovereign.

56. It was only in the simplest condition of society that the King could really be also judge in all matters of litigation. At a very early period this function of sovereignty would be delegated to persons whose duty it was to decide disputes and punish offences. The wise, and learned, and elderly persons, who sat with the King to assist him with their advice, would be deputed by him to decide cases in his absence. But this change in the person of the judge would not materially affect either the character of the office, or the exercise of the function. The same repetition of cases would occur : by deciding them successively in the same way, the subject judge, just like the sovereign judge, would give currency to certain rules, and these rules would come to be looked upon as law.

Judicial making of law not a usurpation.

57. The process by which law is made by judges in the exercise of their judicial function has been undoubtedly misunderstood. It has been said, that the exercise by judges of the legislative function at all, is a usurpation. If by the exercise of the legislative function be meant the evolution of law by the process above described, this statement is the very reverse of truth. A judge who merely substitutes for his own opinion the concurrent opinion of others is no breaker of the law. The only

result of saying that judges could make no law, would
be to say, in effect, in a large number of cases, that there
was no rule of law applicable to the purpose in hand,
and to leave the judge entirely uncontrolled.

58.   I do not, however, mean to represent that judges
in England and her dependencies have done no more, than
simply bow to the authority of their predecessors, rather
than hazard an opinion of their own.   Curiously enough,
whilst shrinking from any avowal of the exercise of
legislative functions, by referring everything to the
'Common Law,' and thus clothing every rule made by
th.m in language, which assumes for it an antiquity
greater than that of any Act of Parliament, judges have in
reali-y exercised the power of legislating to a very large
extent.   Whether too largely, and whether this mode of
m iking laws has on the whole been beneficial or not, are
questions which cannot be fully considered in this place.
Where the regular process of legislation has been so
inadequate as ours has been, to meet the growing wants
of society, in respect of many of those matters which daily
come under the notice of Courts of Law, some such
expedient was inevitable ; and it could hardly be expected
that judges would examine with very great nicety the
limits of an authority, the exercise of which provoked
neither jealousy nor remark.   It is not unnatural, for
example, that they should apply the same remedy to cases
where the law had become obsolete, as to cases where no
law existed.

Objections to the mode in which this function has been exercised.

59.   A very much more important question has been
raised, as to the correct appreciation of the process of
making law by judicial decision.   Austin has minutely
criticised this process, but the published Lecture which
contains these criticisms is, as is so frequently the case
with the scanty remains we have of the writings of that

Character- istics of judiciary law.

eminent jurist, made up of two independent fragments ;
and it is of course, therefore, not summed up into any final
conclusions. It appears to me that the essential difference
between the generation of law by judicial decision and by
express legislation lies in two of the characteristics of judiciary law noted by Austin,—namely, that it is *ex post facto*,
and that it is always implicated with the peculiarities of
the particular case in which it is applied. All the objections which can be raised against judiciary law may be
traced to one or both of these characteristics ; its bulk, the
difficult of ascertaining it, its inconsistency, and so forth.
To the combination of these two characteristics may be
also traced its great, though possibly its only advantage—
that of flexibility, or capacity of being adapted to any new
combination of circumstances that may arise. Were the
judges in England compelled, as in Italy, France and
Spain, and as has been attempted in India, to state
separately and fully what French lawyers call the *motives*,
and Spanish lawyers the *points* of their decisions—that is
to say, their findings in fact and the rules of law which
guide them—there would be a complete revolution in the
history of English case law. The law being stated in
distinct propositions, altogether separate from the facts,
would be easily ascertained. This, coupled with our
notions as to the authority of prior decisions, would render
a conflict so conspicuous, as to be almost impossible. The
law would soon become clear and precise enough ; but so
far as judicial decision was concerned, it would become
absolutely rigid. It is because English judges are absolved
from the necessity of stating general propositions of law,
and because, even when these are stated, they are always
read as being qualified by the circumstances under which
they are applied, that our law remains bulky and uncertain, but has also, in spite of our respect for precedent,

remained for so long a period flexible. Whether it
would be found possible to combine our practice as to
the generally unquestionable authority of prior decisions,
with the practice of laying down in every case abstract
propositions of law separate from and independent of the
particular facts, is an experiment which, as far as I am
aware, has not yet been tried. The High Court at
Calcutta has gone somewhat near it, by requiring even
its own members, when they differ in opinion on a matter
of law, to refer the difference to the arbitration of a
majority of the whole Court. This sometimes leads
to the enunciation of propositions of law ·in an abstract
form, which it is made imperative on all the members of
the Court, and of course on all the inferior Courts, to
accept, until overruled by the Privy Council[1].

60. The nature of the process of reasoning which has *Process of reasoning by which it is extracted.*
to be performed in order to extract a rule of law from a
number of decided cases by elimination of all the qualifying circumstances, is a very peculiar and difficult one.
The opinion of the judge, apart from the decision, though
not exactly disregarded, is considered as extra-judicial, and
its *authority* may be got rid of by any suggestion which
can separate it from the actual result. Unless, therefore, a proposition of law is absolutely necessary to a
decision, however emphatically it may have been stated,
it passes from· the province of *auctoritas* into that of mere
literatura. Curiously enough it is not the opinion of
the judge, but the result to the suitor which makes the
law.

61. Paley has called the process by which law is *Competition of opposite analogies.*
extracted from a series of decisions the competition of

---

[1] See Rule of High Court of Calcutta of July, 1867, in Mr.
Broughton's Civil Procedure, p. 710 (fourth edition).

opposite analogies[1]. Austin considers that this process is
not necessarily confined to the extraction of law from
judicial decisions, but that it may as well be employed
in the application of ascertained rules of law to particular
cases. But, as I have said, it is the peculiarity of English
judges that they do not think themselves bound to distinguish these two operations, and that they very frequently perform them simultaneously. They, in fact,
determine the law only *by applying it.* And I think
Paley's description of forensic disputation and judicial
decision is both forcible and accurate. ' It is,' he says,
' by the urging of the different analogies that the contention of the bar is carried on ; and it is in the comparison, adjustment and reconciliation of them with one
another, in the discerning of such distinctions, and in the
framing of such a determination as may either save the
various rules alleged in the cause, or, if that be impossible,
may give up the weaker analogy to the stronger, that the
sagacity and wisdom of the court are exercised.'

62. It is scarcely, perhaps, necessary to observe that
the function of judges, which consists in thus making
laws by successive decisions, is altogether distinct from
their function of direct subordinate legislation before
adverted to[2].

Third source
of law—
Commen-
taries.

63. Closely connected with the law which emanates
from a series of judicial decisions is the law which is
derived from the commentaries of great jurists. These

---

[1] *Moral Philosophy*, vol. ii. p. 259. Austin seems to have
thought at first that Paley was speaking only of the application and
not the extraction of law. (Lect. xxxvii. p. 653.) But he afterwards changed that opinion. (Fragments, p. 1031.) Very likely
Paley did not, any more than is usual with our judges, distinguish
the two processes.

[2] *Supra,* sect. 46.

are also expounders of the law, and their works are constantly read and referred to in courts of justice, and have
the very greatest weight.

The authority of a commentator cannot, however,
like that of a judge, be traced immediately to the
Sovereign, and, as a general rule, a commentary when it
first appears, is only used as an argument to convince, and
not as an authority which binds. But just as judges by
successive decisions give currency to a rule of law, so by
successive recognition they establish the authority of a
commentator; till at last the opinions which he has
expressed count for as much, or even more, than the
opinions of the most eminent judge. This is the case
with such commentaries as those of Lord Coke, Lord
Hale, and Littleton in England, the Dayabhaga, the
Mitacshara, the Hedaya and the Futwa Alumgiri in India.

64. Between commentaries and judicial decisions there
is a distinction of form which it is important not to overlook. Judicial decisions are, as we have seen, by their
very nature concrete ; all the judge professes to do is to
decide the case before him ; and the principle of law
which guides him has very often to be extracted with
much labour and difficulty. But the commentator not
unfrequently deals with matters entirely in the abstract.
He lays down propositions of law capable of being applied
to a whole class of cases ; he infers one principle from
another ; he foresees new combinations and provides for
new results. A commentary of this character, when once
its authority is established, is far more comprehensive than
any number of volumes of reports ; but very few treatises
of that kind on English law, and scarcely any modern
ones, have attained the necessary standard of reputation.

Difference in form between commentaries and judiciary law.

65. At each step we take in enumerating the sources

of law, the mode of derivation becomes proportionately more obscure. The function of judges in making the law is far less easy of comprehension than that of the legislator ; that of the commentator is again a degree less clear. We now come to a case in which the law at first sight seems to be made by neither Sovereign nor judges, but by the people themselves, at their own will and pleasure.

66. This kind of law is what passes under the name of custom. It would be impossible here to dispose of all the vexed topics of discussion which have arisen on this subject. But some of the obscurities which hang about it may be removed, and, at least, it may be indicated where the difficult ground lies.

67. Custom in its general sense signifies the uniformity of conduct adopted under similar circumstances on many successive similar occasions. Thus burning the dead is said to be a custom of Hindoos ; polygamy is said to be a custom of Mahommedans ; sitting on chairs is said to be a custom of Europeans ; wearing pigtails is said to be a custom of Chinese.

68. By a custom in its legal sense we mean precisely the same sort of thing, but with a narrower application. The law does not concern itself about all customs, but only about those the observance of which is enforced, or the observance of which by the parties themselves affects their legal position. Thus in some districts of England it is the custom for one man at certain times of the year to turn his cattle to graze on the lands of another. This is a custom which the law would enforce. So it would also recognise the custom of polygamy amongst Mahommedans as affecting the right of succession.

69. All that is necessary for the growth of a custom is that people should have a tradition of what their

fathers did before them, a knowledge of what their neighbours are doing around them, and a common conviction
that what is so done is right. Uniformity of action is the
certain result of such a condition of things, and such
uniformity of action, when it has settled down into a rule,
will be called a custom.

70. It has been usual to found the authority of a
custom upon what is called the *consensus utentium*—that
is, upon the mere fact of its observance by those who have
adopted it ; so as to make a rule of law which originates in
custom independent of the sovereign authority. Austin,
in his 29th and 30th Lectures, has no doubt shewn that
this is erroneous. But it does not follow from this, as it
appears to me, that customary law is to be treated
merely as a branch of judge-made law, and not as an
independent source of law. Custom is a notion older
than law itself. Long before, and even long after tribunals had a clear notion of law, decisions were given
according to the custom. This might simply be the
custom of the tribunals itself, or judge-made law ; but it
was no doubt also frequently the custom observed by
those persons with whose habits the judges were best
acquainte l, or in the district where they had jurisdiction.
The old village courts (Schöffengerichte) mentioned by
Savigny[1] no doubt based their decisions entirely upon
such customs, though the practice of drawing up records
of their opinions (Weisthümer) probably gave in time a
decided preponderance to the judicial over the popular
element[2]. I cannot speak from personal knowledge as to

Authority of custom—not a branch of judiciary law.

---

[1] System of Modern Roman Law, sect. 30.

[2] This tendency—that is, the tendency to substitute written rules
of law for the *arbitrium* of the judges—appears everywhere, even
in lay tribunals : '*de constitutionibus autem rusticorum ne penitus
memoriae decedat, necesse est ut scribatur.*' But the written law

the fact, but I believe that the village courts (punchayets) which exist to this day in Madras do precisely the same thing. Tribunals of this kind have scarcely ever any other conception of law than the established custom of their district[1].

71. Of course, amongst more advanced nations, where the tribunals are entirely under the influence of professional lawyers, the reference to custom as a source of law is much more rare, and is somewhat embarrassed by the idea of law as the express or tacit command of a sovereign authority. Yet even here, I think it is scarcely a correct conception of the influence of custom upon law, to treat it as based entirely upon judicial assent. It is a generally recognised duty of judges to be guided by custom; and it is remarkable that, whenever the legislature of this country has defined the special duties of the courts in India in reference to natives, it is to the law and *usages* of Hindoos and Mahommedans, and not to the law alone, that they are directed to conform[2]. So too by the Hindoo law itself, it is laid down as a distinct principle that even the revealed law may be modified by custom[3].

A custom does not necessarily imply an exception. 72. A custom is generally spoken of as if it were an exception to general law, and it is true that most of the rules of law which now pass under the name of custom are exceptional in character; but it would be a great mistake to suppose that this is the general character of customary law. Very many customs which have become law are in no way exceptional; and a very considerable

being found too hard, there has generally been a subsequent reaction in favour of unwritten law.

[1] Compare the account of the growth of the common law given by Sir William Erle, in his Essay on Trades Unions, p. 47.

[2] See the 21 Geo. III. ch. lxx. sect. 17.

[3] Menu, ch. viii. s. 41; see infra, sect. 78.

proportion of the universal rules of law in every country
are only customs sanctioned by law. When, however, such
universal customs become undoubted law, they usually lose
the name of custom; they are called by the ordinary term
law, and their origin is lost sight of. Thus the ordinary
rules of inheritance are called the *law* of inheritance, and
we reserve the name 'custom' for such rules of inheritance as are exceptional; such as the succession in England
of all the sons in equal shares, or the succession in India
of the eldest son alone. But most of the rules of inheritance originated in custom, the only difference being that
some, being general, are called law, whilst others, being
exceptional, are called custom. It is plain, therefore, that
the adoption of customs into the law does not necessarily
interfere with its uniformity; it only does so when a
custom is recognised which is not universal.

73. In recognising, therefore, and importing into the
law customs which are universal, judges are liberal; but
they are jealous of admitting customs which are exceptional to the ordinary law: and the jealousy naturally
increases, in proportion as the antagonism between the ordinary law and the custom becomes more distinctly marked.

74. Some persons would make the enumeration of the
sources of law stop here; indeed, I have already carried
it one step further than Austin would carry it. On the
other hand, many writers would insist, that we have yet
to consider three of the most important sources of law;
the divine law, the moral law, and the law of nature.

Whether there are any other sources of law.

75. By divine law I mean the body of rules set
by God to man through a peculiar process of communication called 'revelation[1].' Nearly all nations claim to be

Divine Law of various nations.

---

[1] Rules of conduct, not actually revealed, may also be referred to
a Divine Author, and, I believe, are sometimes called divine, but

possessed of some such revelation, but the nature of it differs considerably; and the relation which these revealed rules bear to law, in the proper sense of the term, also varies very greatly.

Christians.

76. Christian nations lay claim to nothing more than a revelation of certain doctrines of religion and certain very general rules of morality. The Author of the Christian faith, though repeatedly appealed to for that purpose, always refused to interfere in questions of a political character, or to lay down specific rules of conduct.

Greeks and Romans.

77. The Greeks and Romans had scarcely any notion of a divine revelation at all, in any sense which we should attach to the term. The divine communications which they received were rather in the shape of advice or warnings how to act on some special occasion. If it was supposed that there had been at any time persons, who spoke habitually under divine inspiration, these were not sages who directed the conduct, but poets who stirred the feelings and imagination of their hearers.

Hindoos.

78. The Hindoos, whilst they too have been largely influenced by a mythic poetry of supposed divine origin, have also a very distinct notion of a revelation of the will of God. And this extends not only to the laying down rules of moral propriety and religious observance, but to the conduct of the ordinary affairs of life. But this revelation was neither complete nor final. That it is not the first is obvious upon the most cursory inspection. And the modification of these rules, in order to meet the various necessities which may arise, is distinctly approved of by Menu, who enjoins a king 'who knows the revealed law to inquire into the particular laws or usages of districts,

---

I am at liberty to restrict the expression 'divine law' as I have done, and as it is convenient to do : comprising the unrevealed rules, as is more commonly the practice, under moral law, or law of nature.

the customs of trades, and the rules of certain families,
and to establish their particular laws[1].' And even the
possibility of antagonism between the divine precept, and
existing rules of social conduct as established by positive
law, was recognised in a very remarkable manner, in the
animated controversy which took place in India concerning
the distinctive doctrine of the Bengal school as to the
power of the father to dispose of the family property[2].

79. The Mahommedan revelation is much more recent, Mahommedans.
and though any one reading the Koran for the first time
would hardly suppose that it was so intended, it has
nevertheless been adopted by Mahommedan nations as
the basis of their social and political institutions; but the
most important of these are rather inferences from its
spirit, than exact applications of any specific rule to be
found therein. Wherever specific rules are found, and
there are a few as regards minor matters, they have been
for the most part observed with scrupulous exactness.

80. Buddhists likewise claim to have received their Buddhists.
separate divine communication, but I think it is mostly
confined to moral and religious matters.

81. No nation ever carried its notions of a divine Jews.
law so far as the Jews. For a very considerable period
they claimed to be under the direct personal government
of God Himself, who was in constant communication with
them. It appears, however, that they found this form of
political society (if such it can be called) highly inconvenient, and the traces of the struggle to obtain a different
political constitution are clearly to be found in the Bible;

---

[1] Menu, ch. viii. sect. 41; 'if,' adds a commentator, 'they be not
repugnant to the law of God.' But Menu did not think this
precaution necessary.

[2] See the Dayabhaga of Jimuta Vahana, ch. ii. sect. 28, 29,
referred to in Strange's Hindoo Law, vol. i. p. 23.

where [1] we are told that the Jews desired to have a king
'like all the nations;' and, though they are rebuked
for their ingratitude, their prayer is at last granted. But
for various reasons, which it is not necessary here to
particularize, the Jews, as a nation, never arrived at a
clear separation of divine law and the law set by human
authority.

Erroneous notions as to conflict between divine and human laws.

82. Now to deny that the commands which have been
thus given to ourselves, to Jews, to Mahommedans, to
Buddhists and to Hindoos, have been a source of law,
would, as it appears to me, be to deny that mankind has
had any religious belief at all; nor do I think there
would have been any difficulty about the matter, if Blackstone and some other English lawyers had not suggested
ideas of a most false and mischievous character. Blackstone, speaking of laws generally, and laying down what
is apparently intended as a rule for our practical guidance,
has asserted that precepts which emanate from God are
superior in obligation to any other, and that no human
laws are of any validity, if contrary to these[2]. He would
thus apparently make divine law the primary, and,
where it exists, the exclusive source of law; placing it
even above the expressly declared will of the sovereign
body itself.

83. The proposition is not the less objectionable,
because it is capable of being read in a sense in which
it is not untrue. If Blackstone meant that a conscien-
tious man, with a firm and well-grounded conviction that
there existed a conflict between a particular divine and

---

[1] 1 Samuel viii. 5.

[2] Blackstone shifts his ground so often that it is difficult to fix
him to any precise statement, but this is what I understand him to
mean at pp. 42 and 43 of his Introduction. The same statement
is broadly repeated in Fonblanque on Equity, p. 8 (fifth ed.).

a particular human precept, ought to obey the first and
not the second, he was enunciating an empty truism,
only applicable perhaps once or twice in the history of a
nation, and wholly foreign to the subject which Blackstone had then under consideration—namely, the nature
of laws in general.

84. The absurdity of Blackstone's position, if intended
as embodying a principle of general application, will be
seen at once by attempting to apply it. If a judge were
to say, 'I find so and so in an act of parliament, but in
my opinion the divine precept is otherwise, and I decide
according to the divine precept,' he would be certainly
overruled by the court of appeal, and probably declared
unfit for his office.

85. It seems to me indeed that the fundamental
error lies in treating the conflict between divine and
human laws as an ordinary one, which the lawyer must
be constantly prepared to meet. Nothing can be further
removed from the truth. In every country which
acknowledges a revelation, almost every precept of the
law, which has emanated from a divine source, has
been over and over again acknowledged by the human
sovereign authority. The Koran and the Shasters are
the law of the Mahommedans and Hindoos respectively
in India. The precepts of the Bible have been applied
to the institutions of daily life by ourselves, to as great
an extent as the difference of circumstances will admit;
and there has been a tendency rather to strain, than to
contract the application of the Jewish law to the wants
of modern society. So far from a conflict between human
and divine law being an ordinary occurrence, it is hardly
possible that such a conflict should arise. The very existence of the rule of positive law goes far to disprove the
existence of the conflicting divine precept. A sovereign

body is not very likely to promulgate laws which all, or even a large majority of its subjects would believe to be contrary to the commands of a Being of infinite power, wisdom, and goodness. It is far more probable, that any supposed antagonism is the suggestion of ignorance, or presumption. How a case of real antagonism is to be dealt with, should it arise (and, rare as it is, no one will assert it to be impossible), is a question as unfit to be considered in a treatise on law, as the somewhat similar question—when is a nation justified in rising in rebellion against its rulers?

86. It may, indeed, happen to an advocate or a judge, that his own opinion of what is enforced by a divine precept is in conflict with some rule of positive law, which he is called upon to support. But no one would pretend that the law was in any way affected by the private opinions of those whose duty it is to administer it. Thus there are some Christians who believe that, for reasons founded on divine commands, the marriage tie is indissoluble. But this would not justify a judge who thus thought in refusing to pronounce a sentence of divorce in case of adultery. A large majority of qualified men have thought that there is no such divine prohibition, and have made the law accordingly.

87. So there are to be found Mahommedans who consider that God has forbidden the taking of money for the use of money; but the judges, with the general consent of a vast majority of Mahommedans, have long been in the habit of giving interest on loans of money to Mahommedan lenders; and it would be preposterous for a single individual to set up his opinion against this overwhelming opposition.

Use made by lawyers of divine law.
88. What use the lawyer may at any time make of the divine law is clear enough. The judge, who derives

his power to pronounce upon the law from the sovereign authority, is obliged to decide, even when all his efforts to discover a rule of positive law have failed, or where there are rules which conflict, or where the interpretation of the rule is doubtful. It is a perfectly safe assumption in such cases, that the sovereign power, if it had declared its will in the form of a positive law, would have done so in conformity with the divine precept. And a judge who acts upon the divine precept in such cases, is fully within the limits of his authority. He is doing that which a sovereign judge would undoubtedly himself do under the circumstances, that is, he is deciding the case according to that which is believed to be right and just. So much of divine law has, however, been incorporated into positive law, that even in this way the lawyer has very seldom to resort to it.

89. With regard to the moral law and the law of nature, it would be impossible to say whether or no we would enumerate either or both of these amongst the sources of law, until we had assigned to those terms some more definite meaning than is commonly done. That there are rules of conduct regularly observed amongst men, and which to a considerable degree influence positive law, which are yet, neither positive law, nor the revealed commands of God, is undoubtedly true; such, for instance, as the rules which regulate the intercourse of nations, the laws of war, and constitutional practice. But there is, I think, hardly any rule which a lawyer has been, or would be, called upon to accept upon the ground that it belonged to the moral law, or the law of nature. Speaking very generally, these two expressions comprehend the same rules of conduct, but they refer them to different sources; that which the 'moral law' derives from some innate faculty of distinguishing

Moral law and law of nature.

right from wrong, the 'law of nature' refers to the disposition of man in an uncorrupted state[1]. But the moment a difference of opinion arises as to what the rules are which are to be derived from either of these sources, no further attention is paid to them. There is something almost absurd in my asking *you* to accept a thing as right, because *my* moral sense tells me it is so, or because *I* think that it can be traced to nature. Bentham[2] has said that such expressions as moral sense and law of nature are only pretences, under which powerful men have concealed from themselves and others the exercise of arbitrary power, by making a sham appeal to some external standard, when they are really consulting only their own wishes. This may be true of potentates. But though a lawyer might also choose to avail himself of these or similar expressions, he would really be driven, in every case, to support himself by an appeal to an external standard, and one of a very substantial sort, namely, the common consent of mankind. Now this is obviously only custom on a wider basis. Where the law is silent or obscure, that which mankind at large has regarded as right, is a guide it would be presumptuous to neglect, whatever may be the influence which has led us in that direction—our moral faculties, or our uncorrupted nature.

90. The history of these expressions exemplifies this in a very remarkable manner. The general idea of a law of nature is, as is well known, due to the Greek philosophers of the Stoic school. 'According to nature'

---

[1] I am not sure that persons who refer the existence of rules of conduct to utility or experience, would not use the term 'moral law' to describe them. But the term generally implies the existence of an innate faculty.

[2] *Fragment on Government,* chap. ii. sect. 14; vol. i. p. 8 of collected works.

expressed their idea of moral as well as material perfec-
tion[1]. But by what test did they discover what was and
what was not according to nature? Simply by that of
uniformity. What was the same to all and amongst all
they accepted as natural; whatever varied, they rejected[2].
So too the Roman lawyers, before they had learnt the
Greek philosophy, had, as is well known, evolved from
actual observation of uniformity a body of law, which,
under the name of *jus gentium*, or law common to all
nations, they very extensively applied. When they
adopted the notion of a law of nature, they did not
abandon these rules, or change them a single whit.
There was no necessity to do so ; for the law of nature is
only (as has been said) the law common to all nations
seen in the light of a peculiar theory[3].

91. So too the very expression 'moral law' marks
unmistakeably, that the source from which this law was
actually derived was the same observation of identity.
The word *mos*, from signifying what is customary, has
come to signify what is right. It was to explain the
phenomenon of a common agreement upon this point,
that an innate faculty was suggested : and whenever
this faculty is called in question, it is only by pointing
to this phenomenon that its existence can be proved, or
its extent measured.

92. Nor, I may observe, would it make any difference Principle of
so far as regards the matter now under consideration, utility.
were we to drop these terms altogether, and substitute
the principle of utility in their place, as those would
have us do who have most strongly attacked them. Of
whatever use it may be, politically speaking, to establish

[1] Maine's Ancient Law, p. 54 (first ed.).
[2] Grote's Plato, vol. iii. p. 510, n.
[3] Maine's Ancient Law, p. 50 (first ed.).

clearly in men's minds that the greatest happiness of all
is the true guide of action, the test of conformity to this
principle can be no other than public opinion[1]. The
principle of utility, separated from experience and resting
on a bare assertion of the good or evil tendency of a
particular line of conduct, is just as powerless to convince,
and just as apt to serve as a disguise of arbitrary power
as either nature or a moral sense.

93. In whatever dress, therefore, we may choose to
put our sentiments, I do not think the lawyer need go
beyond actual experience. Whatever rule of conduct
he is called upon to observe, outside of divine law and
the declared ascertained commands of the sovereign
authority, must be supported by a custom of, at least,
very considerable generality : but this alone is a sufficient
recommendation, and further inquiry as to why it became
so is superfluous.

Equity.   94. Hitherto I have only considered the general use
which might be made of a moral law or law of nature,
namely, to supply the *lacunæ* of a positive law. But the
law of nature at Rome and the moral law in England
have, under the name of equity, had a very much more
extensive and more immediate application. For a full
and clear explanation of the method by which, upon an
assumed natural principle of equality, the Roman lawyers

[1] Bentham admits this. He says : 'Those who desire to see any
check whatsoever to the power of the government under which they
live, or any limit to their sufferings under it, must look for such
check and limit to the source of the Public Opinion Tribunal,
irregular though it be, and, to the degree in which it has been
seen, fictitious : to this place of refuge, or to none ; for no other
has the nature of things afforded. To this tribunal they must on
every occasion appeal.' Securities against Misrule adapted to a
Mahommedan State, sect. 1 ; vol. viii. p. 562 of collected works.

managed to get rid of dogmas and distinctions which belonged to the strict law of Rome, but which were not found in the law common to all nations, I must refer the student to the chapter on 'Equity' in Sir Henry Maine's Ancient Law. Our own notion of equity is so far identical with this, that the moral law comes in as an avowed remedy for the inconvenience and inapplicability of an already existing system. But the origin of English equity is in that early stage of history when the idea of law was very incomplete, and the exercise of the judicial function had not been clearly separated from the ordinary exercise of sovereign authority. The decrees of the Court of Chancery were in their origin founded on a sort of dispensing power residing in the Sovereign by virtue of the prerogative. It was the King's conscience which was moved by an injustice, and because it was one which was not remediable by the ordinary law, the Chancellor received a commission to remedy it, sometimes from the King himself, but sometimes also from parliament[1]. Of course it was easy to pass from this to a general commission to redress grievances for which the strict rules of law supplied no adequate remedy, without noticing that thereby power was given to the Court of Chancery practically to fix the limits of its own jurisdiction, by determining in what cases the deficiencies of the common law rendered it necessary for itself to interfere.

94 *a.* Notwithstanding this, equity has to a great extent lost in England that feature, which at first sight it would seem easiest to preserve, namely, its elasticity. Sir Henry Maine[2] considers that this is due to courts of equity having originally adopted certain moral principles, which have been carried out to all their legitimate con-

Why equity has become comparatively rigid.

---

[1] Spence's Chancery Jurisdiction, vol. i. p. 408.

[2] Ancient Law, p. 69 (first ed.).

sequences, and which fall short of the corresponding ethical notions of the present day. I venture to think that it is also due, in part at least, to the very different conception of law itself by modern lawyers, and to the great importance which is now attached to the stability of law, and to the necessity, in order to secure it, for a complete separation of legislative and judicial functions. I do not, of course, canvass the acute and truthful generalization that equity precedes legislation in the order of legal ideas, but I would base it on a far more general principle than the preliminary assumption of fixed ethical rules.

95.   Consider the matter from the opposite point of view. Equity precedes legislation in legal history. Why? Because the idea of law as an inflexible rule without the possibility of modification, is wholly unsuited to the early notions of the functions of courts of justice. According to a notion which extends far down into our own history, and which even now very largely exists in the popular mind, the function of judges is not so much to enforce the rigid commands of a Sovereign, as to redress grievances. To this relation of ideas I shall have again to refer. The complete inversion of this conception is marked by the treatise of Austin. The first steps towards it were taken in the respect paid to precedent. Until it was complete, it was impossible to separate the province of law from the province of morality. Both ideas are comprehended under the term 'justice.' The flexibility and adaptability to special circumstances, which are the very essence of the remedial functions of courts of equity, conflict with the idea that the rules to be administered are rules of law, and with the conception of law which now prevails in jurisprudence.

96.   The elasticity of equity now depends on the same cause which gives flexibility to the common law :—that it

is law made by judges in the course of judicial decision ;
that it is *ex post facto* and concrete ; and not, like an Act
of Parliament, prospective and abstract[1].

97.   A very curious problem with reference to equity is In India.
being worked out in India. We scorn the exclusive maxims
of the Roman Law, and we emphatically profess to extend
the protection of law to all classes of the Queen's subjects
alike. Nevertheless, there are in India enormous gaps
in the law. It is not too much to say that there are
considerable classes of persons whose legal rights are,
with reference to many very important topics, entirely
undefined : and there are many topics affecting all classes
on which it would be scarcely possible to lay down a
single principle, which there would not be some hope of
challenging with success. It has been supposed that in
India these gaps are to be filled up by the judge deciding
the case according to ' equity and good conscience.'
And it has even been said, that all the rules of law
which a judge has to apply in India are subject to ' equity
and good conscience.' But though in the present state
of Indian Law some such maxim and some such expedient may be necessary, it is well to be on our guard
against the dangers to which it may lead. Constantly
criticized by an able bar, always closely watched by a
jealous public, generally dealing with suitors who have
the energy and means to resent injustice—the equity
judges of England and of Rome have been under a
restraint as effective, if not as obvious, as the judges of
common law. Under these restraints, and with ethical
ideas generally accepted in an homogeneous society, as in
England, equity may do, and no doubt has done, very
useful work. But in a country like India, where these
restraints are almost wholly wanting, and where it is

[1] See supra, sect. 59.

perfectly possible (not to speak of minor antagonisms) that in successive courts of appeal a Hindoo, a Mahommedan, and a Christian might have to sit as judges in the same case, the attempt to apply a system which has only been extensively applied in two countries of the world, might seem somewhat hazardous[1].

Written and unwritten law.

98.　A curious classification of law, which has some bearing on the questions we have been now considering, has become current in England, and this it is desirable to notice. The law directly made by the supreme or subordinate legislative authority, is called *written* law; the rest of law, from whatever source it may be derived, is called *unwritten* law.

99.　This distinction[2] has nothing whatever to do with that which the words would seem to indicate; that is to say, with the circumstance whether the law has been, in fact, reduced into writing: indeed, as we have seen, nearly all the sources of law are writings. It is an arbitrary use of words which is hardly justifiable, and which, if not explained, is likely to mislead.

---

[1] The difficulty of transferring the ideas of European systems of law, together with all their traditional modifications, into Indian courts, is illustrated by a line of argument which I have more than once heard. It is said (and truly said in a certain sense), that all courts of law in India are courts of equity also, and that the law must therefore be administered equitably. And (it is urged) it would be inequitable to apply strictly the rules of procedure, where they would press hardly on particular litigants. No one would think of claiming any special favour on such a ground in the English Court of Chancery. But it is not so easy to explain to a person wholly ignorant of the history of the terms, why, with the principles which they profess to adopt, courts of equity do not more frequently than any other courts relax the rules of procedure which they have once laid down.

[2] Austin, Lect. xxviii.

CHAPTER III.

RELATIONS WHICH ARISE OUT OF LAW.

100. We have hitherto considered what we mean by the term 'law,' and where it is to be found. We now proceed to consider the relations which arise out of it.

101. Every law is the direct or indirect command of the sovereign authority, addressed to persons generally, bidding them to do or not to do a particular thing or set of things; and the necessity which the persons to whom the command is addressed are under to obey that law is called an *obligation* or *duty*. Duty and obligation.

102. The words 'obligation' and 'duty' do not belong exclusively to law. It is frequently said that we are under an obligation to such a one, meaning only that we have received a favour from him, for which we ought to be grateful: or we say that a man's position in society obliges him to do this or that; or that it is our duty to revere God, or to love our parents.

103. Of course in this place, when we speak of obligation or duty, we refer only to such obligations and such duties as arise out of the express or tacit commands of the sovereign authority which we obey.

104. 'Right' is a term which, in its abstract sense, it is in the highest degree difficult to define. Fortunately, where the term is used to describe a particular relation or class of relations, and not as an abstract expression of Right.

E

all relations to which the name may be applied, it is far
easier to conceive. Nor is it impossible to explain some
of the ideas which the term connotes; and this is what
I shall attempt to do here.

105. Every right corresponds to a duty or obligation;
no right can exist unless there is a duty or obligation
exactly correlative to it. On the other hand, it is not
necessary that every duty or obligation should have its
corresponding right. There are, in fact, many duties or
obligations to which there is no corresponding right[1].
For example, there are duties imposed upon us to abstain
from cruelty to animals, to serve certain public offices
when called upon, and to abstain from certain acts of
immorality; but there are no rights corresponding to
these duties, at least none belonging to any determinate
person. If it is asserted that a right exists at all in the
cases I have put, it must be meant that it belongs to
society at large; but I think rights are generally considered as belonging to particular persons.

106. Of course, as every right corresponds to a duty
or obligation, and as every duty or obligation is created
expressly or tacitly by the sovereign authority, so rights
are created expressly or tacitly by the sovereign authority
also. And as the term duty or obligation connotes the
idea that its observance is capable of being, and will be
enforced by the power which creates it, so also the term
right connotes the idea of protection from the same source.

107. Rights have sometimes been described as a
faculty or power of doing or not doing. A faculty or
power of doing is undoubtedly the result of some rights;
for instance, the right of ownership enables us to deal
with our property as we like, because others are obliged
to abstain from interfering with our doing so. But in its

---

[1] Austin, Lecture xii. p. 356 (third ed.).

abstract sense we should hardly, I think, identify the right with this faculty or power.

Moreover, to speak of the faculty or power of not doing, in the same sense as we speak of the faculty or power of doing, involves a confusion of ideas which it is most desirable to avoid.

108. Right is also very often confounded with liberty, as in the popular expression, so common in political writers, 'the rights and liberties of the subject.' The liberties here spoken of, however, may be nothing more than those rights which correspond to the duty or obligation imposed upon others to forbear from certain acts ; which acts would interfere with our *liberty* in the abstract sense of that term. But very often the phrase expresses in a confused manner that extent of freedom from all kinds of duty and obligation, which, in the opinion of the writer, ought to exist in a well-regulated state.

109. It is essential to every legal duty or obligation, and therefore to every right, that it should be specific. This follows from the essential quality of a legal duty or obligation—that it is the result of a command. A command must by its very nature be specific. It must be addressed to determinate persons bidding them do a thing, with such certainty that it may be ascertained whether or no it has been obeyed. Thus we may say, in popular language, that it is the duty of parents to educate their children, but we cannot thereby signify a legal duty. All we mean is, that it is one of the precepts of morality that they should do so. Before it can become a legal duty, a command to that effect must issue from the legislature ; and should this command only make education in general terms compulsory, then all the other particulars, the ages at which the children are to be sent to school, the period they are to remain, the penalty to be incurred by

Rights. duties. and obligations are specific.

not doing so, and so forth, will have to be settled by a subordinate authority, that is to say, some such body as a School Board, constituted for the purpose, or, in default of any such body, by the tribunals which administer the law.

Sovereign body has no rights, and is not subject to duties or obligations.

110. It being moreover the essential nature of a duty or obligation that it is the result of a command, it follows that it is necessarily imposed upon some person other than the person who issues the command. No man, except by a strong figure of speech, can be said to issue commands to himself. Every legal duty or obligation, therefore, is imposed by the sovereign body on some person other than itself.

111. It is equally true, though it is a truth by no means so easy to grasp, that every right belongs to a person other than the sovereign body which creates it. This, like most truths which result directly from fundamental conceptions, is scarcely capable of demonstration, yet it would not, I think, have ever been brought into doubt, had it not been for a slight confusion of language, which I shall endeavour to remove.

112. Though the sovereign authority cannot confer upon itself a right against a subject, it may impose upon a subject a duty or obligation to do a specific thing towards itself, as, for instance, to pay a certain sum of money into the Government treasury; and this will result in a relation very closely analogous to the ordinary one of debtor and creditor. A tax or a fine imposed upon a subject is indeed constantly spoken of as a debt to the Crown, and recovered by a process analogous to that by which ordinary debts are recovered.

113. But between the so-called rights of the Sovereign to a tax, or a fine, and the right of a subject to receive a debt from a fellow-subject, there are essential differences.

The subject holds his right to recover his debt, and can only exercise and enjoy that right at the will and pleasure of another, namely, the Sovereign who conferred it upon him. The sovereign power, on the other hand, which imposed the tax or fine, is also the power which enforces it. Moreover, the right to payment of a debt, which is possessed by the subject, is not only dependent on the will of another for its exercise and enjoyment, but it is limited by that will; and nothing but the external sovereign power can change the nature of the legal relation between debtor and creditor. Whereas, in the case of a tax or fine, although the Sovereign has expressed in specific terms, and therefore for the moment limited the duty to be performed towards itself, it follows from the nature of sovereignty, that by the sovereign will the duty may be at any moment changed. And though there is no difficulty in conceiving the *duty* which would arise upon each successive command, it is impossible to conceive a *right* of so fluctuating a character;—not because a right cannot change as easily as a duty or obligation, but because we cannot conceive a right as changing at the caprice of its holder.

114.   Looking to the habit that prevails of enforcing those duties or obligations which the sovereign body has directed to be performed towards itself, by a procedure nearly similar in form to that in common use for the enforcement of duties or obligations which have to be performed by subjects towards each other, we should readily understand, that the former class of duties and obligations, as well as the latter, had come to be considered as having correlative rights. Nor, when confined to such duties and obligations as the payment of taxes or fines, would there be any objection to the extension of the term 'right,' by a sort of fiction, to the claims of the Crown.

It is, however, with reference to political discussions that the distinction becomes of importance. Knowing the respect which men have for legal rights, and the feeling which all men have that legal rights ought to be secure, politicians, especially the partisans of authority, constantly base the claims of the sovereign body on the simple assertion that they are rights. Nor (as in a phrase to which I have already adverted) are the partisans of liberty, when it serves their turn, reluctant to assert, that the people have rights against the Government; though it is more easy to strip off from these (so-called) rights the appearance of being founded in law. I think, if both sides were ready with the answer, that these are only rights in the sense of being sanctioned by morality, or the general usages of mankind; and that they are not rights in the sense in which we speak of rights of property and personal security; then, I think, the assertion would lose a great part of its force, and the discussion would be reduced to its true political ground, namely, what is expedient for the welfare of the people at large.

115. Austin sums up the characteristics of right, on which I have last insisted, as follows [1] :—'To every legal right, therefore,' he says, 'there are three parties : the sovereign government of one or a number which sets the positive law, and which through the positive law confers the legal right, and imposes the relative duties : the person or persons on whom the right is conferred : the person or persons on whom the duty is imposed, or to whom the positive law is set or directed.'

115 a. Every right, duty, and obligation exists, as has been said, in respect of some specific object. This object

---

[1] Lect. vi. p. 291 (third ed.).

may be either a thing or a person. Every right belongs
to a person, and every duty or obligation is imposed upon
a single person or several persons at once. The terms
'person' and 'thing,' therefore, form an important
element in the conception of every right, duty, and
obligation.

116. The word thing includes all animate and inani- Things.
mate objects of sense which are not persons. But besides
this, which is the ordinary and popular meaning of
the term, that which is not yet in existence may be the
subject of rights, and as such. is called 'a thing.' Thus
the ship which is not yet built but which the ship-builder
has promised to build, the coming year's crops, the easement of light and air, the unpaid debt, may all be subjects
of rights, and are spoken of as things.

To mark this distinction, things are divided into cor- Corporeal
poreal and incorporeal. The distinction must not be and incorporeal.
overlooked; for, as we shall see hereafter, some rules of
law depend upon it.

117. Another classification of things on which rules of Moveable
and im-
law are founded is into moveable and immoveable. These moveable.
terms might seem to mark a physical distinction only, but
it is not always very precisely ascertained. In some cases,
indeed, the physical distinction is clear enough, and the
legal distinction corresponds with it. Thus land is clearly
enough both physically and legally immoveable. But it
would be difficult to assign a reason in many cases for
classifying a thing either as one or the other; as, for
instance, a share in a railway company. Things not in
existence are generally considered as belonging to the
class which their ultimate form indicates. Thus a debt is
a moveable thing, but the interest in land which the next
taker will enjoy after the death of another is considered as
an immoveable thing.

Persons.   118. Persons are human beings capable of holding rights, and liable to perform duties and obligations.

Birth.   119. Every human being at his birth acquires some rights, though he rarely, for reasons which will be explained hereafter, can so soon commence to incur obligations, and some time must always elapse before he is liable to perform duties.

It is generally considered necessary in order to constitute birth, that there must be complete separation of the child from the mother, and life in the child after separation; it makes no difference how short a time the child lives after this.

Death.   120. For practical legal purposes death is an event which cannot be for a moment doubtful. But besides the cessation of physical existence which is generally signified by the term, there is known to some systems of law a sort of conventional death, or, as it is sometimes called, a civil death. This used to be considered in Europe as taking place when a man made certain religious vows and became a monk. Under the Hindoo law there was at one time something very similar to this in the case of the jogee, who renounced the world and lived by mendicancy. An outcast also was under the Hindoo law so completely considered dead, that the usual funeral ceremonies were performed for him[1]. But the effect of expulsion from caste is greatly modified, if not altogether removed, by the Act XXI of 1850 of the Indian Legislature.

In these cases the fictitious death rarely extends so far as totally to extinguish the rights, duties, and obligations of the persons feigned to be dead. It chiefly concerns those rights under which a man possesses, or can claim property. But the persons feigned to be dead would

---

[1] Menu, ch. ii. ss. 183, 184; Strange's Hindoo Law, vol. i. p. 160.

remain amenable to the law, and, as regards their person, under its protection.

121.   The capacity to hold rights, and the liability to perform duties and obligations, is the creature of the sovereign power, and is subject therefore to every species of modification, and even to total extinction.   So that whilst some men have been reduced to a state of slavery in which the law treats them only as property[1], or the subjects of the rights of others, other men have procured for themselves immunities and privileges which put them almost beyond the reach of the ordinary law.   But in England, and countries dependent upon England, and in most other civilised countries, these inequalities have to a great extent disappeared; and the capacity to hold rights, and the liability to perform duties and obligations is, for all full-grown men, members of the same political society, pretty nearly alike.   Except as regards certain public functions, the capacity and liability of unmarried women is very nearly the same as that of men.   The capacity and liability of married women is generally, to some extent, limited : it is greatly so in England; less so in India, not only among Hindoos and Mahommedans, but also among Europeans married and living in that country, in consequence of the provisions of the Indian Succession Act.   The capacity and liability of persons under a certain age is less than that of a full-grown person ; and the capacity and liability of persons of unsound mind is also limited. *Modified capacity and liability.*

122.   An alien, that is, a person who belongs to a different political society from that in which he resides, stands in a position altogether different from that of his *Aliens.*

---

[1] See 'Smith against Gould,' Lord Raymond's Reports, p. 1274, where the judges refused to apply this doctrine to a negro slave in England, overruling some prior cases to the contrary.

neighbours. He is not in the habit of obedience to the
same sovereign authority as they are. In times of peace,
however, the position of aliens in most modern civilised
countries has been substantially assimilated to that of
the members of the political society in which they reside :
but in time of war, these rights, of necessity, in a great
measure cease.

Juristical
persons.

123. There is a modified use of the term 'person'
amongst lawyers which, from its importance and peculiarity,
requires considerable attention. Besides human beings,
who are generally understood by the word 'person,' we
find that certain abstractions, or entities, or whatever you
may choose to call them, are spoken of as holding rights
and being liable to duties and obligations. Thus the
City of London, a Bank, the Government of India, an Idol,
a Railway Company, are frequently spoken of as holding
property, as bringing and defending suits, of making contracts, and so forth, as if they were ordinary men. This is
of course a pure fiction. There is no person here to whom
these rights belong, or who incurs these obligations. In
the case of the Idol there is no human being to whom the
right or obligation could possibly be referred ; and even in
the case of the Government, or a Company, it makes no
difference that these are composed of individuals ; for
these individuals have *personally* nothing to do with the
right or obligation in question. Everything, however,
proceeds exactly the same, or very nearly the same, as if
a real living person were concerned. There is a fictitious
person, or, as I prefer to call it, a *juristical person* (to
distinguish it from a real person), to which all the rights
are supposed to belong, and upon which all the duties or
obligations are imposed. A great many juristical persons
are in England called corporations, but the term is not for
general purposes a satisfactory one, and I cannot, therefore,

substitute it for the somewhat pedantic expression I have
chosen[1].

124. Generally speaking, a juristical person is an
aggregate of individuals who have been joined together
to prosecute some common object, as a company of shareholders for the purpose of carrying on a trade. But this
is not always so; for instance, an idol necessarily implies
the idea of singularity. Moreover, all aggregations of
individuals having a common object are not juristical
persons. For instance, such associations as the British
Parliament, a literary club, or a religious sect are not so.

125. When an aggregate of real persons is incorporated, and forms a juristical person, it is very important
to perceive clearly that the rights, duties, and obligations
of the juristical person do not belong to, and are not
imposed upon the individuals collectively. This is what
distinguishes aggregates of persons which are, from aggregates of persons which are not, juristical persons. Thus,
if eight or ten persons enter into an ordinary trading
partnership, the stock-in-trade belongs to them jointly;
they themselves have jointly the custody and control of it;

[margin note:] How corporate bodies
differ from
a partner-
ship.

[1] I have adopted this expression from Savigny, who has discussed
the nature of juristical persons at considerable length. (System of
Modern Roman Law, ss. 85 sqq.) Thibaut uses the expression
'Gemeinheit,' which Mr. Lindley translates 'corporation.' But
Thibaut's original definition of a 'Gemeinheit' would hardly coincide
with the definition of a corporation in the English law. From Mr.
Lindley's translation it would appear that this definition was
modified by the author in the later editions, but I have not been
able to ascertain its exact terms. It would seem, however, that
Thibaut, instead of calling a person of this kind, as Savigny does,
a 'juristical person,' would call it 'a *moral* person.' See Thibaut's
System of Pandects Law, General Part, s. 113 of the translation
by Lindley. This is the last abuse of a term already, I should have
thought, sufficiently ill-used. I am surprised, however, to find the
same expression in the generally excellent Italian Civil Code (s. 2).

and they sell and dispose of it as they please. On the
other hand, each is individually liable for the debts of the
concern. But when a number of persons are formed into
a juristical person, such as a railway company, the individual shareholders, as such, have neither the custody nor
control of any part of the property of the company ; they
cannot, as such, dispose of it in any way whatever : nor
can they be sued for any debts which the company has
incurred [1].

Cannot be created except by Sovereign.

126. It is a general rule that juristical persons cannot
be created without the assent, express or implied, of the
sovereign authority [2]. This is a very strict rule of English law ; and the power which, in India, Hindoos and
Mahommedans claim of creating juristical persons for
religious purposes to any extent they please, is in conflict
with the ideas of all other civilized nations.

Status.

127. Every person possesses a vast number of rights,
and is liable to a vast number of duties and obligations.
Every person also has, as we shall see hereafter, certain
capacities and incapacities to do acts by which his rights,
duties, and obligations are affected. When the rights,
duties, and obligations of any one person, together with
his capacities and incapacities, are viewed as a whole, they
are designated by the term 'status.'

Condition.

128. Sometimes we have to consider and speak of, as
a whole, not all the rights, duties, obligations, capacities,
and incapacities of a person, but a certain section of them
only ; to which therefore, for the sake of brevity, it is also

[1] Compare the frequently quoted maxim of Ulpian, '*Si quid
universitati debetur singulis non debetur, nec quod debet universitas
singuli debent.*' Dig. Bk. III. tit. iv. l. 7. s. 1.

[2] This was a rule of Roman law, and has been copied by all
modern European nations. See Dig. Bk. XLVII. tit. xxii., and
the Italian Civil Code, annotated by Cattaneo and Borda, s. 2.

convenient to assign a name. These smaller aggregates of rights, duties, obligations, capacities, and incapacities, may, I think, be aptly termed 'conditions.' Thus we speak of the condition of master, father, husband, servant, son, wife, and so forth; meaning thereby the rights, duties, and obligations, capacities, and incapacities of a person when he stands in that particular relation.

129. There is this marked distinction between this use of these two words. When we use the word status, we generally wish to keep out of view the particular character of the rights, duties, obligations, capacities, and incapacities of which it is made up. Whereas, on the contrary, when we use the word condition, we generally wish to mark and keep in view a similarity in the composition of the particular aggregate, wherever it is found. Thus, when I speak of the condition of a father, I generally mean to indicate those rights, duties, obligations, capacities, and incapacities which are common to all fathers alike.

130. There has been a great deal of discussion about the true meaning of the terms status and condition; and their use has been greatly impaired by the uncertainty attaching to them. I have substantially adopted that meaning which has been assigned to them by Austin in the Introductory Outline to his Course of Lectures. It is true that he does not in words draw the distinction which I have drawn between status and condition; but he uses it nevertheless.

131. Sometimes it is necessary to speak of, as a whole, a number of rights, duties, and obligations, which do indeed belong to one person, but which, not being all that are comprised under the term status, cannot be described by that word; and which, not being the same or similar in all persons, cannot be called a condition. For instance, *Juris universitas.*

the rights, duties, and obligations which on a man's death pass to his heir, or on his insolvency pass to the official assignee, are often considered and spoken of as a whole. Such aggregates of rights, duties, and obligations were called by Roman lawyers *juris universitates.* It is impossible to translate this term, and I do not venture to propose a new one; though it would be undoubtedly useful if such a one could be found.

132. Before quitting this discussion on the nature of persons and things, in the legal sense of the terms, I will advert to a classification founded on those terms, which has been the source of some confusion.

Law of persons and things. 133. Making the various combinations which are possible, we see that we may have (1) rights of persons over persons; (2) rights of persons over things; (3) duties or obligations of persons to act or forbear in respect of persons; (4) duties or obligations of persons to act or forbear in respect of things. Laws which concern, or which chiefly concern, the rights, duties, and obligations of persons in respect of persons, have been sometimes classed together and called the law of persons; and laws which concern, or which chiefly concern, the rights, duties, and obligations of persons in respect of things, have been likewise classed together and called the law of things.

Rights of persons and things, an erroneous classification. 134. I cannot discover that this classification of laws has been turned to much purpose, and it would have been scarcely worth while to mention it, had it not been that by slightly changing the terms in which this classification is expressed, Blackstone has introduced an egregious error. He speaks not of the law of persons and of the law of things, but of rights of persons and of rights of things [1]. Rights of persons there are undoubtedly; for all

[1] Analysis (passim) prefixed to the earlier editions of the Commentaries.

rights are such. There may be also rights *over* things, and rights *over* persons ; but rights *of*, that is, belonging to, things, as opposed to rights *of*, that is, belonging to, persons, there cannot be.

134 *a.* In English law, at any rate, the law of persōns and the law of things is so mixed up, that no use can be made of this classification so long as our law retains its present form. We do not in England possess any legislative provision, or body of legislative provisions, which professes to be systematic ; whilst Blackstone, whose treatise professes to be such, and who has been followed by the general body of English lawyers, has misunderstood the distinction. Even in India, where an attempt has been made to enunciate the law in a systematic form, it does not seem to have been found possible to preserve it. Thus, in the Penal Code, the law at once imposes on persons the duty to forbear from assault, and punishes a breach of that duty by fine or imprisonment, or both. The duty to forbear from assault belongs to the law of persons, and the liability to suffer punishment also; but the obligation to pay a sum of money belongs to the law of things. It seems to me indeed very doubtful, whether a system of law could be so contrived as to make any use of this distinction.

135. Having thus discussed the nature of persons and things in the sense in which those terms are used by lawyers, I revert to the consideration of rights, duties, and obligations ; and I proceed to shew how, with reference to certain special qualifications of them, they have been classified.

136. Sometimes a right exists only as against one or more individuals, capable of being named and ascertained ; sometimes it exists generally against all persons, members of the same political society as the person to whom the

Rights *in rem* and *in personam.*

right belongs; or, as is commonly said, somewhat arro-
gantly, it exists against the world at large. Thus in the
case of a contract between A and B, the right of A exists
against B only; whereas in the case of ownership, the
right to hold and enjoy the property exists against persons
generally. This distinction between rights is marked by
the use of terms derived from the Latin : the former are
called rights *in rem ;* the latter are called rights *in personam.*

The term ' right *in rem* ' is a very peculiar one; translated literally it would mean nothing. But it has an
arbitrary meaning which is made perfectly clear by two
passages in the Digest of Justinian. In Book iv. tit 2.
sec. 9, the rule of law is referred to—that what is done
under the influence of fear should not be binding : and
commenting on this, it is remarked, that the lawgiver
speaks here generally and ' *in rem,*' and does not specify
any particular kind of persons who cause the fear ; and
that therefore the rule of law applies, whoever the person
may be. Again, in Book xliv. tit. 4. sec. 2, it is laid down
that, in what we should call a plea of fraud, it must be
specially stated whose fraud is complained of, ' and not *in
rem.*' On the other hand, it is pointed out that, if it is
shewn whose fraud is complained of, it is sufficient ; and it
need not be said whom the fraud was intended to injure ;
for (says the author of the Digest) the allegation that
the transaction is void, by reason of the fraud of the
person named, is made ' *in rem.*' In all these three cases
in rem is used as an adverb, and I think we should
express as nearly as possible its exact equivalent, if we
substituted for it the English word ' generally.' In the
phrase ' right *in rem* ' it is used as an adjective, and the
equivalent English expression would be a ' general right ;'
but a more explicit phrase is a ' right availing against the

world at large;' and if this, which is the true meaning of the phrase 'right *in rem*,' be carefully impressed upon the mind, no mistake need occur.

The term 'right *in personam*,' on the other hand, is capable of literal translation. It is the converse of a right *in rem*; that is to say, it is a right available against a particular person or persons.

137. This is a convenient place to point out a distinction with regard to the use of the term obligation, which it is desirable to keep in mind. When that term is used in its wider sense, it is, as already mentioned, synonymous with duty; that is, it signifies the binding force of law upon the members of a political society generally. But the term obligation is frequently used to express, not the binding force of law generally, but the necessity we are under of doing a particular act for the benefit of a particular person; or, to use more technical language, the term obligation, in this, its secondary sense, is used correlatively, not to a right *in rem*, but to a right *in personam*.

Obligation as opposed to duty.

138[1]. Duties and obligations are either to do an act, or to forbear from doing an act. When the law obliges us to do an act, the duty or obligation is called positive; when the law obliges us to forbear from doing an act, then the duty or obligation is called negative. Thus 'thou shalt do no murder' is a negative duty or obligation; but 'fulfil your contract' is a positive one.

Positive and negative duties and obligations.

139[2]. Duties or obligations are further divided into relative and absolute. Absolute duties and obligations are those to which there is no corresponding right belonging to any determinate person or body of persons; as, for instance, the duty or obligation to serve as a soldier, or to pay taxes. Relative duties or obligations are those to

Relative and absolute.

---

[1] Austin, Lect. xii. p. 356 (third edition).   [2] Ib. p. 357.

F

which there is a corresponding right in some person or definite body of persons; as, for instance, the duty or obligation to pay one's debt.

140 [1]. Duties and obligations are also divided into primary, and secondary or sanctioning. Primary duties and obligations are those which exist *per se*, and independently of any other duty or obligation ; secondary or sanctioning duties and obligations are those which have no independent existence, but only exist for the sake of enforcing other duties or obligations. Thus the duty or obligation to forbear from personal injury is a primary one ; but the duty or obligation to pay a man damages for the injury which I have done to his person is secondary or sanctioning. The right which corresponds to a primary relative duty or obligation is called a primary right. The right which corresponds to a secondary or sanctioning duty or obligation is called a secondary or sanctioning right.

141. The series of duties and obligations in which are comprised the original primary one, and those which exist merely for the purpose of enforcing it, very often, indeed generally, extends beyond two. Thus I contract to build you a house ; that is the primary obligation. I omit to do so, and I am, therefore, ordered to pay damages ; that is the secondary obligation. I omit to pay the damages, and I am therefore ordered to go to prison ; that is also called a secondary obligation, though it comes third in the series. And if, as we are at liberty to do, we look upon the obligation to pay damages as now the primary one, the expression is not incorrect. The terms primary and secondary will thus express the relation between any two successive terms of the series.

142. The secondary or sanctioning duties or obliga-

---

[1] Austin, Lect. xlv. p. 787 (third edition).

tions which enforce primary absolute obligations are
themselves always absolute ; that is to say, there is no
right to enforce such duties or obligations belonging to
any determinate person or body of persons other than the
sovereign body.

143. On the other hand, secondary or sanctioning
absolute duties and obligations are used to enforce primary
relative duties and obligations also.   Thus the primary
relative duty or obligation of a servant to his master is
frequently enforced by the provisions of the criminal law,
by means of the obligation to suffer a fine or imprisonment ;
and as these relative duties or obligations have, generally
speaking, each their relative secondary or sanctioning duty
or obligation also, they are in such cases doubly enforced.
Thus if a man's property be wilfully injured, there arises
the absolute duty or obligation to suffer the punishment
for mischief or trespass, and the relative duty or obligation to make compensation to the party injured.

144. Secondary or sanctioning absolute duties or
obligations are for the most part the pains and penalties
imposed by the criminal law.   I shall have occasion to
discuss hereafter how far they are resorted to in civil
procedure [1].

144 a. Primary relative duties and obligations correspond
either to primary rights *in rem*, or to primary rights *in
personam*.   Those which correspond to primary rights *in
rem* are for the most part negative ; that is to say, they
are duties or obligations to forbear from doing anything
which may interfere with those rights.   Their general
nature may be best seen by considering the nature of the
rights to which they correspond.   Thus there are the
large classes of rights comprised respectively under the
terms ownership, possession, personal liberty, and personal

---

[1] Infra, sect. 437 sqq.

security ; which are all primary rights *in rem*, and the corresponding duties are to forbear from acts which infringe those rights. Primary rights *in personam* are chiefly those which are created by contract. The rights comprised in the relations of family, of husband and wife, of parent and child, guardian and ward, and other similar relations, are partly primary rights *in rem*, and partly primary rights *in personam*. Thus the right of a father to the custody of his child is a right *in rem ;* the conjugal rights of a husband over his wife are rights *in personam*.

145. Secondary or sanctioning relative duties or obligations, which arise on the non-observance of primary ones, are for the most part penalties and forfeitures which are enforced by civil as distinguished from criminal procedure [1].

Criminal and civil. Public and private.

146. The proper use to be made of these distinctions would be in a systematic catalogue of duties or obligations. Classifications somewhat analogous to these are indeed in use, though no such systematic enumeration has (as I shall presently shew) yet taken place. Thus law generally has been classified into public and private, and into criminal and civil. Austin [2] has, however, shewn how unsatisfactory these classifications are. They are probably founded on an imperfect conception of the distinctions to which I have just now adverted. It is indeed possible to say of some duties or obligations that they are criminal, and of others that they are civil ; but this, for the most part, is only the case where they are secondary or sanctioning ; and in fact this classification amounts to little more than the recognition of the distinction between criminal and civil procedure. The distinction of laws into public and private has rather

---

[1] But see supra, sect. 144, and infra, sect. 437.

[2] Lect. xvii. p. 416 (third edition).

reference to the object for which they are imposed, than the
nature of the duties and obligations which they create.
And many laws generally accounted private, as for
instance laws which regulate personal security, scarcely
differ in their ultimate object from many laws generally
reckoned as public, as for instance the laws which relate
to police. The ultimate object in each case is the protection of individuals. Even the laws which protect
the person of the Sovereign only exist for the benefit of
the members of the political society by securing peace
and order. In fact, we find, when we attempt to make
use of these terms for purposes of classification, that
there are numerous topics which might be just as well
included in one as in the other of the divisions which
they mark.

147. In speaking of those duties or obligations which Sanctions.
have no independent existence, I have resorted to the
somewhat clumsy expedient of calling them 'secondary or
sanctioning,' in order to keep in view both their characteristics,—that they exist only for the sake of enforcing other
duties and obligations, and that they enforce these duties
and obligations by means of a sanction.

148. It is desirable to conceive clearly the nature of
a sanction. A command, as Austin has pointed out[1], 'is a
signification of desire, but a command is distinguished
from other significations of desire, by this peculiarity—
that the party to whom it is directed is liable to evil from
the other in case he comply not with the desire.' And,
as every law is a command, every law imports this liability
to evil also, and it is this liability to evil which we call
by the name of sanction. Duty or obligation is hence
sometimes described as obnoxiousness to a sanction, and

[1] Lect. i. p. 91 (third edition).

t is no doubt a correct description from one point of view.

149. The operation of the sanction is also clearly explained by Austin; and it is this[1]—'The party obliged is averse from the conditional evil which he may chance to incur in case he break the obligation : in other words, he wishes or desires to avoid it. But, in order that he may avoid the evil, or may avoid the chance of incurring it, he must fulfil the obligation—he must do that which the law enjoins, or must forbear from that which the law prohibits.'

150. I shall have to consider the nature of sanctions hereafter[2] more in detail, and shall endeavour then to reconcile this view of law in general with that which seems at first sight inconsistent with it—namely, the actual operation of courts of law. For unless this can be done, our analysis is somewhere deficient.

[1] Lect. xxii. p. 459 (third edition).
[2] See chapter xi.

CHAPTER IV.

Primary Duties and Obligations.

151. Duties and obligations are created in all cases by the sovereign authority, but they may be created either expressly or tacitly ; directly or indirectly. Any one however may ascertain, by attempting to enumerate them, to how very small an extent primary duties and obligations have been expressly stated : and even where an express statement has been attempted, the terms employed are frequently so vague as to render the expression almost useless.

Primary duties and obligations rarely expressly stated.

152. The primary duties and obligations which have been expressed are chiefly those the breaches of which are called crimes. But even here the form of the expression is a definition, not of the primary duty or obligation, but of the breach of it. It is nowhere said in positive law, 'thou shalt not steal,' but whoever does such and such an act is guilty of theft ; we are nowhere bidden by the sovereign authority not to kill, but whoever causes death under certain circumstances is guilty of murder, or manslaughter, or culpable homicide. The expression is in these cases certainly not the less effectual, and I now only draw attention to the form of it as remarkable.

Form of expression.

153. None of the ordinary duties and obligations of daily life are anywhere expressed, and most of them are not very distinctly implied. We should look in vain for any direct expression of the sovereign authority fixing accurately the

Not very clearly implied.

mutual duties and obligations of parent and child, husband
and wife, guardian and ward ; forbidding the performance
of acts hurtful to the person, property, or reputation of
others ; or commanding us to pay our debts, and perform
our contracts. These duties and obligations are for the
most part tacitly imposed upon us : and it is only when a
breach of these duties and obligations is complained of,
that any attempt is made to ascertain them with exactness ;
and even then the inquiry almost invariably assumes that,
if the sovereign authority had expressed itself, it would, as
in the case of crimes, have defined the breach of duty or
obligation, and not the duty or obligation itself.

Not stated
by Black-
stone.

154.   Take for instance those duties and obligations
which correspond to the right of ownership, of personal
liberty and personal security. Even a commentator like
Blackstone, who professes to set before his readers a complete and exhaustive view of the English law, scarcely
touches upon them at all. He does not, and could not
wholly overlook them. He appears to consider (rightly
enough) that the discussion of them would properly fall
under the head of the rights to which they correspond[1].
Considering that such rights would belong to a man even in
a state of nature (though he omits to tell us how they would
be secured) he calls them absolute ; and if it were possible
that a man in a state of nature could have any rights in a
legal sense, there is not the least reason why they should
not be so called ; though of course the word ‘absolute’
would then mark an antithesis different from that which
I have used the word to express. But what does Blackstone, after having given them this name, tell us about
these rights? He plunges at once into the consideration of political liberty ; of magna carta, habeas corpus,

---

[1] Commentaries, vol. i. p. 124.

taxation, the prerogative, and the right to carry arms. Not a word about rights in any legal sense ; that is, rights corresponding to duties and obligations imposed upon individuals in relation to individuals. At one time he refers vaguely to such rights, but only with an observation that their nature will be better considered when he comes to treat of their breach. Turning to the Third Book, which treats of ' Private Wrongs,' we find that nearly the whole book is taken up with a description of the different Courts of Law and Procedure. Even when he professes to discuss the wrong, or violation of the right, which, of course, presumes an antecedent inquiry into the nature of the right, his attention is absorbed almost entirely by distinctions between the forms of action, suitable for enforcing the remedy which the party wronged has against the wrong-doer. Nearly all that Blackstone has to say anywhere, besides this, about ownership, or, as he would call it, property, relates to the transfer of it, and the various modes in which the rights comprised under that term may be apportioned. The nature and extent of the rights themselves are passed over nearly in silence[1].

155. Other writers have escaped the confusion into

---

[1] Though the scantiness of expression to which I here advert is a feature of general jurisprudence, this tendency to confound the rights which protect person and property, so far as they are the subject of civil procedure, with the forms of pleading, is, I think, a peculiar feature of English law. It would not be convenient here to trace the origin of this confusion, but it will suggest itself to any one who reads the account given in books on pleading, of the ' original writ,' and the ' action on the case.' See Stephen on Pleading, seventh ed., chap. i. and the note *ad finem*. With the narrow notions of courts of civil procedure on this subject in early times, we may contrast the healthier maxim of the criminal law, that where a statute forbids the doing of a thing, and provides no special sanction, the doing of it is always indictable. Bacon's Abridgement, Indictment (E).

which Blackstone has fallen between the legal rights of subjects as against each other, and the (so-called) constitutional
rights of subjects against the government; but no writer,
whose opinion is acknowledged as authoritative in courts
of law, has yet attempted to put into an express form those
duties and obligations, which we all acknowledge the necessity to observe, and upon which we depend for the security
of person and property. No such writer has attempted to
ascertain, with anything approaching to accuracy or com-
pleteness, what constitutes a wrong, or breach of such
duties and obligations. Even where the sovereign authority has taken upon itself the task of promulgating its
commands in a complete form, by means of a code, we find
that little progress has been made in this respect. Thus the
French Civil Code, while it abstains from defining rights, is
no more explicit on the subject of delicts than Blackstone
on the subject of civil injuries, to which they correspond.
We are told that whoever causes damage to another by
any act, is under the obligation to repair it[1]. It will be
observed that here also the expression is of the secondary
obligation only, and so vague as to give us scarcely any
assistance in ascertaining the primary obligation even by
inference.

This absence of clear expression on the part of the
sovereign authority of the duties and obligations which
it desires to have performed, has caused people sometimes
to forget the principle stated at the outset of this chapter,
that all legal duties and obligations are created by the
sovereign authority alone.

156.   It must not, however, be hence inferred that the
legislative functions of the sovereign body, or of its delegates,

[1] Code Civil, s. 1382. I shall discuss this definition more fully
hereafter. See sect. 182.

are inactive. Laws are being made every day, and these
all assume that the primary duties and obligations, of
which I have been speaking, and to which they constantly
refer, are known, though they have not been defined.

157. The sovereign authority in making new laws
always avoids, as far as possible, disturbing existing
rights, duties, and obligations. Even if it is necessary
to introduce a general change in the law, which would
otherwise have that effect, this is generally avoided by
declaring the change to be prospective: as, for instance,
in the Wills Act, which only applies to wills which have
been made since the act was passed.

158. The limit of the arbitrary power of the sovereign
authority to impose upon us any number of new duties
and obligations, and to deprive us to any extent of our
rights as often as it pleases, is to be sought, not in legal
rules, but in political maxims. The lawyer is bound to
admit that such laws, if made, would be valid. But the
politician knows that no Government in a free country
dare make such laws, except just so far as public utility
imperatively requires it. Public utility does require that
every one should surrender a small portion of his income
in the shape of taxes; public utility even sometimes
requires that a man should surrender altogether, for public
purposes, the property he has inherited from his ancestors,
for a railway for instance, or a public building; and the
sovereign authority makes him do so. But no exercise of
such a power beyond the strict requirements of public
utility is tolerable.

159. Many acts which have the form of the exercise of
arbitrary power are tolerated because in substance they
are not so. Thus the grant of letters patent for the
exclusive use of an invention assumes the form of a
special creation of a right by the Sovereign, in favour

Marginal notes: Legislation generally prospective. — Limitations or arbitrary exercise of legislative power.

of an individual. It has, however, nothing about it which is arbitrary and uncertain. The individual who grants the patent only carries out the provisions of the Legislature. Titles and distinctions are also frequently conferred by the sovereign authority on individuals, but they carry hardly any privileges, and are of little legal importance.

CHAPTER V.

LIABILITY [1].

160.   LIABILITY is the word which I use to express the condition of a person who, by breaking a primary duty or obligation, has become liable to a secondary one. In every inquiry as to liability two questions arise : first, has a primary duty or obligation been broken ? secondly, what is the secondary duty or obligation which arises from the breach ? If we keep this very simple statement of the nature of the inquiry steadily in view, we shall avoid a great deal of confusion.

Liability, what used to express.

Two branches of inquiry.

161.   I propose to examine some of the leading terms and phrases current upon this subject. They are to be found scattered in commentaries, reports, and acts of

---

[1] It will probably occur to the reader that, if law were systematic and complete, this chapter would assume a totally different character and proportion. The two preceding chapters would, under a slight change of form, contain an exhaustive description of primary duties and obligations, and this chapter would only discuss the secondary duties and obligations which arise upon their breach. But (even if this were possible) I should certainly fail in the object I have in view, if I deviated so far from the existing system. I might, as will appear in the sequel, discuss contract with reference to the primary obligations which arise upon it, but in all other cases nothing short of a complete reconstruction of jurisprudence will enable us to discuss primary duties and obligations, except by the inverse process of considering when they have been broken.

parliament. There are two elements of great difficulty in this examination. One is that these terms and phrases are frequently used in an artificial sense greatly differing from their ordinary one; the other is that this artificial meaning is itself variable.

Division of liability into *ex contractu* and *ex delicto.*

162. The first current notion with which I shall deal is that which treats all liability as arising out of a contract, or out of a delict; or, to use the English phrase, out of a contract, or out of a tort.

163. In order to understand the meaning and value of this classification, we must get as clear an idea as we can of the terms in which it is expressed. I will, therefore, first consider what is meant by the term ' contract,' and the expression 'obligation which arises out of a contract.' For this purpose I shall make use of the inquiry into the meaning of the term contract contained in Savigny's System of Modern Roman Law [1], of which the following is a paraphrase.

Savigny's definition of contract.

164. 'The idea of contract (says Savigny) is familiar to all, even to those who are strangers to the science of law. But with lawyers it is so frequently brought into play, and is so indispensable by reason of the frequency with which they have to apply it, that one might expect from them an unusually clear and precise conception of it. But in this we are not a little disappointed.

165. 'I will try (he says) to shew what a contract is, by the analysis of a case which no one can doubt is one of true contract. If then with this view we consider the contract of sale, the first thing that strikes us is several persons in presence of each other. In this particular case, as in most, there are precisely two persons; but, frequently, as in a contract of partnership, the number is quite

---

[1] Sect. 140.

uncertain ; so that we must adhere to plurality in this
general and indeterminate form, as a characteristic of contract.   These several persons must all have come to some
determination, and to the same determination ; for, so
long as there is any indetermination, or want of agreement,
there can be no contract.   This agreement must also be
disclosed ; that is, the wishes of each must be stated by,
and to each, until all are known ; for a resolution which
has been simply taken and not disclosed will not serve as
the basis of contract.

166.   'Moreover, we must not neglect to observe the
object which is aimed at.   If two men were to agree to
. assist each other reciprocally, by example or advice, in the
pursuit of virtue, science, or art, it would be a very odd
use of the term to call this a contract.   The difference
between such cases and the contract of sale, which we
have selected as the type, is this : In the latter, the object
which the parties have in view is a legal relation ; whereas
in the former, the objects are of quite another kind.   But
simply to say, that the object which the parties to a contract have in view is a legal relation, does not go to the
root of the distinction.   When the judges of a court of
law after a long discussion agree upon a decree, we have
every one of the characteristics hitherto noted, and it is a
legal relation that the decision has in view ; but yet there
is no contract.   The bottom of the distinction is, that the
judges have before them a legal relation to which they
are no parties.   In the case of a contract of sale the legal
relation which the parties contemplate is their own.

167.   'These characteristics may. be summed up in
the following definition.   A contract is the agreement of
several persons in a concurrent declaration of intention,
whereby their legal relations are determined.'

168.   It will be observed that this definition of con-

English
definitions
of contract.

tract includes not only those agreements which are a promise to do, or to forbear from some future act, but those
also which are carried out simultaneously with the intention of the parties being declared. English writers are
not very clear upon this point. While on the one hand
they would seem in practice to treat as contracts only
those agreements which bind us to do, or to forbear at
some future time ; yet we find, on the other hand, that
in their definitions of contract they take the widest
possible ground, rejecting all the limitations suggested
by Savigny, and making, in fact, the two words 'contract'
and ' agreement' synonymous.

Thus it has been proposed by the very highest authority
(the Indian Law Commissioners) to define a contract as
' an agreement between parties whereby a party engages
to do a thing, or engages not to do a thing [1].'

Distinction
between
contract and
performance
of a con-
tract.

169.   From some expressions in passages subsequent to
that which I have quoted, Savigny appears to treat the
performance of a contract as itself a contract. Thus, if I
rightly understand him, he says that the agreement for
the sale and purchase of a house is one contract, and the
consequent delivery of possession by the vendor to the
purchaser is another. This, with deference to so great
an authority, I venture to doubt. I think there is here a
confusion which is exceedingly common between contract,

---

[1] Second Report (1866), p. 11. English writers have not generally
attempted to define contract. The French Civil Code (Art. 1101)
defines it as a convention by which one or more persons create an
obligation (s'obligent) towards one or more other persons to do, or
not to do something. The Italian Civil Code (Art. 1098) defines it
as ' the agreement of two or more persons to establish, regulate, or
dissolve between themselves a juridical bond (un vincolo giuridico).'
The authors of the New York Civil Code are as vague as ourselves,
only a little more brief. They define a contract as ' an agreement
to do, or not to do a certain thing.' (s. 744.)

and transfer or conveyance, which Austin has several times pointed out in the course of his Lectures[1].

170. Subject to this modification (and for our present purpose it is not an important one) I think Savigny's analysis of contract may safely be adopted. The essential distinction between it, and the definition current in those countries which have adopted the Code Napoleon, is this : Savigny defines contract solely with reference to the contemplation of the parties : if the parties intend to declare their legal rights *inter se*, he calls it a contract, whether or no it has the effect intended is not considered[2]. The Code Napoleon, on the other hand, makes it of the essence of the definition of contract that an obligation is thereby created. For instance, if I were to promise a voter ten pounds for his vote, that would be a contract according to Savigny ; but, as no legal obligation would result from it, it would not be a contract according to the definition of the French Code. The Italian Code nearly accords with Savigny's definition.

171. The advantage of Savigny's definition is, I think, that it keeps more clearly before the mind the true mode in which the legal relation arises. When the parties have expressed their desire to create the legal relation, then arises the totally distinct question, whether the sovereign authority will recognise it as such. Supposing the parties to the contract to be of full capacity, and that the legal relation contemplated would not conflict with any command of the Sovereign, express or tacit, it will generally result from the agreement. It is, however, required in

How the legal relation arises.

---

[1] See Lecture xiv. and the notes to Table II., pp. 587, 1005 (third ed.).

[2] I gather this from the general tenor of Savigny's observations, and, I think, it is also implied in, though not expressly affirmed by, the definition.

some cases before the contract is made binding, that it should be accompanied by certain solemnities, as they are called. As, for instance, that it should be made in the presence of witnesses; that it should be in writing; or signed; or registered.

Effect of omitting solemnities.   172. A distinction exists with regard to the effect of omitting these solemnities which is sometimes embarrassing. The legal relation is sometimes recognised for some purposes, and not for others: or perhaps it ought to be said, in some cases, though the legal relation is recognised, impediments are thrown in the way of making any use of it. Thus the legislature sometimes says, that unless the solemnities have been performed the contract shall not be given in evidence; sometimes, that no action shall be brought upon it; sometimes, that it shall have no effect. There has been the greatest difficulty in ascertaining the precise effect of these obscure and vague expressions.

Intention of parties to contract.   173. From the slovenly mode also in which parties to a contract, in the hurry of business or from carelessness, frequently express themselves, great difficulties arise in ascertaining what legal relation the parties intended to create. It is with reference to this inquiry that it is said, 'the intention of the parties governs the contract.' But the difficulty of ascertaining the intention still remains. The person to whom the promise is made, or promisee, as he is called, may say that he intended one thing, and the promiser may say that he intended another. In which sense is the promise to be taken? Paley discussing this question says: 'It is not the sense in which the promiser actually intended it, that always governs the interpretation of an equivocal promise; because, at that rate, you might excite expectations which you never meant, nor would be obliged to satisfy. Much less is it the sense in which the promisee actually received the promise; for,

according to that rule, you might be drawn into engagements you never designed to undertake. It must, therefore, be the sense (for there is no other remaining) in
which the promiser believed that the promisee accepted his
promise[1].' Austin[2], remarking on this passage of Paley,
says that if this rule be adopted, should the promiser
misapprehend the sense in which the promisee accepted
the promise, either the promisee will be disappointed, or
he will get more than he expects: and he suggests that
the true guide is the understanding of both parties.
Paley's two first propositions are undoubtedly correct.
Austin's criticism, however, on what Paley considers as
the only other possible alternative is, as undoubtedly,
sound. But with the greatest respect for so high an
authority, it appears to me that Austin, in his own suggestion, merely falls back on the old difficulty; for the
difficulty only arises when the parties aver that they understood the promise in different ways, which in every
equivocal promise is, of course, possible.

174. The practical solution of the difficulty is, I
think, simple enough. Austin rightly points out that
there is a distinction between the intention of the parties,
and the sense of the promise. But this distinction hardly
avails anything for our present purpose. Even the sense
of the promise may be different to different persons; the
promiser may consider that his words bear one sense, the
promisee may consider that they bear another; and a
stranger may consider that they bear a third. There is

How ascertained in practice.

[1] Paley, Moral Philosophy, book iii. part i. chap. v. See
Archbishop Whateley's note, in which I find he arrives at the
same conclusion as I do, namely, that the result of a promise may
be different from what either one party intended, or the other
expected.
[2] Lect. xxi., note, ad finem.

but one way out of this difficulty. The judge, who has to decide what legal obligation has resulted from the transaction, may fairly use all these as a guide to his own conclusion. Having first ascertained the terms in which the parties expressed themselves, he may hear what each party says as to their true interpretation, and what each respectively says he intended by them; he may also consider what interpretation would be put upon them by an uninterested man of ordinary understanding. He may even go further, and consider the surrounding circumstances, so far as they throw light upon either the sense of the promise, or the intention of the promiser, or the expectation of the promisee. But after all he must put upon the words his own interpretation; and from the sense which he attaches to the words he must *presume* the intention. So that the current phrase 'the intention governs the contract' is really only true to this extent; that it governs the contract, where both parties are agreed what the intention was. Where there is a dispute as to the intention, the contract (strictly speaking) is governed by the intention, as it is presumed from the sense which, under all the circumstances, the judge thinks fairly attaches to the promise.

175. For instance, suppose you wrote me a letter offering to buy 'my bay horse, if warranted sound, for one hundred pounds,' and that I accepted the offer; whereupon I sent the horse to you with a written warranty as a fulfilment of the bargain. If we were to dispute, whether the warranty I offered you was such a warranty as was contemplated, the court would hear what you and I had to say as to the meaning of the contract, and our respective intentions and expectations; but would in all probability decide, that the sort of warranty which I was bound to give was the usual warranty in such

cases; that being the warranty which a man of ordinary sense and understanding would expect under the circumstances. The judge might be able to form an opinion without further inquiry whether the warranty was such, or not; but he might not; and if he could not do so, he would inquire from experienced persons what sort of warranty is usually given in such cases. And whatever sense experienced persons usually attach to the word 'warranty' when dealing in horses, the court would attach to it in this case, and decide that that was the warranty intended, whatever protest you might make, that that was not what you expected, or I might make, that that was not what I intended.

176. If, indeed, after having agreed to purchase my *bay* horse, you wanted to make out that your intention was to purchase my *brown*, the court would scarcely listen to you. Suppose, however, that I have two bay horses, and you insisted you had bought one, whilst I insisted you had bought the other. On the words of the promise itself it would be impossible to discover, whether we really intended the same or different horses; and, if the same, which. But a very little further inquiry would probably clear up the whole matter. It might turn out that, of my two bay horses, you had had one sent to you to look at; that you had offered me seventy-five pounds for this bay horse, and that I had insisted on having one hundred. And if nothing had ever passed between us about the other horse, and your offer of a hundred pounds for my bay horse followed close upon this negotiation, there would be no doubt at all, that you would be considered to have bought that horse which had been sent to you for inspection. And the judge would come to this conclusion, not because he is certain that was what I, or you, or both of us understood or intended. He has no means of ascertaining that. He

concludes that no reasonable man would suppose that in that letter any other horse was referred to, and he fixes upon that horse accordingly.

177. This, I think, is the practical method which tribunals adopt for deciding, in cases of dispute, what obligation has resulted from a contract. For this purpose they generally adopt certain maxims of interpretation[1], which, however, generally conclude with a protest that these maxims must always yield to the evident intention of the parties. What is here called the 'evident intention of the parties' is that presumed intention which, as I have said before, the judge takes from the interpretation, which interpretation may possibly conflict with one or another of the generally accepted maxims.

Contract not the source of obligation.

178. From this examination of the term 'contract,' we see that it is an occasion upon which the sovereign authority creates a primary obligation, according to the presumed intention of the parties. The contract itself is not, as the common expression 'an obligation which arises out of, or is created by, contract' might, at first sight, seem to indicate, the source of the obligation. It is the sovereign command which creates the obligation—in other words, which gives to contracts their binding force. This command is nowhere expressed. It is tacitly understood as a general rule in most civilized countries, that contracts will be enforced, and only the exceptions from it are expressed.

178 a. A contract is the simplest and at the same time the most frequent occasion for the creation of a primary

---

[1] See Chitty on Contracts, ch. i. sect. 3. par. 4, where these maxims are collected. It is common to transfer the maxims for the interpretation of wills, conveyances, and contracts from one to the other without very careful discrimination; but I doubt whether the interpretation of these three classes of documents proceeds upon precisely the same principles.

obligation. There does not appear to me to be any reason
why all the circumstances upon which that creation would
take place should not, even in the present state of jurisprudence, be accurately defined. The result of this would
be, as I have already suggested, to reduce the question of
the liability which arises from a breach of contract to
considerations of the simplest character [1].

179. If we revert now to the division of liability into Delict or
that which arises out of contract, and that which arises tort.
out of delict or tort, we shall find it necessary next to consider the meaning of the word 'delict' or 'tort.' It is,
however, far more difficult to assign any distinct meaning to
this word 'tort,' or to its corresponding Latin expression
'delict,' than to the word 'contract.' All are agreed that
it expresses some kind of breach of duty or obligation, but,
as I have already pointed out, lawyers generally, when
treating of this part of their subject, pass very lightly
over the consideration of the duty or obligation which is
broken, and English lawyers address themselves chiefly to
the procedure to which the party is amenable. And
although in almost every English law-book, and in some
Acts of Parliament, we find it stated or assumed, that all
ordinary cases which come before the Courts of Common
Law may be divided into actions of contract and actions
of tort, or, as it is sometimes put, actions of contract and Actions of
actions independent of contract [2], yet I know nothing more tort.
difficult to grasp than the distinction on which this classification is founded. Indeed, if we accept some accounts
of that distinction, it is difficult to believe that it exists
at all.

180. If, for instance, we turn to the description of torts

[1] See the note to the heading of this chapter.
[2] Smith on Contracts, p. 1; Bullen and Leake on Pleading, third
ed., p. 273; 15 and 16 Vict., chap. 76, Sched. B.

by a very able modern writer [1], what we are there told
is, that a tort or a wrong, independent of contract, involves
the idea of the infringement of a legal right or the violation of a legal duty. But is not a breach of contract both
an infringement of a legal right and a violation of a legal
duty? Further on we are told that one class of actions of
tort are founded on infractions of some private compact, or
of some private duty or obligation, productive of damage.
But are not actions for breach of contract founded on that,
which is at once the infraction of a private duty or obligation, and also of a compact? Again, though we are
reminded that tort differs essentially from contract, yet I
have in vain endeavoured to discern what the essential
difference is. On the contrary, I find it stated, that the
same transaction may give rise to an action of tort and an
action of contract. True, it is said that an action of tort
cannot be maintained for a breach of contract, but only
where the tort complained of *flows* from a contract. But
what sort of special connection is expressed by the word
' flowing' I am unable to conceive.

181. It is easy enough to see that the learned author
is not here expressing his own ideas on the subject, but
struggling to gather up into a consistent whole the vague
and contradictory language of various authorities ; whereas
the mere collocation of these authorities must satisfy any
one that such a struggle is hopeless.

French defi-
nition of
delicts.

182. The idea which attaches to the word delict, as
used by continental lawyers, is scarcely more definite
than that which attaches to the word tort. I am not
aware of any attempt to define it very accurately; but
there is in the French code a chapter headed ' Delicts,'
which would lead one to suppose that we should there find

---

[1] Broom's Commentaries on the Common Law, book iii. ch. i.
pp. 658, 676, 677 (first ed.).

a description of the things which are called by that name. I have already referred to the form of expression used in this chapter [1], and all I am able to infer as to its meaning is, that a delict is said to be the act of one man which causes damage to another, provided it be done intentionally, negligently, or imprudently. But, as I shall have occasion to shew hereafter, these expressions, if used to indicate what acts are delicts and what are not, are altogether inadequate, and to a great extent inappropriate or useless.

183.   I must also observe that even were the nature of *Delict or tort not the source of obligation.* delict and tort ever so clearly ascertained, it will not be exactly true to say that the secondary or sanctioning duty or obligation arises out of a delict, or out of a tort. As in the case of contract, the delict or tort will only be the occasion upon which the duty or obligation arises ; the existence and the nature of the duty or obligation depend entirely upon the will of the sovereign authority.

184.   Moreover, were the terms contract and delict ever *Obligations ex delicto are secondary only. Those ex contractu are primary.* so clearly defined, there is obviously this further objection to the classification, so common amongst lawyers of the French school, of obligations generally into those which arise from a contract, and those which arise from a delict.   The first branch of it has reference only to

---

[1] Supra, sect. 155.   The clauses of the Code Civil are as follows :—'Art. 1382. Tout fait quelconque de l'homme, qui cause à autrui un dommage, oblige celui par la faute duquel il est arrivé à le reparer. Art. 1383. Chacun est responsable du dommage qu'il a causé, non seulement par son fait, mais encore par sa négligence, ou par son imprudence.' It will be seen that I construe Art. 1383 as containing, by implication, a limitation on the extreme generality of Art. 1382, and that I translate ' par son fait' (somewhat boldly I admit, but I cannot understand what else is meant by it) by ' intentionally.'   Pothier's two definitions do not quite agree with the Code or with each other.   See Introduction Générale aux Coutumes, sect. 116 ; Traité des Obligations, sect. 116.   See also Les Codes Annotés de Sirey, par P. Gilbert, Paris, 1859, and infra, sect. 219, note.

primary duties or obligations : the second branch of it only to secondary or sanctioning ones. Nor is this at all a fanciful criticism. When duties or obligations are spoken of generally as arising, either out of contract, or out of delict, it is impossible to avoid seeing that, under this form of expression, it has been altogether forgotten that, behind the obligation which arises from the delict, and which is only a secondary or sanctioning one, there must always lie a primary duty or obligation, of which the delict is a breach ; and the nature of which must be always ascertained before it is possible to say whether or no a delict has occurred.

185. Lastly, the division is, in another respect, obviously incomplete. Whatever may be the idea which attaches to delict or tort, as opposed to contract, it is obvious that there are many duties and obligations which do not arise in any way out of contract; breaches of which are, nevertheless, not usually called delicts or torts. For instance, suppose certain taxes to be imposed by the sovereign authority, and these taxes (as is very often the case) to be farmed out to an individual, with a right to recover them by distress of goods. Neither the primary obligation to pay the taxes to the farmer, nor the secondary obligation to suffer the distress, will find any place in this classification. The omission to pay the tax would not, in the ordinary sense of the word, be called a delict, and the obligation to pay the tax certainly does not arise out of a contract. So too, in India, the obligation of a shareholder to repay to his co-shareholders the amount of Government revenue, which they, or either of them, have paid on his behalf, in order to prevent the estate being sold, has been declared not to be an obligation which arises out of contract. On the other hand, one would scarcely, in common language, describe this omission as a delict or tort.

Obligations may be neither ex contractu nor ex delicto.

186. The existence, indeed, of duties and obligations which cannot be said to result, either from a contract on the one hand, or from a tort or delict on the other, is acknowledged in rather a peculiar way, by speaking of duties and obligations which arise out of quasi contract, or out of quasi delict. This, however, is really only as much as to say, that there are certain obligations which we cannot make fall within either of our divisions; the events upon which they arise being admitted to be neither contracts nor delicts, but being represented to be either something like contracts, or something like delicts or torts; which, as Austin has pointed out, is merely creating a sink, into which every event which gives rise to an obligation, but which is neither a contract nor a delict, is thrown without discrimination [1].

187. We also generally find that authors, when treating of the nature of wrongs (that is, breaches of primary duties or obligations), divide them into wrongs, which are civil injuries, and wrongs which are crimes. But this division, though proper enough for some purposes, is based upon distinctions which are wholly unimportant when we are ascertaining liability. If in the present day this division points consistently to anything, it is not to any distinction in the primary duties and obligations which have been violated, but to the mode of procedure adopted to enforce the secondary duty or obligation, which arises on the breach of the primary one. If the court where the act is punishable be a court of criminal procedure, it is considered criminal, and is called a crime or an offence. But nevertheless, there is still some difficulty about distinguishing civil injuries and crimes upon this, as indeed upon any other principle. Courts exist, such

Civil injuries and crimes.

___
[1] Fragments, vol. ii. p. 945 (third edition).

as the court of petty sessions in England, and of the
inferior magistrates in India, of which the proceedings
are sometimes considered to be civil, sometimes to be
criminal, and sometimes intermediate between the two.
Thus proceedings to remove a pauper, or to get rid of
a private nuisance, are clearly civil; just as a summary
conviction for theft is clearly criminal ; but whether proceedings to compel a father to support his bastard son are
civil or criminal has been found somewhat difficult to
determine. The English law seems to treat them as
criminal, but very analogous proceedings in India have
been considered as civil. The French code divides all
breaches of duty or obligation which are not of a purely
civil nature into *crimes* (specially so called), *delicts* (using
in a narrower sense the same word as is also used generally to describe civil injuries), and *contraventions of
police ;* these are all comprised within the Penal Code, and
the latter class contains some matters which we should
class as civil injuries.

Origin of
distinction
between
civil injuries
and crimes.

188. Whilst, too, we find that in modern times the
division between civil injuries and crimes is fluctuating
and uncertain, we observe that in the earlier stages of
society, if it existed at all, it was based on entirely
different notions[1]. To exact for all injuries both to
person and property a payment in money to the person
injured appears to have been the first form of *legal*
liability for injuries to private persons, alike in Greece,
in Rome, and among the Teutonic tribes. The first
idea of criminal law, as distinguished from this, seems
to have grown out of the punishment by the sovereign
authority of offences directly against itself. And the
impulse to the more general development of criminal

[1] Maine's Ancient Law, ch. x. ; Kemble's Saxons in England,
ch. x.

law in modern times seems to be due, in this country,
to an extension of this last notion. It is supposed by
rather an odd fiction that by every offence the 'King's
peace' is disturbed, and his 'dignity' offended. And it
was formerly necessary in all cases that it should be so
stated in the indictment ; not only where acts of violence
had been committed, but even where the offence charged
was such as obtaining goods by false pretences, or selling
ale on a Sunday. Modern writers still attempt to preserve a somewhat similar notion, when they tell us that
civil injuries are an infringement of rights belonging to
individuals considered as individuals; whereas crimes are
breaches of public rights and duties belonging to the
whole community[1]. However, the examples given above
sufficiently shew that this distinction is not adhered to.

189. At other times the mental consciousness of
wrong on the part of the person who does the act
appears to be made the test of criminality. We are
often told that in order to commit a crime a person
must have a guilty mind. No doubt, too, there has been
a readiness to bring all acts, which are in the general
estimation of mankind *wicked*, within the criminal law.
But a very slight experiment will shew that neither is
this a test which has been consistently applied to distinguish civil injuries from crimes[2].

190. Moreover, all these terms and distinctions, founded
as they are upon differences, either in the occasion on
which duties and obligations are created, or upon the
mode in which they are enforced, are very likely to lead

Nature of
duties and
obligations
not depend-
ent on the
occasion of
their crea-
tion.

[1] Blackstone's Commentaries, vol. iv. p. 5; quoted in Broom's
Commentaries, p. 869 (first ed.).

[2] See Russell on Crimes, vol. i., whence it appears that an indictment will lie for neglecting to forward an election writ (ch. xvii.),
and for removing a dead body, however innocently (ch. xxxvii.).

one to suppose that the nature of duties and obligations,
either primary or secondary, is in some way dependent
thereon. But this is not so. For instance, the duty
I am under to abstain from acts, which would interfere
with the enjoyment of your property, may arise upon an
express contract between you and me, or may depend,
without any contract, solely on your right of ownership.
Certain rights with their corresponding duties and obligations do, indeed, for the most part arise upon contract ;
certain other rights with their corresponding duties and
obligations do, as it so happens, for the most part arise
independently of contract. Breaches also of primary
duties and obligations which are the subject of civil procedure are, as a fact, generally followed immediately by
consequences of one kind ; whilst breaches of primary
duties and obligations which are the subject of criminal
procedure are, as a fact, generally followed immediately
by consequences of another kind. But there is nothing
in this which is either necessary, or even constant. There
is hardly any duty or obligation usually arising upon
contract which might not arise independently of it ; and
a very large number of rights, with their corresponding
duties and obligations, arise partly upon contract, and
partly not ; indeed, we have seen how the attempt to
discriminate between duties and obligations by the occasion which creates them has completely failed. So we
shall see hereafter that the consequences of all breaches
of duty or obligation are in a great measure ultimately
the same, whether their consequences be civilly or criminally pursued.

No general
rules for
ascertaining
liability
exist in
jurispru-
dence.

　191. It is hardly necessary for me to remark on the
barrenness of the results thus far obtained—which are nevertheless all that I am able to glean from any of the usual
sources—as to the general nature of liability. Assuming

Savigny's analysis of the conception of contract to be accepted, and the meaning of the term to be well settled in law (which, by the way, is rather a liberal assumption), it may be said, subject still to the settlement of a few minor details, that the nature of obligations which result upon a contract is pretty well understood; and then, as I have before remarked, the question of liability is very nearly solved. But with regard to all liability which does not result from a true and proper contract, we have hitherto got nothing but a few very unsatisfactory distinctions and definitions.

192. Failing, therefore, codes or treatises on law, where we might expect to find the information we require prepared for us in a general form, we must turn to the actual practice of the law, and see how judges do, in fact, deal with the question of liability. For that question has to be determined by them every day; and it need hardly be insisted on, that every such determination presumes a law or rule in general terms upon which it is based; and if we could only extract all such rules, we should have solved, so far as it is capable of being solved, the question under consideration.

Questions of liability, how dealt with in practice.

193. I therefore proceed to examine the phrases in common use among lawyers, when they wish to give their reasons, why liability exists in some cases and not in others; and also the various terms by which they describe events which give rise to liability, and by which they distinguish events which do not give rise to it. I shall not, in so doing, advert any further to liability which results from a true and proper contract, as that has been, as I have shewn, treated by them after a more satisfactory method.

194. We generally find that those acts, which, when

considered with reference to the secondary obligation which results from them, we call torts, are, when considered with reference to the nature of the act itself, called **Injury.** injuries; and a good deal is made of this word 'injury,' as if it, in itself, told us a good deal about the matter. We are told over and over again, that in order that a man should be liable for any damage, on the ground that it is a tort, there must be injury. But what is injury? All we know of it is that it is the infringement of a right. I believe also that injury is for the most part used in the special sense of an infringement of one or other of those rights which relate to property, or personal security, or reputation. But what are those rights? I have never yet found them described even superficially. If we knew them, then we should also know the duties and obligations to which they correspond, and our difficulty would be solved.

Qualifying adverbs. 195. When something more definite than this is attempted, we generally find that the act or omission, which is said to be an injury, is qualified by some adverb which is apparently intended to indicate that which constitutes the required test of liability. Amongst such adverbs I find the following :—fraudulently, dishonestly, maliciously (avec préméditation, avec de guet-à-pens), knowingly, intentionally, wantonly, malignantly, rashly, negligently, wilfully, wickedly, imprudently, and clumsily (par malad-resse). So also I find such adverbs used as forcibly, with a strong hand, violently (avec violence et voies de fait), riotously, tumultuously, or in large numbers (par attroupe-ment). Again, for the same purpose I find such expressions made use of as wrongfully, feloniously, unlawfully, illegally, injuriously, and unjustly[1].

---

[1] Many of these adverbs also make their appearance in Codes, and other legislative productions, but I think they mostly originated

196. I have purposely selected these adverbs, as well from the descriptions of those acts relating to person, property, and reputation, which are called crimes, as from the descriptions of the similar acts, which are called delicts or torts, without any attempt at discrimination. For criminal liability, in almost all such matters, contains within it civil liability also, combined with some additional element; and it is chiefly as applied to acts relating to person, property, and reputation, that I am about to attempt to ascertain the meaning of these adverbs.

197. Considering these adverbs closely, it appears to me that they may be divided into three classes, which are indicated by the order in which I have enumerated them: as follows— *What these adverbs express.*

First, those which are, apparently, intended to express the condition of mind of the person who does the act.

Secondly, those which are, apparently, not intended to characterize the act simply as the occasion of a secondary or sanctioning obligation, or (to use a popular, though less correct expression) to characterize it simply as punishable, but which are intended to express what is commonly called an aggravation—that is to say, to mark the act, as giving rise to a special secondary or sanctioning obligation of a serious kind.

Thirdly, those which are, apparently, intended to express something, but really express nothing at all; being only so many different names for the very thing the nature of which we are trying to discover.

198. The terms of the second class can be of no assistance to us here. We are considering not the nature of

with judges. At any rate I have been desirous to gather together every mark of liability that can claim authority, from whatever source it may proceed.

H

the secondary duty or obligation which arises from the breach, but what constitutes the breach itself.

Mental element in definition of liability. 199.   The adverbs of the first class, therefore, are those from which we have to derive our conception of liability. These, though they all refer to the state of mind of the person at the point of time when his conduct has to be considered, do not all describe that state of mind from the same point of view.   There are certainly two—'knowingly' and 'intentionally'—which only describe a simple condition of mental consciousness, the exact nature of which I shall hereafter consider.   The rest, or most of the rest, combine with this (which I shall venture to call, for the sake of brevity, the purely mental element) a conception of another kind.   They more or less imply that the state of mind under consideration is, when tried by some standard which the author of the expression has in view, not what it ought to be.   What this standard is, it is extremely difficult to discover, but it is something in the nature of a moral standard.

Austin's investigation of it. 200.   What I have called the purely mental element in liability has been investigated by Austin; availing himself for this purpose of the prior labours of Locke[1] and Brown[2].   It is greatly to be regretted that Austin did not exhaust the subject of legal liability; but he has rendered, nevertheless, great service by clearing away a vast amount of preliminary difficulty.

201.   We must for the present suspend our judgment upon the question, how far the liability of men for their acts or omissions depends on the state of their mental

---

[1] Lect. xxii. p. 462 (third ed.).   He refers particularly to the chapter on 'Power' in the Essay on Human Understanding, Bk. II. ch. xxi.

[2] Lect. xviii. p. 425 (third ed.).   Brown's Enquiry into the Relation of Cause and Effect, particularly Part I. sect. 3.

consciousness at the point of time when their conduct has
to be considered. There is no chance of correctly estimating this, until we have formed definite conceptions of
the meaning of the various terms by which that state is
expressed. But these terms also presume that men have
a certain control over their conduct, and (in part at least)
describe the state of mind, in reference to the determination which has been taken, as to how that control shall be
exercised. It is, therefore, necessary also to investigate
the nature of this control.

202. Austin, in his Eighteenth Lecture[1], has drawn our attention to the fact that, if we examine ourselves, we perceive that we can exercise control over certain parts of our bodies. The moment (he says) I conceive the wish, certain parts of my body will change their state for certain other states, provided the body be not diseased, and the desired change be not impeded by any external obstacle. This control (he observes) does not extend to all parts of the body; not even to all parts of the body which do continually change their states; for the motion of the heart is not affected by a wish conceived that it should stop or quicken[2]. So the passage of an electric current, or contact with a galvanic battery, will cause motions of my arms and legs over which I have no control. Nor does this control extend to the mind: in other words, my mind will not change its state for any other state when and so soon as I desire it. Try (as Austin says) to recall an absent thought or to banish a present one, and you will find it frequently a long and troublesome matter; and sometimes indeed that it is impossible, although your mind is perfectly sane, and there is no external obstacle[3].

Limited control over our bodily movements.

203. Limited, however, as is our control even over our bodily motions, it is only through our bodily motions

Only through our bodily move-

---

[1] Third ed. p. 423.   [2] Ib. p. 425.   [3] Ib. p. 426.

ments that we can perform acts. that we can do an act. There is no conceivable means by which a silent and motionless man can do an act. He must put in motion the muscles of his mouth to speak, or of his limbs to move. Strictly speaking, therefore, the beginning and end of human control over acts is this— there being certain bodily movements which we can immediately produce at pleasure, we may wish any one of those movements, and it will immediately follow.

Bodily movements, how connected with wishes which precede them and consequences which follow them. 204. We very rarely, however, put any parts of our bodies in motion merely for the sake of producing that motion. The wish which immediately produces the bodily movement is generally the result of an antecedent wish to attain a certain object, but which wish is not, like the wish for a bodily movement, satisfied directly it is conceived. Thus I pass near a fruit tree ; I am hungry, and I wish to eat of its fruit. My wish to eat of the fruit prompts me to go through a variety of bodily movements which I expect will ultimately satisfy that wish. I raise my arm to seize the fruit, I pull it from the branch on which it grows, I bring it to my mouth, I bite it and chew it, and at last swallow it. All these bodily movements were wished, but they were wished, not as an end, but as means to an end ; namely, to appease the painful sensation of hunger.

205 [1]. The wishes which produce bodily motions as, and so soon as, they are wished, or, in other words, which consummate themselves, are sometimes called, for the sake of distinction, volitions. The wishes which generally precede volitions, and which are fulfilled by means of these bodily movements, are called motives [2].

Series of motives and means may be indefinitely extended. 206. The series of volitions, and of motives antecedent to volitions, and the series of means which lead ultimately to the end which I have in view, may be indefinitely extended. Thus, in the case just put, the fruit may be out of my

---

[1] Austin, Lect. xviii. third ed. p. 426.   [2] Ib. p. 428.

reach, and then a wish will arise for a ladder by which I may get at it ; this wish will cause me to go and search for a ladder, and I shall conceive volitions for such motions of my limbs, as will carry me to a place where I think it likely that I shall find one ; for such further motions of my limbs as will have the effect of placing the ladder, when found, upon my shoulders, will bring me back to the tree, place the ladder in position, and mount me on it. Again, the desire for the fruit may not be a desire to eat it, but to carry it away to a distant country and there to sell it ; and I may have come from that country on purpose to look for this fruit, prompted by a desire for gain ; and for that purpose may have made a long and difficult journey lasting many months. My wish for the money which I shall gain may have been prompted by a previous wish to make a fortune, in order to enable me to marry, or to buy a particular estate, or to attain any other object of human desire. And it is obvious that this series of wishes and means may be carried on in either direction ad infinitum.

207. The words ' motive ' and ' end ' are not applied exclusively to the extremes of the series ; but they are applied to the extremes of any part of the series, which at the time may be under contemplation. Thus, suppose our traveller in search of his fruit desires to penetrate into a certain country where he thinks it is to be found ; but being opposed in his attempts to land there, he resorts to violence in order to get rid of that opposition ; and in so doing kills one of his opponents. Here, the people of the country, not knowing wherefore he came, and only adverting to this part of his proceedings, would speak of his wish to land as his *motive* for killing his opponent, of landing as the *end* which he had in view, and of his killing his opponent as the *means* to that end ; though

in reality his ultimate end was still a long way off, and his primary motive commenced much earlier.

208 [1]. Any one of a series of events which are regarded as the result of our bodily movements is called an 'act.' Perhaps in strictness the word 'act' ought to be confined to those bodily movements which immediately follow volitions; but common language and convenience justify the extension of the term to the consequences of those bodily movements. Indeed the use of the word is more comprehensive still; for not only is each of the events which results from our bodily movements called an act, but the whole series of events resulting in the end is spoken of as an act; the successive steps of the operation not being enumerated. Thus, if by a long and complicated plot I succeed in procuring your death, I am said to murder you; the whole series of events which lead to your death is called a murder; and that murder is spoken of as my act.

209. When I thus speak of your death as my act, I consider your death as if it resulted from my exclusive agency. But it is very rare that an event is, strictly speaking, the result of the act of one single individual. Very likely your death would not have occurred, but for circumstances over which I had no control. Thus I may place a cup of poison where it is probable that you will come; and I may so place it as to make it probable that, if you come, you will take it up and swallow it. But I may trust entirely to accident, or to your known habits to bring you to that place. Nevertheless, if you should come to the place, and swallow the poison and die, your death would be said to be caused by my act. Even if any one else had by his act caused you to come to that place, your death would

[1] Austin, Lect. xix. pp. 417, 432 (third ed.).

still be said to be my act. Thus we see that in this
way the same event might be spoken of as the act of
two different persons.

210 [1]. If we consider further any case of motive, voli- States of
mind of a
person who
does an act.
tion, bodily movement, and consequences of that bodily
movement, we shall perceive the following distinctions.
Suppose yourself again under the tree wishing for the
fruit, which is beyond your reach. For the moment we
need not consider any ultimate object you may have in
view, but may take the desire to obtain the fruit as your
motive, and the obtaining it as your end. In order to
get it, you pick up a stone and throw it at the fruit,
hoping thereby to knock it off the branch to which it
is attached, so that it may fall within your reach. You
wish that from the act of throwing the stone certain consequences should follow, and you think it likely that
they will follow; in other words, you wish to bring the
fruit within your reach, and you think it likely that by
throwing the stone you will do so.

211. Again, at the same time that you throw the
stone at the fruit, you see that you are also throwing it
in the direction of an open space of ground, where people
are constantly passing and repassing; and though you
have no wish to cause hurt to any one of those persons,
you think it likely that you may miss the fruit and
do so.

Or, again, you may see that you are throwing the stone
in the direction of that place; but you may conclude, after
thinking about it, that the stone is not likely to fly to so
great a distance, or that no one will just at that moment be
passing there.

Or you may see the place and the people, but it may
never occur to you to consider, whether the stone which

---

[1] Austin, Lect. xx. pp. 433, 439 sqq.; Lect. xxi. pp. 449 sqq.

you throw at the fruit may in any way injure any one of them.

Or you may not take the trouble to look round and see, whether there are any persons in the direction in which you are throwing the stone or not.

212. We see that there are here six cases :—

1. The case in which you contemplate the event (bringing the fruit to the ground) as a consequence of your act which is likely to happen ; you wish the event may happen, and you wish it as an end.

2. The case in which you contemplate the event (hitting the fruit) as a consequence of your act which is likely to happen, and you wish that it may happen ; but you wish it, not as an end, but as means to an end.

3. The case in which you contemplate the event (hitting a passer by) as an event which is likely to happen, but you do not wish it to happen, either as an end, or as means to an end.

4. The case in which you contemplate the event (hitting a passer by) as a consequence of your act, but you conclude, on insufficient grounds, that it is not likely to happen.

5. The case in which you do not contemplate the event (hitting a passer by) as a consequence of your act, although you are aware of the circumstances which render that event likely.

6. The case in which you do not contemplate the event (hitting a passer by) as a consequence of your act, because you do not take the trouble to observe the circumstances which render that event likely.

213. I have taken a different case from that taken by Austin [1], in order to shew that this analysis will apply equally well to any case of the kind ; and also

---

[1] See Lecture xix. p. 434 (third ed.).

because it is necessary for me to carry the illustration somewhat further than he does. His example, as far as it goes, is much the neater of the two.

214. Though I have enumerated six cases, they do not correspond to as many different states in the mind of the actor. In the first three cases these states are (for our present purpose) identical. Following Austin's example [1], I describe them by one name—*intention;* that is to say, I include under that name the three cases in which the consequences are expected [2], whether they be wished or no. Upon the same authority, I call the state of mind in the fourth case, *rashness;* and, in the fifth and sixth, *heedlessness:* including under the last term both the case in which the consequences are disregarded, and the case in which they are not known, for want of observation.

Intention, rashness, and heedlessness.

215. Next, instead of considering the state of mind of a person who does an act, let us consider the state of mind of a person who omits to do an act. A man does not provide himself with sufficient money to support his wife and children. He may have spent all his money expressly in order that it might not be forthcoming for that purpose; and he may have done this, either as an

States of mind of person who abstains from an act.

---

[1] Lect. xix. p. 436.

[2] I use the word 'expected' without any reference to the degree of probability, to cover all cases in which the consequences have been contemplated, and not rejected as unlikely. If it were necessary to distinguish between these degrees of probability, we should have to invent corresponding terms to describe states of mental consciousness intermediate between intention and rashness, for which no names at present exist. But I know of no case in which liability is in any way dependent on them. At first sight it would seem to be made so by the distinction between murder and culpable homicide contained in the Indian Penal Code (sections 209, 300). But it appears to me that this distinction does not really depend on the difference in degrees of probability. (See App. A.)

end, in order to injure his family, or as means, in order
to throw the burden of their support upon some other
person. Or he may have spent his money in pleasure,
knowing and recollecting that this would be the result,
but indifferent to it. Or he may have spent all he had,
because he rashly expected that a relation would die and
leave him money. Or, lastly, he may have been utterly
careless, and never have thought about the matter
at all.

216. We see, therefore, that we may put the same
alternatives of intention, rashness, and heedlessness in the
one case as in the other. Whatever, therefore, be the
nature of the event which gives rise to liability, whether
it be the doing of an act (breach of a negative obligation),
or the not doing of an act (breach of a positive obligation),
the state of mind of the party liable is described by one
or other of these terms.

217. So far, therefore, as regards that element exclusively, which I have termed the purely mental one, it seems
to me that the adverbs of the first class enumerated above
must more or less accurately express, either intention,
rashness, or heedlessness ; these three comprising, according to Austin's analysis, which has never yet been dis-
puted, all the possible states of mind of a person doing
or abstaining from an act.

Negligence:
what it
means.

218. In my separate examination, with the help of
this analysis, of the adverbs enumerated in the above list,
I shall confine myself to those most frequently in use,
and to which something like a precise meaning has been
attributed. By far the most important of all of them is
that which expresses, that the person, when he does or
omits the act, is negligent. A whole chapter of the topics
most frequently discussed in litigation turns entirely upon
the word 'negligence'. Books have been written on it,

and hundreds of reported cases are wholly taken up with
the discussion of it.   It is, therefore, of the last importance thoroughly to examine it.

219[1].   When negligence expresses a state of the mind   How op-
                                                          posed to
(for, as I shall shew hereafter, it does not always express intention.
a state of the mind at all), it is opposed to intention ;
and it expresses without distinction either of the two
conditions of mind which we have called rashness and
heedlessness, but more generally the latter.   It is also
used with reference to the not doing as well as the
doing of an act.   Thus it is said that death, ensuing
in consequence of the malicious omission of a duty, will
be murder, but that death, ensuing in consequence of
the omission of a duty which arose from negligence,
will be only manslaughter[2].   By malicious[3] omission
of a duty I understand to be meant, that we omit to
do an act which we are commanded to do, that we
advert to the consequences of the omission, and that
we expect these consequences to ensue, though not necessarily desiring those consequences, either as an end, or
as means to an end.   By negligent omission of a duty
I understand to be meant, that we omit to do an act
which we are commanded to do, without adverting to the
consequences, or, if adverting to them, expecting on insufficient grounds that they will not ensue.   So we find
it said, that negligence alone is not a sufficient cause of
action without a breach of duty[4], which I understand to

---

[1] Austin, Lect. xx. p. 444 (third ed.).

[2] The distinction between murder and manslaughter is thus drawn
in the case of the Queen against Hughes, by Lord Campbell delivering the considered judgment of five judges.   See Dearsley and Bell's
Crown Cases, p. 249.

[3] See infra, sect. 226.

[4] This is the language of Sir William Erle delivering the judgment of seven judges in the case of Dutton against Powles ; see Law

mean—that where consequences ensue upon an act or
omission which we did not intend, then it is not sufficient
that we heedlessly disregarded those consequences, or
rashly expected that they would not ensue; for in
order to constitute liability there must be disobedience
to a positive command.

Later expo-
sitions of its
meaning.

220.   But in the latest and most authoritative exposi-
tions of the term negligence, we find that it is declared to
describe, not the actual state of mind of the party who
does or does not do the act; not the absence from his
mind of certain ideas which might have led him into
a different course of action or inaction, which state of
mind he might have avoided, and which ideas he might
have recalled by a proper use of his faculties—not in short
that which I understand by the word heedlessness; not,
again, the hasty and ill-grounded expectation that results
will not follow, which I understand to be expressed by
rashness; but the absence of care, of diligence, and even
of skill; and moreover, not the absence of that care,
diligence, or skill, which the party under the circumstances was able to exercise, but of that care, diligence, or
skill, which under the circumstances the law requires.   So
that whatever be the exact nature of the qualities to
which we ascribe these names, the *actual* state of mind
of the person is not at all what is considered.   Thus
it is said that the ' action for negligence proceeds upon

Journal Reports, vol. xxxi. Queen's Bench, p. 191.   We shall see
hereafter how small a place this leaves to negligence.   Compare the
observations of Sirey on the Code Civil: ' Dans l'application de
l'article 1382 et pour savoir quand il y a *faute*, il faut se souvenir
que la loi entend par là l'action de faire une chose qu'on n'avait
par le droit de faire.' ·It is curious to observe how regularly lawyers
in every country, when pushed upon any of these terms, fall back
upon the barren generality, that they express what the law forbids;
quod non jure factum.   (See Digest, Book ix. tit. 2. sect. 5. par. 1).

the idea of an obligation towards the plaintiff to use care, and a breach of that obligation to the plaintiff's injury[1].' And more explicitly still, 'a person who undertakes to do some work for reward to an article, must exercise the care of a skilled workman ; and '—not his inadvertence, or even his neglect to use such skill as he possesses, but—'the absence of *such* care is negligence.'

221. It is obvious in these cases, particularly the last, which is the language of a judge celebrated for the acuteness and accuracy of his legal perceptions, that the term 'negligence' is used to express something wholly independent of the state of mind of the person whose act or omission is under consideration. The workman's negligence consists, not in heedlessness of the act he is doing or omitting, or of its consequences; not in his omitting to use all the care of which he is capable; but in his omitting to use the care which a skilled workman would use, whether he is capable of it or not. It is simply the omission to perform a positive duty, and in this particular case a positive duty which arises upon a contract. As the phrase is, the workman, when he undertakes the work, *spondet peritiam artis;* he promises to use the ordinary skill of his craft.

Modern interpretations of the term negligence.

222. The latter use of the term negligence is perfectly in accordance with ordinary language. We constantly speak

---

[1] This is the language of Lord Penzance in his considered judgment delivered in the case of Swan against The North British Australasian Company ; see Law Journal Reports. New Series, vol. xxxi. Exchequer, p. 437. The next quotation is from the judgment of Mr. Justice Willes, in the case of Grill against The General Iron Screw Colliery Company ; see Law Reports, Common Pleas, vol. i. p. 612. Of course with a shifting term like 'negligence' it would be possible to find it used in a variety of shades of meaning, but I have confined myself to the passages most frequently quoted in the current treatises, as containing the accepted definitions of negligence.

of a person who breaks a positive duty as neglecting
that duty, intending thereby only to express that he
has not performed the act which he was commanded
to perform, without any regard to the state of mind
which preceded the non-performance. And as a question
of terms it is only necessary to be careful to avoid sliding,
without perceiving it, from this meaning of the word negligence into that other meaning of it, where it expresses
rashness or inadvertence; as so easily happens when a word
has several meanings not wholly disconnected.

Negligence
in the later
sense of no
use in ascer-
taining
liability.

223. But then we must consider what is the result of
this second definition of negligence. What does it tell us
to say, that a man is liable for negligence, in this sense
of the word negligence? As it appears to me, for our
present purpose, just nothing at all. To say that a man is
liable for negligence, and to define negligence as the omission to do that which the law requires, only brings us
back by a very circuitous route to that which we have
above said ought to be the first step in the inquiry,
namely, what is the duty which the law imposes upon us.

224. Now, as I have already pointed out, in a very
large class of cases the discussion of liability turns exclusively upon the question, whether or no there has been
negligence. If then it is true, that the word negligence
in these discussions means no more than the later authorities to which I have referred represent it to mean, then
it is obvious that this discussion simply revolves in a
circle. What is a tort? The breach of a duty or obligation. What constitutes such a breach? Negligence.
What is negligence? The breach of an obligation. In
this way we shall never arrive at a result.

225. I do not mean to say, either of negligence, or of
the other similar terms, that they do not give us any information as to what the obligation is, in some cases. I

only wish now to get rid of the self-deception that we can
get at the obligation simply by talking about what constitutes negligence. I shall state hereafter, what I consider
to be the result of this analysis of terms in common use.

226. Malice is another term very frequently used as if Malice.
it expressed something from which liability may be inferred. It points directly to the state of mind of the
person, and probably it originally expressed pretty nearly
the same thing as malevolence, that is, the motive (in the
estimation of the speaker a bad one) which induces a party
to act, or abstain from acting. It has been thence transferred to intention, and in the best known definitions[1] of
malice it is scarcely distinguishable from intention; and it
is applied, not only to cases where the consequences of an
act are desired as an end, but where they are desired as
means, and even to cases where they are merely adverted to
and expected, without being desired at all. When used in
this extended sense, the badness of the motive which
prompts the act is altogether lost sight of, for it is obvious
that a man may even desire to kill, as an end, or as means
to an end, or he may do an act which he knows to be likely
to cause death, without desiring to kill, from motives
which are altogether good, and yet be guilty of a crime.
Cases of mistaken patriotism, of excess in the use of the
right of self-defence, or in the exercise of power by con-
stables and other persons similarly situated, afford very
frequent examples of this kind.

227. The difficulty of obtaining a clear idea of what 'Malice in
is meant by the term malice is also greatly increased by   fact' and
the use of the phrase 'malice in law.' If, for instance, I   'malice in
erroneously suspect you to be a thief, and I communicate   law.'

---

[1] See Russell on Crimes, by Greaves, fourth ed., vol. i. p. 668 note,
whence it appears that the accepted definition of malice is 'a wrongful act done intentionally without just or lawful excuse.'

my suspicions to another, not in any way intending to
injure you, or thinking it likely that I shall injure you,
but because I, erroneously, think it my duty to do so,
there can, of course, be no malice in any reasonable
sense of the word. And this is admitted in such cases by
saying there is no 'malice in fact.' Nevertheless lawyers
persist in such cases in saying that there is ' malice in
law.' Obviously the state of the law which they approve,
and which they wish to apply, is that of a primary obligation not to publish statements injurious to the character
of another, except in certain specified cases, of which that
under consideration is *not* one. They desire that this obligation should be in no way dependent on my belief as to
the truth of my statements, or on my desire or expectation that you may be injured by them. Nevertheless, the
forms of procedure still assume the contrary; you are
bound to state that I acted maliciously; and after it
has been most carefully inquired into and ascertained that
there was no malice in the matter, the judges still hold
me liable by telling me that there was ' malice in law.'
What, of course, this really means is, that there are
circumstances under which I am liable for false statements affecting your character independently of malice,
but it would be far better, and save endless confusion, if,
instead of doing this by interposing the phantom called
' malice in law,' we said so plainly. To arrive at our
point by this circuitous route is just as if the court,
desiring to relieve a debtor from the obligation to pay
a debt, were to tell him he would be considered as having
paid it if he sent his creditor a cheque drawn in full form
on his bankers for no pounds, no shillings, and no pence.

Other similar cases.   228. We meet with many other similar cases; thus
we have legal or constructive fraud as distinguished from
actual fraud—a most embarrassing term; notice in law,

or constructive notice, as distinguished from actual notice. Any one acquainted with the history of English law knows exactly how this has occurred. To have said that malice, or fraud, or notice, were not necessary, in cases where they had been generally thought necessary, would have been too much like an avowed innovation. For though it is, as I have shewn above, a duty imposed upon English judges, within certain limits, to make new laws, it is against the tradition of their office ever to avow it. By saying, therefore, that there is malice in law, or fraud in law, they pretend that there is malice, or fraud, or whatever else they think unnecessary, when there is really none at all.

229. Knowledge, or, as it is barbarously called, the 'scienter,' is frequently made the criterion of liability. But it is generally very difficult to ascertain what sort of knowledge is referred to. Thus, in one of the very few attempts which the legislature has made to define offences with precision[1], we find it laid down that a man is guilty of culpable homicide who does an act with the intention of causing death, or with the intention of causing such bodily injury as is likely to cause death, or with the knowledge that he is likely by such act to cause death. Now if by 'knowledge' is here meant, the condition of mind in which a man knows death to be likely, and adverts to it, then knowledge is identical with intention, and the phrase in question is superfluous. But if, on the other hand, a man is to be considered as having knowledge of all that he has power to recall to his mind, if he adverted to it, then the definition of murder would be extended in a most alarming manner. Any heedless act would render a man guilty of that crime ; for heedlessness of necessity includes knowledge to this extent—that a man cannot be said to

---

[1] Indian Penal Code, sect. 299. See App.

I

disregard consequences, which he would not have expected even if he had adverted to them.

<small>When important.</small>

230. Of course knowledge of a fact may be of very great importance, as evidence, in determining liability, and also because the nature of many primary duties and obligations is such, that they are only imposed upon us when a certain state of facts has been brought to our knowledge, or, as it is technically termed, upon our receiving notice. Thus, if I have a cow which I am driving along the road, and it runs at you and injures you, I am generally not liable; but if it has been brought to my knowledge that the cow has a propensity to run at people, or, as Lord Hale puts it, 'if I have notice of the quality of the beast,' then I am liable.

<small>Dishonesty.</small>

231. Dishonesty is a word a good deal used in some modern legislation. As far as I am able to discover, it signifies the state of mind in which a man knows, and adverts to the fact that he is committing, and, therefore, intends to commit, a breach of the law.

<small>Wantonness.</small>

232. Wantonness is used, as far as I can gather, to express those cases in which consequences are desired as an end, but the motive to the act is not one of the ordinary passions of revenge, or lust, or avarice, or the like; but rather (as the phrase is) the love of mischief for mischief's sake. Its use, as an expression which characterises liability, has no doubt arisen from the confusion between motives and intention, which we have already noticed in the case of malice.

<small>Fraud.</small>

233. Fraud, though it is a term frequently used in such a way as to suggest that it is a test of liability, has not, as far as I am aware, been authoritatively defined. Bentham[1], however, who generally took very considerable pains to ascertain the precise meaning

[1] See Bowring's edition of Collected Works, vol. vi. p. 292 n.

of terms, thinks it embraces the idea of falsehood or
mendacity. And I understand falsehood to be the
moral characteristic which, after much debate, has been
decided to be necessary in order to constitute liability for
fraud. Nevertheless, say the books, to constitute fraud it
is not necessary to shew that the parties making the
assertion knew it to be untrue ; it is enough that the
person making it did not believe it to be true[1]. It is difficult to understand a distinction founded on the difference
between knowledge and belief. One can easily understand a rash assertion, assumed to be true on insufficient
grounds, or a heedless assertion, made without considering
at all whether it is true or not ; and there are not wanting
indications that want of care in making assertions may,
under some circumstances, render a man liable. But
such statements could hardly be called false or mendacious.
Moreover the distinction which philosophers draw between *believing* and *knowing* is very subtle, and by no
means universally recognised. Sir William Hamilton
has said that knowledge is a certainty founded upon in-
tuition, belief is a certainty founded upon feeling ; but
James Mill applies the term belief to every species of
conviction[2].

234. What I think was intended is this. When a
man makes a direct assertion, he very often impliedly also

[1] This is not the exact language of Lord Wensleydale, who was
the author of this distinction ; but the distinction is (as I understand it) made to turn, both in the original and in the quotations of
it, upon the difference between knowledge and belief. See the
judgment of Lord Wensleydale in the case of Taylor against
Ashton, in Meeson and Welsby's Reports, vol. xi. p. 415 ; Smith's
Leading Cases, sixth ed. vol. ii. p. 94 ; Addison on Torts, third ed.
p. 828.

[2] See James Mill's Analysis of the Human Mind, ed. 1869, p.
343, note by J. S. Mill ; and An Examination of Sir William
Hamilton's Philosophy, by J. S. Mill, chap. v.

asserts that he has, to the best of his ability, exercised his judgment, and believes the assertion to be true. Thus, if I say, 'Mr. A has a good constitution,' there is here a direct statement of fact concerning A's health, and also, in many cases, as for instance, if the question were put to me by an office about to insure A's life, an implied statement, that I have exercised my best judgment in the matter, and have come to that conclusion. This implied statement will be mendacious, should I not have given the matter any careful consideration; or should I have considered it and not come to any conclusion; or should I have considered it, and not come to that conclusion which my statement involves.

235. Whilst discussing the various terms which have been used to express liability, I will advert to two phrases in common use, which are sometimes placed in apparent opposition to the terms which we have been considering. These two phrases express not quite the same thing, but things nearly similar. Thus it is said of certain acts that the question of liability is not one of negligence, but that a man does them *at his peril;* so also it is said in certain cases that he is liable, not for fraud, but because there is a *warranty.* What I take to be aimed at in the first of these two phrases is, that there is some act which the law does not forbid, some act from which there is no primary duty or obligation to abstain, but for which, if a man does it and harm ensues, he will be liable. For instance, a man is said to accumulate water in a reservoir on his land at his peril; which apparently means that it is not unlawful for the landowner to accumulate water in the reservoir, but if the reservoir bursts and the water floods his neighbour's land, he must make him compensation. I have some doubt whether this is the true view of the law; and whether a man is not generally prohibited from doing that which is in

Doing a thing at peril.

fact dangerous; though of course it is very often impossible
to discover the danger till after the event has happened.
But, even if he is not, it would only come to this; that as
regards certain acts the primary duty or obligation is not to
abstain from them, but only to compensate persons who
are damaged by them. It is in this view that the duty or
obligation in the case above put has been often compared
to that which is expressly undertaken by an insurer.

236. A warranty, properly speaking, is in form an Warranty.
undertaking that certain events will happen, or will not
happen; have happened, or have not happened; but it is in
reality a promise to make compensation for the loss occa-
sioned by their happening or not happening. Such a
warranty is a contract; the obligation is one which arises
on the agreement of the parties; and such contracts are
very often entered into as ancillary, or supplemental to
contracts of sale, or other similar transactions. But the
word 'warranty' is not confined exclusively to transactions which are properly called contracts. Whenever
it is incumbent upon a person, from any reason whatever,
to take upon himself the consequences, should a statement which he makes not be true, he is said to warrant
the truth of the statement; whether this duty or obligation be imposed by contract between the parties, or
in any other manner. And when it is said that a party
is liable for a breach of warranty, as distinguished from
saying that he is liable for a fraudulent representation,
I understand it to be affirmed that there is some primary
obligation upon him, not only to state nothing except
that which he believes to be true, but also to take the
consequences of stating anything which in fact is not true.

237. Upon a review of this analysis of the meaning of Terms which
the terms, which are in common use to express what con- express the
state of

stitutes liability, I think it is quite clear that they are only legitimately used as a test of liability, so far as they are contained in the command itself which expresses the primary duty or obligation, said to have been broken. Until, therefore, the exact expressions of these duties and obligations have been determined by the legislature, or ascertained by judicial authority, we cannot say with precision how far this is the case. So far as regards most of those duties and obligations, breaches of which are the subject of procedure in civil courts, we shall probably find that the liability (which I may call civil liability) depends, not upon whether the consequences were intended, or even contemplated by the party whose conduct is to be considered; still less upon whether or no that conduct conforms to any moral standard; but upon whether a command has been obeyed, which either in absolute terms requires certain acts or omissions, or is qualified by being restricted to acts or omissions which are unreasonable, imprudent, unskilled, dishonest, or the like. I must not set a foot or drop a twig upon your land; I must not lay my little finger upon your person. And whether I do so advertently or inadvertently, intentionally or heedlessly, is of no importance. If the trespass, or assault, is my act, I am liable to you for it; the primary duty or obligation being simply to abstain from doing such an act. When, in consequence of our being brought into contact, as by employment, or invitation, or as fellow workmen, or fellow travellers, or the like, many acts which would have been before wholly prohibited, now become lawful under certain conditions. Hence our relative duties and obligations come to assume a more complex form; and when, as happens in most cases, instead of a simple duty or obligation to abstain from the act, there is a duty or obligation to bring to the doing of it a due

amount of care, skill, diligence, prudence, or the like; then
it is the absence of this care, skill, diligence, or prudence,
which determines the liability. Still, therefore, the test of
liability is not the actual condition of mind of the person
whose conduct is being considered; the inquiry is not
whether he brought to bear all the care, skill, diligence
and prudence of which under the circumstances he was
capable; but whether the care, skill, diligence, or prudence
which he brought to bear, comes up to that standard, which
under the circumstances the law requires. The *law* never
gets nearer than 'the care of a skilled workman,' 'the
prudence of a man guided by those considerations which
ordinarily regulate human affairs[1],' 'a reasonable amount
of diligence,' 'proper skill,' and so forth.

238. But where a command is expressed in terms no
more definite than to require that a man's conduct shall
conform to what is ordinary or reasonable (and I am unable even by suggestion to push the law into terms of
greater precision), then the test of conformity to this
standard is in the breasts of those persons who form the
tribunal which has to decide upon the liability.

239. Moreover, whilst an act, forbearance, or omission
is frequently an occasion of liability, without reference
either to the actual state of mind of the party who acts,
forbears or omits, or its moral quality, neither the actual
state of mind, nor its moral quality will ever alone determine the liability. A particular application of this principle
is expressed in the rule which we have already referred to

*Never alone
sufficient to
determine
liability.*

---

[1] See the judgment of Mr. Baron Alderson in the case of Blyth
against The Birmingham Waterworks Company, reported in the
Law Journal Reports, vol. xxv. Exchequer, p. 212. It is adopted
by Mr. Justice Brett in his judgment in the case of Smith against
The London and North-Western Railway Company, Law Reports,
Common Pleas, vol. v. p. 102.

for the purpose of illustrating one of the meanings of the term negligence[1]. However malignant may be the motives which influence my conduct ; however disastrous may be the consequences which I expect to result from it ; however rash or heedless it may be ; I shall not be liable unless I have transgressed certain limits ; which limits, if we are strangers, are marked out by those same primary duties and obligations to abstain altogether from certain acts before referred to, the breach whereof alone, without any further consideration, renders me liable ; and which, if we are related, are marked out by the relation. I have a fine spring of water on my land. For some years I have allowed it to run off in the direction of a neighbouring village, the inhabitants of which have come to depend on it mainly for their supply of water ; from the most malignant motives, and hoping and expecting thereby to bring famine and sickness into the village, I dam up the stream in that direction, and turn it into another, where it is entirely useless to them. Am I or am I not liable? The answer depends simply on whether the inhabitants of the village have gained a right to the water ; in other words, whether I am under a primary duty or obligation to abstain from any act which deprives them of it. If they have not gained that right, and I have not incurred that duty or obligation, I am not answerable under the law. If they have gained that right, then, however useless the stream may be to them ; though my object was to supply another village which was perishing for want of water ; though I may even have been misled by a scientific opinion that the supply of water was sufficient for both villages—I shall still be liable.

240. So in the questions which so frequently arise between persons related to each other as master and

---

[1] Supra, sect. 219, ad finem.

servant. The servant may be exposed by the master to great danger which might be avoided, yet, if the servant knew of the dangerous nature of the employment, the master is not liable for any accident that may happen. Here it would be difficult, on moral grounds, to defend the conduct of the master in thus exposing his servant to danger, even with his own assent; and, as the master ex hypothesi knows of the danger, he must at least disregard the consequences, if he does not intend them. What draws the line is the master's duty as defined by the law. It is not the legal duty of the master to preserve his servant from risk in all cases in which it is immoral to expose him to it; nor is the master made liable either because he expects, or rashly hopes to avoid, or heedlessly disregards, the consequences of the exposure; the law simply makes it his duty to take certain precautions to preserve his servant from risk, when the risk is one which he knows of, but which his servant does not [1].

241. The terms which mark, independently of its moral quality, the state of mind of the party supposed to be liable, are very often legitimately used in ascertaining what is called criminal liability; that is, in ascertaining the liability which arises from breaches of duties and obligations, which are the subject of criminal procedure. As I have before remarked, the same general duty or obligation may be enforced by a criminal, and also by a civil sanction; but in such a case the criminal sanction is not generally applied to all breaches of the duty or obligation,

In what cases these terms most frequently useful.

[1] See and compare the cases of Riley against Baxendale, Exchequer Reports, vol. vi. p. 445; Paterson against Wallace, Macqueen's Scotch Appeals, vol. i. p. 751; Seymour against Maddox, Queen's Bench Reports, vol. xvi. p. 332; and Skipp against The Eastern Counties Railway, Exchequer Reports, vol. ix. p. 226. The comparison and analysis of the judgments in these cases is an instructive exercise.

but only to certain kinds ; and it is just these kinds which such terms are used to mark. And as there are criminal sanctions as well as civil sanctions, so also there are different kinds of criminal sanctions or punishments ; and the law not unfrequently makes liability to different kinds of punishment depend on the state of mind of the person charged : in other words, the terms which mark this state are used to distinguish crimes from civil injuries, and also to distinguish the different species of crimes. I drive in the street without taking that amount of care which the law requires every one to take, and without exercising that degree of skill which the law requires every one to exercise who drives in the street, and thereby inadvertently kill a man ; I am liable to pay damages to his family. I drive over him intending to kill him ; I am guilty of murder. I carelessly leave my child without food ; I am liable to be imprisoned for doing so. I leave him without food intending that he should thereby die ; I am liable to be hung. I strike a blow intending to cause grievous hurt ; I am liable to one punishment. I strike a blow intending to cause hurt, but not grievous hurt ; I am liable to another. I strike a blow which I ought not to strike, but without intending to hurt, and I am liable to a third.

The primary duty or obligation must always be determined. 241 *a.* For any other purpose these terms are almost entirely useless. Whether or no we are liable, does not generally depend upon our state of mind when we act or abstain from acting ; it does not depend on our motives, nor does it depend on our intention, rashness, or heedlessness ; it depends on the act or the omission to act. When pressed, therefore, we are obliged, as we see has been done in the case of negligence, to explain away these terms in a manner, which only throws us back upon the original and inevitable inquiry—what is that

which the law bids or forbids us to do?—and leaves that
inquiry unsolved. But it cannot remain so. Until that
inquiry is solved it is useless to attempt to answer the
first question of liability—has a primary duty or obligation
been broken? Do whatever you will, not a single lawsuit
can be brought to a termination until this question be
answered. The answer to it may be assumed or admitted,
but it must be given in every case; and, in so far as it is
a proposition of law, in abstract terms. The answer to this
question is the law which every tribunal has to administer;
which the judge must lay down to the jury, and which the
jury must adopt. And exactly to the extent to which the
terms adopted by the judge are vague; exactly to the extent to which the duty or obligation is expressed by
reference only to an imaginary standard,—to this extent
will the decision of the case be handed over to the jury,
who will then, under the name of fact, decide upon the
law also.

242. Indeed I am strongly inclined to think that the Why the subject has not been cleared up.
reason, why lawyers have shrunk from testing accurately
the conventional phrases which they use as to the nature
of liability, is, that it lays too bare the truth, that the
nature of many primary duties and obligations are only
determined by reference to such an imaginary standard.
For if it is once acknowledged, that the duty or obligation
in question is thus indeterminate, the distribution of functions which is at the basis of our legal system is altogether
disturbed; indeed, the distinction itself between questions of *law* and questions of *fact*, upon which that distribution is based, in a great measure disappears; and the
jury, with whom rests the ultimate affirmance or negation
of liability, is emancipated from much of their theoretical
control. The real object of a good deal of the ingenuity
which has been displayed in eluding the true question, in

cases of the kind on which I have been observing, is, I
think, to avoid this result. It has been felt that it would
be dangerous to hand over to the inexperience of juries
the uncontrolled decision of cases of this description. By
the process of granting new trials for misdirection, setting
aside verdicts as against evidence, entering nonsuits because there was no evidence, and so forth, the judges,
whilst professing only to discuss propositions of law, do
really enter upon a consideration, which they are driven,
when pressed, to admit to be a proper function of the jury
—namely, the decision whether the conduct of the party
has conformed to that standard, which the law has *not*
defined further than I have above stated. I am very far
from saying that this interference, if I may so call it, has
not been beneficial, and even necessary ; but I think it
well worth consideration, whether some method of avoiding
the evil contemplated could not be found, which would be
at least as effectual, and which would not have to be
arrived at by a train of reasoning which contains a good
deal both of confusion and artifice.

CHAPTER VI.

Grounds of Non-liability.

243. The rules of law which impose certain secondary obligations, upon persons who commit breaches of primary obligations, are subject to a certain set of exceptions, which are usually classed together under this head. The several grounds upon which a person will not be held liable to the secondary obligation, though he has committed a breach of the primary one, are insanity, ignorance or mistake, intoxication, infancy, and duress.

244. Insanity—under which term I include all dis- Insanity. orders of the intellect of a grave character—has been little discussed with reference to its general effect on liability; it has been almost always discussed exclusively with reference to the particular effect of it on those secondary duties or obligations which are the subject of criminal procedure, or (as we might say) with reference to its effect on criminal liability only. This no doubt is its most important aspect, and I should be stepping too far out of the ordinary methods of discussion were I not to follow the same route.

245. The ideas current on the subject of insanity Modern ideas of it. have undergone very considerable modification of late years. Indeed it is only in recent times that the subject has received anything like the consideration which it deserves. Attention was first drawn to it by the horrible

sufferings endured by insane persons in confinement.
It apparently used to be thought that every insane person,
who had physical strength and liberty to use it, was
dangerous, and that the only way of rendering him harmless was by forcible restraint. The idea seemed to be
that insane persons were under some sort of external
impulse, which drove them to commit acts (as the phrase
was) against their will. It is now known that, with rare
and temporary exceptions, insane persons are susceptible
of very much the same kind of influences as other persons.
They can be made to feel the effects of discipline, and
can appreciate, in a very considerable degree, the painful-
ness of reproof and the pleasure of approbation. The
consequence is that, in the best asylums, the patients are
scarcely ever under physical restraint.

How they
affect
liability.

246. This discovery, though it has greatly mitigated
the sufferings of persons subject to this calamity, has undoubtedly opened a new and difficult inquiry, whenever it
has to be decided, whether or no the insane person is
legally responsible for his acts. This mode of treatment
clearly shews that the moral and intellectual qualities are
hardly ever entirely effaced. The insane have in a great
measure recovered their liberty, but with it also they
ought to resume, in part at least, their responsibility.

Peculiar
character of
criminal
cases.

247. It may be perhaps doubted, whether the recognition of this responsibility has kept pace with the increasing tendency to treat abnormal conduct as indicating some
form or other of mental disease. It is also unfortunate that
the law of insanity should have been to so great a degree
fashioned upon the practice in criminal cases: for this
practice is rather the result of a series of compromises,
than an application of principles which are scientifically
correct. The effect of setting up a plea of insanity in answer
to a criminal charge is generally almost as disastrous

to the accused, as if he were to admit his guilt. Insanity
itself is a stigma ; and accused persons, if found insane,
are liable to be imprisoned for an indefinite time ; whereas
convicts are only imprisoned for a specified period. Hence
it follows, that few persons care to set up this defence
except in capital cases, in which this defence is frequently
insisted upon, strenuously enough ; but even here, for the
most part, only in that class of cases, in which murders have
been committed under the influence of violent passion,
without any attempt at concealment, and where any other
defence is therefore hopeless. Now this is just the very
class of cases in which the question of insanity presents
itself under peculiar difficulties. The violent excitement
under which the accused is labouring produces an extra-
vagance of conduct very like that produced by insanity :
indeed anger itself is so like madness as to be pro-
verbially identified with it.

248. The question which, on principle, it would seem True ground
ought to be decided upon a plea of insanity, is that which liability.
is suggested by the only reason which can be given for
holding insane persons not to be punishable. They are
not punishable because the prospect of punishment would
not in their case have its usual deterrent effect. As
Austin[1] says, a sanction operates as a motive for the fulfilment of an obligation : the party obliged is averse from
the conditional evil, which he may chance to incur in case
he breaks the obligation ; and in order to avoid that evil,
or the chance of incurring it, he must fulfil the obligation : so that every sanction acts upon the desires of the
person obliged. And Lord Coke, in the third part of his
Institutes[2], also bases the infliction of punishment on its
deterrent effect ; and he considers that punishment inflicted
upon an insane person, would be so generally deemed in-

---

[1] Lect. xxii. p. 459 ; Lect. xxv. p. 497 (third ed.).   [2] p. 6.

human and cruel as rather to make men desperate than
to deter them from crime. I will not now stop to consider whether Lord Coke's reasoning is quite correct. It
is at any rate clear that, on the deterrent principle of
punishment, the admission or rejection of the defence of
insanity ought to depend upon the answer to the inquiry
—whether or no the accused person can be considered
capable of estimating the consequences to himself, in the
shape of punishment, which would result from committing
a breach of the law? If he is so, the prospect of the
punishment, which the law has apportioned to the breach,
ought to have its deterrent effect upon him, and to inflict it
would scarcely seem capable of being considered inhuman
or cruel.

Essentials of crime generally not wanting,

249. I must also observe that the general non-liability
of insane persons cannot be rested on the absence of any of
the essential elements of crime. It is indeed possible that a
man's intellect may be so disordered, that he may altogether
fail to perceive the consequences of his acts, whether to
himself or to any other person. But in the majority of
cases this is not so. All the essentials of a crime will be
found to be present, if we examine it, in nearly every case.
Even the furious madman who kills his keeper because he
is refused his liberty, conceives a wish, which prompts him
to do a certain act, in order that he may accomplish the
end which he has in view. He *intends* his keeper's death
as means to that end, and every condition of the crime
of murder is fulfilled.

Mode in which question submitted to jury.

250. But whatever may be the true ground on
which the excuse of insanity is based, it cannot by any
possibility be that which the form of the inquiry
assumes, when the accused person is alleged to be insane.
The law requires that the question should be put to the
jury in this singular form :—had the accused sufficient

reason to know that he was doing an act that was wrong[1]?
What gave rise to this form of putting the question it is
not very easy to discover. The capacity of distinguishing
right from wrong has hardly at any period been accepted
as a general test of insanity. Probably this form of
putting the question is due to the notion which (as
already mentioned) lurks in our criminal law, but which
is never boldly asserted, and is sometimes emphatically
denied, that the moral quality of the act determines the
liability to criminal punishment.

251.   It must be remembered, however, that this question has always to be answered in criminal cases by a
jury—a tribunal which generally comes to the task
without any previous training, and which is wholly incompetent to discuss with nicety the very peculiar and
difficult question, which the law requires to be placed
before them. Probably, therefore, what really happens is
that, consciously or unconsciously, the jury give their verdict
according to their opinion upon a much more general
question—namely, whether, under all the circumstances,
the prisoner ought to be punished : and, where their decisions are not distorted by a special dislike of the punishment provided for the offence (as sometimes occurs in capital
cases), the result is perhaps as good as any to which, in
the present state of science, it is possible to attain[2]. It
would probably, however, be better still, if the question
were submitted by the judge to the jury in a somewhat

(marginal note: How dealt with by them.)

[1] See the answer of all the judges, except Mr. Justice Maule, to
questions put by the House of Lords, at the end of the answer to
the second and third questions. These questions and the opinions
of the judges thereon were printed by the House of Lords on
19th June, 1848; they are to be found in most works on Criminal
Law.
[2] See the somewhat similar observations of Lord Hale, Pleas of
the Crown, vol. i. p. 32.

different form, so that his own remarks might be more intelligible, and more direct upon the point upon which their determination actually turns. And at any rate the decision of a jury has this negative advantage; that, if unsatisfactory, it forms no precedent; on the contrary, the public condemnation which follows it, serves as a guide and warning, for some time at least, against similar errors.

Insanity as a ground of non-liability in contracts.

252. The question of non-liability upon a contract, because of the insanity of the party sought to be made liable, arises in a great many different ways. It may happen that the intellectual faculties are so obscured, and the judgment so disordered, that the agreement, which is the foundation of the contract, cannot have taken place; and there being no contract, there will be no primary obligation, and therefore no liability to a secondary one. But in many cases the condition of the insane person may be such as to enable him fully to understand the negotiation, and the ultimate result. When a man orders five hundred coats from his tailor, or ten thousand pairs of boots from his bootmaker, he may have lost all notion of number and quantity; but he may not; and he may be induced to give the order under the insane delusion, that he can speculate profitably in some large government contract for such articles. Yet, though there is here a complete contract, according to our definition, the insane person would not be liable, because the law excepts some of the contracts made by insane persons from the general rule that contracts will be enforced. It is only some of the contracts, and not all the contracts, made by insane persons which are thus excepted. If the contract is for the supply of articles of ordinary use and consumption, or for doing work, or any other service suitable to the rank and position of the insane person, it is generally considered valid and binding. Thus an insane person has been held liable

to pay his tailor for clothes, his bookseller for books, an attorney his fees, his servants their wages, and so forth. In one case even the purchase of an annuity by an insane person, not known to be so, it being a fair and reasonable transaction, was held to be valid. But the sale of an estate under similar circumstances has been held void.

253. How far a person who is insane would be held responsible, in courts of civil procedure, for his acts or omissions independently of contract, is a matter in which one is surprised to find our law books nearly silent. Lord Hale lays down, however, a sweeping rule, which would entirely shut out this defence in such cases—that no man can, in matters of this sort, plead his own *mental deficiency* [1]. *Insanity as ground of non-liability in other cases.*

254. Ignorance and mistake are generally classed together, and the considerations which apply to them are pretty nearly the same. If it is necessary to distinguish them, I understand ignorance to be, not to know of the existence of facts which do exist; mistake, to be the supposition that facts exist, which do not. *Ignorance or mistake.*

255. Where a man does an act which is a breach of a primary obligation, he may be ignorant of, or mistake the consequences of the act; or he may by mistake believe that the case is an exceptional one, and that circumstances exist which render the act lawful. This last is a very common case. *Ground of non-liability.*

256. Ignorance of the consequences of an act, or mistake as to the consequences which are likely to arise, of necessity render it impossible for a man to intend or disregard those consequences; a man so ignorant cannot, therefore, by any possibility, commit any crime which involves such intention or disregard.

---

[1] Pleas of the Crown, vol. ii. p. 16.

Ignorance not a defect of the will.

257. Blackstone[1] says, if a man intending to kill a thief in his own house, by mistake kills one of his own family, this is no criminal action. But Blackstone's explanation of this is most extraordinary; and to me, indeed, altogether unintelligible. He says, 'for here the will and the deed acting separately, there is not that conjunction between them, which is necessary to form a criminal act.' Nothing can shew more strongly than this confusion in the mind of so eminent a writer the importance of the analysis undertaken by Austin, of the relation between the mental consciousness of the actor, and the act done. It is not very safe to attempt to assign a meaning to such a phrase as 'the will and the deed acting separately,' but I suppose it is another form of the erroneous expression so often met with, 'doing an act against your will.' The true view of the case I take to be this—Acts are produced by the will, by means of motions of our bodily muscles. But this exertion of the will, or volition, is the result of an antecedent desire. Thus, I take up a pistol, aim it at you, and pull the trigger, because I desire to kill you. I desire to kill you, because I believe that you are breaking into my house, and I consider it necessary to kill you in order to protect myself and my family. After I have fired, I find that you are a friend, coming to pay me an unexpected visit. My mistake as to your person has caused me to desire your death, which desire has acted upon my will. The same mistake has also led me to suppose that I was justified in killing you in self-defence.

Ignorance or mistake must not be rash.

258. Blackstone has, of course, assumed that the circumstances were such as to justify the erroneous inference. If I was rash or heedless in concluding you to be a thief, I might be guilty, though of a different crime. For rashness or heedlessness may be a ground of criminal imputation,

---

[1] Commentaries, vol. iv. p. 27.

and then the ignorance which is the result of that rashness or heedlessness cannot absolve me.

259. So again where my mistake is not either rash or heedless, I may yet be liable in some cases. Thus suppose I see in my neighbour's garden something moving in the trees, which I believe to be a wild, but harmless animal. I examine it very carefully, and satisfy myself that it is a wild animal. I fire at it, and it turns out to be my neighbour himself, who is dangerously wounded by the shot. Here I am clearly liable; and why? Because, though my mistake may be a reasonable one, yet, if all that I believed to be true, were true, my act would still be a breach of a primary duty or obligation, and the facts which I supposed to exist would not justify it. But not so in the case put by Blackstone. In that case, if all I believed to be true, were true, there would be an excuse for what would otherwise be a breach of a primary duty or obligation. There is a primary duty or obligation to forbear from taking life, but an exception where life is taken in self-defence. There is a primary duty or obligation not to fire guns into my neighbour's garden, and no exception where the object fired at is a wild animal. I am therefore liable to such consequences as are laid down by the positive law. I should be liable for manslaughter in England, because of the extremely sweeping definition of that crime; perhaps in India I should not have committed a crime, but I should be liable civilly.

Will not excuse an act otherwise unlawful.

260. The effect of ignorance, or mistake, on the primary obligations which arise upon contract, is more complicated; and this complication is in a great measure due to its having been the custom to consider under this head several matters which do not properly belong thereto.

Ignorance or mistake in cases of contract.

261. I have already adverted [1] to the mode which is

Inquiry sometimes

[1] *Supra*, sect. 174.

shut out by rules of interpretation. generally adopted for ascertaining the intention of the parties in case of dispute. It has there been observed, that all a tribunal can do—after deciding upon the evidence what were the terms of the contract; after hearing the statements of both parties as to what each intended; and after inquiring into the circumstances which happened about that time, so far as they throw any light upon the contract—is to put upon the words its own interpretation, and from that interpretation to presume the intention. But in arriving at this presumption judges generally, as I observed, follow certain rules; such, for instance, as that the technical terms of law can never be used in any other than their technical sense, or ordinary words in any other than their ordinary sense, and so forth[1]. So that a man may even find himself fixed with an obligation arising upon a contract, which he did not intend, almost without having had an opportunity of asserting his mistake; and practically the question of ignorance or mistake is thus very often shut out, upon grounds which stand somewhat apart from the general principles upon which that excuse depends.

Non-liability sometimes based on another principle. 262. On the other hand, there are many cases in which this excuse appears to prevail, in which the real ground of exemption is of another kind. Thus, if I enter into a contract in ignorance of the existence of an important fact, or under a mistake in supposing a fact to exist which does not, should the ignorance or mistake be caused by the contrivance of the person in whose favour the obligation is intended to be created, the obligation is considered to be void upon a much simpler principle, namely, of fraud; it being a well-known exception to the general law which bids us to perform our contracts, that it does not apply to cases where the party to whom the promise is made has committed fraud.

[1] Supra, sect. 177.

263. So also there may be cases in which the law
creates no primary obligation upon the occasion of a contract, unless the parties have fulfilled certain requirements
towards each other ; one of which frequently is, not only
to abstain from fraud, that is, from giving false information, but to give all the information which one possesses,
and even sometimes to guarantee the truth of the representation ; the legal obligation being conditional upon
the fulfilment of this requirement, and if it is not fulfilled,
the obligation is not created.

264. I may also add that, in all cases, the law
requires that persons, when they make contracts, should
exercise reasonable care and diligence to guard against
ignorance or mistake ; that is to say, it will impose the
obligation, notwithstanding any ignorance or mistake
attributable to such want of care or diligence.

Ignorance or mistake no excuse if the result of carelessness.

265. The remaining cases are few; but they are the
only ones to be solved by the rules of law which properly
relate to the excuse of ignorance or mistake. Assuming
the mistake or ignorance to be established, and that it is
not due to fraud, or wilful or negligent omission, then
arises the question whether the mistake or ignorance
alone prevents the obligation from existing. We may
divide the cases into two classes: (1) where the promise
has been performed, and the ignorance or mistake is
used as a ground for claiming restitution ; (2) where the
promise has not been performed, and the ignorance or
mistake is used as a ground for alleging that no obligation
exists. Another important distinction which separates
each of these two kinds into two further subdivisions, is
that the ignorance or mistake may be either (1) mutual,
that is, common to both promiser and promisee, or (2)
single, that is, on the part of one only.

Real cases of ignorance or mistake as an excuse in contract.

265 a. The law which is applicable to such cases

English law not very clearly settled.

is not very well settled; at least it is difficult to extract any very clear principles from the multiplicity of reported cases, which are always referred to when this question arises, and which, notwithstanding important distinctions,

Cases where ignorance or mistake is mutual.

are not always very accurately distinguished. This much is clear; that, where the ignorance or mistake is mutual, the promise is not binding on the parties; but if there are any reasons why a simple dissolution of the obligation would not, under the circumstances, be fair, the promiser will be held to his promise, unless he assumes in its place an obligation to do what is just and proper. For instance, there was a case in which the supposed owner of a fishery, after having expended a good deal of money in improving it, let it to a relative. It turned out afterwards, that this relative was himself in reality the owner. The agreement to hire the fishery was considered not to be binding; but the lessee was compelled to repay the sums of money which the lessor had laid out in the improvement of the estate [1].

266. It seems also that in cases of mutual ignorance or mistake, not only would the promise to do a future act be considered as not binding, but if the promise had, under similar circumstances, been performed, there would be a good claim to restitution; the claim being subject to similar considerations as to what was just and proper between the parties.

Ignorance or mistake on one side only.

267. If the ignorance or mistake be single, the general opinion seems to be that the performance of the promise cannot be declined on that ground alone. This is a question which touches closely upon one which has been already discussed, but differs from it. The sense of the promise is here supposed not to be doubtful, but the

[1] See the case of Cooper against Phibbs, reported in Law Reports, House of Lords, vol. ii. p. 149.

intention of the promiser is supposed to be shewn to differ
from the sense. There is in such a case, no doubt, not
any true contract, for a man cannot be said, strictly, to
promise that which he does not expect; but the same
obligation is enforced, and the case is treated exactly as if
a true contract in the sense of the promise existed. One
judge in England, however, certainly seems to take a
different view, and to consider that, if the contract be one
of sale, the ignorance or mistake, even when single, avoids
the bargain.

268. Moreover, whether or no this last opinion be
correct, where the object of the plaintiff is to obtain what
is called a specific performance, that is, to compel a fulfilment of the obligation by a threat of punishment, the
court would have power to fall back on the maxim, that
it is always in its discretion to grant or withhold this
somewhat exceptional relief : and it doubtless would
do so, if the contract was one which, in the opinion of
the court, ought not, in common fairness, to be enforced.
And should the plaintiff in a similar case seek to enforce,
not the original obligation, but only the secondary
obligation to pay a sum of money by way of compensation,
the jury, if they held a similar opinion, would probably
give very trifling damages.

269. In the case of breaches of duties or obligations Ignorance
which are independent of contract, or are so considered, in other
the question whether ignorance or mistake affects the cases.
liability has been hardly ever discussed.

270. A distinction, about which a good deal has been Ignorance
said, is usually drawn between ignorance of law and ignorance
ignorance of fact. It is generally laid down as a universal of fact.
rule of English law, that ignorance of fact excuses all
liability, whereas ignorance of law excuses none. The
rule itself is simple and intelligible enough, and I might

dismiss it without further consideration. But as it
appears to me, that there is some misconception both as to
its real operation, and as to the reasons on which it is
based, I shall make some remarks upon it, with special
reference to its operation in criminal cases.

Erroneous reasoning of Blackstone. 271. Austin[1] has shewn that to affirm, as Blackstone
affirms[2], that every person *may* know the law, is untrue;
and that to argue, as Blackstone argues, that a man's
ignorance of law will not excuse him, because he is bound
to know it, is only to assign the rule as a reason for itself.
Austin considers[3] that the only sufficient reason for the
rule in question is, that ' if ignorance of law were
admitted as a ground of exemption, the Court would be
involved in questions which it were scarcely possible to
solve, and which would render the administration of
justice next to impracticable.'

A rule of convenience. 272. The question, therefore, is reduced to one of
convenience. When we refuse to allow people to set up
their ignorance of law, as a ground of exemption from
liability, it is not because this is a less valid excuse than
ignorance of fact, but because this is an excuse, into
which it would be inconvenient to inquire.

Founded on improbability of defence being true. 273. If we examine further the reasons, why it is said
to be inconvenient to do this, we find that they are two-
fold: that the defence would be set up in nearly every case,
and that it would be impossible to decide, whether it was
true or false. Consequently (I understand the argument
to be) it is a case in which inquiry must be shut out by a
presumption; and it is obviously necessary to presume
that the defence is false, or the law would become

[1] Lect. xxv. p. 497 (third edition).
[2] Commentaries, vol. iv. p. 27.
[3] Lect. xxv. p. 498 (third edition).

powerless. This reasoning falls entirely to the ground, unless the chances of the defence being really false greatly outnumber the chances of its being really true. Unless they do so, the presumption ought to be, as it generally is, in favour of innocence.

274. Now, to estimate this probability, we must understand what is meant by ignorance of law, or (which comes to the same thing, but is easier to estimate), what is meant by knowledge of law. This may mean general knowledge that such and such an act is forbidden by the law, and that doing it will be a breach of duty or obligation, to which some sort of sanction is affixed. Or it may mean a particular and accurate acquaintance with the terms of the law ; with what constitutes a breach of it, and what penalties result from the breach. Or it may mean some degree of knowledge intermediate between these two.

What is meant by ignorance of law.

275. It is a certainty that no man alive possesses this knowledge in the highest degree, as regards all acts. Not even a lawyer could express fully and accurately all the primary duties and obligations of which the breaches are crimes ; but nearly every man possesses it in some degree or other, as regards most acts. Nearly every one above the age of infancy knows, as to nearly every act for which he is liable to be criminally punished, at least this much—that it is forbidden by the law, and that the doing it is followed by some sort of consequences disagreeable to himself. Most men know a good deal more ; they know that violence, and fraud, and dishonesty will be punished by various kinds of restraint and bodily suffering. Even when a new crime is created, as when, by an Act of George the Second [1], it was for the first time made an offence, punishable like theft, to steal a bill of exchange or promissory

---

[1] 2 George II. ch. xxv.

note, though it is quite possible that the first thirty or forty persons punished knew nothing of this change in the law, yet they all knew, that the law had always forbidden them to take this sort of property; that it was a breach of the law to do so; and that the law on this point was enforced by some sanction, though perhaps not a severe one. If, therefore, the knowledge which is presumed, is this sort of general knowledge, there can be little doubt that the presumption is nearly always correct; and so far from thinking it likely that the defence would be set up in every case, I think it would nearly always be considered a perfectly hopeless one.

Whether the rule is not too sweepingly applied.

276. But the matter assumes a different aspect in certain particular cases. For example, it is sometimes permitted to us, and even made our duty, to inflict pain and loss on others. We are perhaps called upon to act in such cases with promptitude and severity, under a combination of circumstances which rarely occurs; of which, therefore, we have little experience; and where legal advice is not at the moment to be procured. But, unless we are judges acting judicially, we are liable to criminal punishment for our acts, even though, with the utmost good faith, we believe ourselves to be bound, in fact and in law, to act as we have done; should it turn out, upon investigation, that our view of the law is incorrect. The Indian Penal Code[1] declares, that nothing is an offence which is done by a person who, by reason of a mistake of fact, in good faith believes himself to be bound to do, or justified in doing it. But it expressly excludes from the advantage of this exception those persons whose error consists, not in a mistake of fact, but in a mistake of law. Nor am I aware that the exception is more favourable in similar cases in England.

[1] Section 76.

This seems to place many persons, especially those responsible for peace and good order, in a very unsatisfactory position. Nor is it easy to see why, as one might say, a judge sitting in court should be excused from knowing the law, and a sentinel on duty should not[1].

277. Somewhat different considerations apply to cases of contract. Where there is a mutual mistake in the law, to hold the parties to the contract, is to hold them to that which neither party intended, when they made the contract; and it certainly is difficult to see why this should be done. And it would be easy to meet the suggestion which Austin makes about the difficulty of proof, by presuming that a person knew the law on the subject on which he was contracting, until he had established the contrary. Where the mistake has been made only by the person who seeks to avoid the obligation, then we have to consider whether we ought to disappoint the well-grounded expectations of one side, or the ill-grounded expectations

---

[1] It seems to me hardly credible that in a work of the highest authority, published only five years ago, the following case should be cited as a precedent, which is to guide us in the present day in the administration of the criminal law. It is alone sufficient to shew that the doctrine on which it is based requires reconsideration. ' The prisoner was sentinel on board the *Achille* when she was paying off. The orders to him from the preceding sentinel were—to keep off all boats, unless they had officers with uniforms in them, or unless the officer on deck allowed them to approach ; and he received a musket, three blank cartridges, and three balls. The boats pressed ; upon which he called repeatedly to them to keep off; but one of them persisted and came close under the ship, and he then fired at a man who was in the boat and killed him. It was put to the jury to find, whether the sentinel did not fire under the mistaken impression that it was his duty ; and they found that he did. But a case being reserved, the judges were unanimous that it was, nevertheless, murder.' Russell on Crimes, by Greaves, fourth edition, vol. i. p. 823.

of the other. It is obvious that the former stands in the more favourable position; and indeed to hold the contract binding in such a case may often be supported without any presumption at all. People are rarely compelled to enter suddenly into contracts about matters with which they have not had some previous opportunity of making themselves acquainted; and to enter into a contract without making inquiries, and taking legal advice if necessary, may be fairly considered as a want of ordinary care.

Roman Law on this subject.

278. It is also desirable to notice that under the Roman Law, which is invariably quoted on this point, the principle was applied in a far less sweeping manner than with us. There was in the first place a general exception in favour of soldiers, of persons under twenty-five, and of persons who were so placed as not to have ready access to legal advice (*jurisconsulti copiam habere*). These were considered as persons who were not expected to know the law (*quibus permissum erat jus ignorare*). Women also were partially excused[1]. Of course, in a matter so purely dependent on social considerations, it is not likely that the rules of Roman Law would serve as a model for any modern state. But, as they are so frequently referred to, it is well they should be understood.

Intoxica-tion.

279. Intoxication is a disordered state of the intellect, produced by eating or drinking something. Blackstone says it is rather an aggravation of the offence than an excuse for criminal misbehaviour; and that the law will not suffer any man thus to privilege one crime by another[2].

---

[1] See the authorities collected by Thibaut in a note to sect. 29 of the General Part of his System of Pandects Law (p. 25 of Mr. Lindley's Translation, first edition).

[2] Commentaries, vol. iv. p. 26. I doubt whether the passage of Lord Coke to which Blackstone refers as an authority for this

The Indian Penal Code says[1]: 'In cases where an act done is not an offence, unless done with a particular knowledge or intent, a person who does the act in a state of intoxication shall be liable to be dealt with, as if he had the same knowledge as he would have had, if he had not been intoxicated, unless the thing which intoxicated him was administered without his knowledge and against his will.' The English rule is intelligible, though the reasoning by which Blackstone supports it is worthless. Drunkenness in itself can hardly be said to be a crime under English Law[2]; and even if it were, it is simply begging the question to say, that when a man pleads drunkenness, he thereby seeks to privilege one crime by another; the whole question being, whether or no that other act is or is not a crime. The Indian rule is very difficult of comprehension. I am not quite sure what is meant by 'a particular knowledge or intent,' but I suppose setting fire to a house is an offence, though *not* done with any particular knowledge or intent; yet it is not at all likely that intoxication was intended to be an excuse in such a case. On the other hand, passing counterfeit coin is clearly an offence in which a particular knowledge is necessary; namely, knowledge that the coin is spurious; and therefore, a drunken man who takes a counterfeit coin, which he would certainly have discovered to be counterfeit if he had been sober, and pays it away without discovering it, is guilty, under this provision, of passing counterfeit coin, knowing it to be counterfeit. But this result seems very remarkable.

Erroneous reasoning of Blackstone.

Rule of Indian Penal Code obscure.

position, has been correctly understood by him. See First Part of the Institutes, p. 247.

[1] Sect. 86.

[2] It is an offence punishable by a fine of five shillings under 21 James I. chap. vii. sect. 3. But simple drunkenness, independently of any other consideration, is very rarely, if ever, punished.

280. Nor is it easy to see why, though the section refers to both knowledge and intention, only knowledge should be presumed, and not intention. The result of presuming knowledge would be to render the drunken man liable in those very numerous cases, in which the nature of the crime is determined by knowledge that certain conse-quences are likely to ensue; but the knowledge that certain consequences are likely to ensue, and the expecta-tion that they will ensue, are hardly distinguishable; and expectation that they will ensue is, according to the opinion of Austin, intention. Perhaps this is an accidental omission.

True effect of excluding the defence of intoxica-tion alto-gether in criminal cases.

281. The question, how far intoxication affects liability, can never, I think, be satisfactorily settled by presuming that things are different from what they really are. If the state of mind, which we call knowledge or intention, is essential to the breach of the duty or obligation in ques-tion, the first consideration will be, whether or no the drunkenness was such, as to have prevented the possibility of such a state of mind. It is perfectly consistent with very great drunkenness, that a man should know and intend the consequences of his acts. A soldier who after a day's hard drinking discharges his musket in the face of his serjeant, may know and intend the consequences of his acts, just as well as the jealous lover who stabs his rival in the arms of his mistress. Indeed it is hardly possible to preserve the physical capacity to execute this sort of crime, without also retaining the low degree of intelli-gence which is necessary to the offence. But, if that is not the case; if the drunkenness is such that no offence can have been committed, or not the particular offence with which the person is charged; then the true effect of presuming knowledge or intention, in spite of the facts, is to make drunkenness itself an offence, which is punish-

able with a degree of punishment varying with the consequences of the act done [1].

282. How far intoxication affects the liability of a man in a court of civil procedure, to make compensation for damage done, has been little discussed. The same distinction would be here necessary as in considering criminal liability. If the primary obligation be such that the state of mind is an element in the breach, then the person pleading intoxication may, or may not, have that state of mind. If he has it, then he is liable like any other person. If he is so intoxicated that he cannot have it, then, if liable at all, he is liable because there is a law, which makes men liable for damage which they do when drunk, independently of any consideration of their state of mind when they did it.

Intoxication in other cases than crimes and breaches of contract.

283. So in cases of contract, an intoxicated man may, or may not, have the degree of intelligence necessary to agree upon the terms of a contract; and this would be a matter of inquiry. But here a different principle intervenes. A man who is intoxicated generally shews it; and there is this exception to the law that contracts will be enforced, that a contract made with a man who is apparently drunk will not be so. The sovereign authority, for good reasons, has decided that people ought not to transact business with persons whose incapacity to exercise sound judgment is thus apparent.

Intoxication in contract.

284. The rules which govern the liability of infants and minors have varied considerably in different countries.

Infancy.

---

[1] It would appear from a passage in Lord Hale that some lawyers have thought that the formal cause of punishment *ought* to be the drunkenness, and not the crime committed under its influence. Pleas of the Crown, vol. i. p. 32. I have not been able to test the authorities to which he refers.

They have had their origin mainly, but not exclusively, in considerations of intellectual deficiency. They have been founded to some extent on the necessity of subjecting young persons to parental or other control; on their physical incapacity to go through certain forms; not unfrequently on their incapacity for sexual intercourse; but the most prominent consideration has, of course, always been the absence of that knowledge and experience, which is necessary to enable any one to appreciate the consequences of his acts. Traces of these principles may be found in the Roman, the English, the Hindoo, and the Mahommedan Law. But it is obvious that an inquiry into liability upon these principles would be both difficult and inconvenient; and consequently, the necessity for this inquiry has been to a great extent superseded, by laying down certain fixed rules as to liability, based simply upon the age of the person sought to be made liable.

Criminal cases.

285. The rules vary somewhat in different countries, and they also vary with reference to the nature of the duty or obligation which is in question. As regards acts which lead to penalties or forfeitures under criminal procedure, a child cannot, under the Indian Penal Code [1], be made liable until he has attained the age of seven years. Above seven years and under twelve the child will not be liable, unless he has attained sufficient maturity of understanding to judge of the nature and consequences of his conduct. This means that he will generally be considered not to have attained that condition; but he may be shewn to have done so. The law of England is substantially the same, except that fourteen years is substituted for twelve. The French Code provides that, wherever the accused is under sixteen years of age, there must be an inquiry into what is called his discernment [2].

[1] Sect. 83. [2] Code Pénal, Art. 66.

As regards those acts which are usually called torts or delicts, the consequences of which are liability to make compensation, or some other obligation of a civil kind, they would probably be dealt with upon the same principles as acts which are punished criminally.

286. As regards contracts, the law is very favourable Contracts. to young persons. Up to a certain age, which in European countries is usually fixed at twenty-one, they are not generally liable to obligations created by way of contract, though they can compel persons who have made promises to them to perform them. But though the minor cannot by his own act incur any obligation, there is generally some person, his father or mother, or a person specially appointed for the purpose, and who in this relation is called his guardian, who can make, under certain circumstances, valid contracts on the minor's behalf. Moreover a minor, on attaining his full age, may ratify, either expressly, or by acknowledging their existence in any other way, any contract made by him when under age. A minor may also generally make a valid contract to pay for the necessaries of life. In India the same general principles apply to contracts made by minors as in Europe. The age of majority is not however fixed with any certainty. There seems to be a general disposition to fix it at eighteen.

287. We now come to another matter, upon which Duress there has been no little confusion, owing to the inconsiderate use of terms. We constantly hear people speak does not of a man doing an act against his will, and lawyers discuss destroy the will. the validity of an act done against the will. But if we use language with the precision which is absolutely necessary in order to deduce legal consequences, and revert to the analysis above given of the relation between the will

and the act (the only one which appears to me to be rational), it will be at once apparent, that to say that a man has done an act against his will, is a flat contradiction. If I thrust a gun into your hand and force your finger on to the trigger, it is I who fire the gun and not you. You do not do an act against your will. You do no act at all. On the other hand, if I present you a document for signature, and inform you that unless you sign it I shall blow your brains out, producing at the same time a pistol to convince you that I am in earnest; whereupon you take up the pen and sign; in that case you sign in accordance with your will, and not against it. What I have operated upon is not your will, but upon the desires which influence your will. I have never deprived you, nor can I ever deprive you, of the power of freely choosing, whether to sign the paper or to be shot through the head. Knowing that you have a strong desire to live, I put you in a position in which, in order that that desire may be accomplished, you must do an act which you otherwise desired not to do. I might be mistaken. Your repugnance to the act might be so great that death would be preferable. Many a woman has preferred death to yielding up her virtue.

288. This will be seen more clearly if we compare this case, which most people would describe as an act done against the will, with a case which would not be so described, but which will be found on examination to stand on precisely the same grounds. I am a prisoner in the hands of a cruel enemy, who I feel certain will take an early opportunity of putting me to death. I have the chance of speaking to you, and promise you a thousand pounds if you will carry a message to one of my friends, who, I feel sure, will come to my aid when he learns my situation. It is exceedingly painful

to me to expend so large a sum of money, which I can ill spare, and I would gladly avoid doing so. But I fear to lose my life, and you will not take less, so I sign a promise to pay that amount. No one could speak of this as an act done against my will; and yet the condition of my will, in this case, is precisely the same as that of yours, in the former case. Each of our wills is influenced by conflicting desires—the desire to live, and the desire to avoid an act; the desire to live preponderates, and we act accordingly.

289. Having removed this misconception, let us see how the improper influence upon the desires, which is called duress, affects the obligations which arise out of an act. As in all other cases, it is only by an examination of the law which creates the primary obligation, that we can discover this. Under what circumstances does the law create obligations upon contracts, which have been entered into by persons under what is termed duress?

290. A great many cases of so-called duress may be got rid of upon a very simple ground. If the act done under the influence of duress be for the benefit of the person who has used the improper influence, the sovereign authority will refuse to lend its sanction to it, on the ground that no one can be allowed to take advantage of his own wrongful act. But there are undoubtedly cases in which a promise will not be enforced, though the promisee be wholly innocent. Thus if a friend of mine asked you to lend him a thousand pounds, and I, wishing his request to be granted, threatened to take your life unless you signed a promise to pay him the money, the promise would not be enforced, although he and I were not acting in concert.

Real cases of duress as a ground of non-liability.

291. The principles upon which the sovereign autho- *Rules which govern these cases.* rity will refuse to create an obligation in such cases have

not been, as far as I am aware, very exactly stated. If a judge has to decide such a case he would generally consider a good deal, what under all the circumstances appeared to be just and proper. Three rules appear however to have been adopted. First, the danger to be avoided must be of a serious kind, that is, danger to life, or limb, or liberty, either to the person himself, or his wife, or his children. Danger of losing one's good character, or of injury to one's property, is not considered sufficiently serious. Nor is the danger of being sued in civil process, or of being charged with a crime. Of course I mean not sufficiently serious to justify the non-performance of a promise made to an innocent person. Should the person who threatens the danger himself seek to enforce the promise, the case would, as I have pointed out, be treated on different principles.

Secondly, it is necessary that the danger should be one which a person of ordinary constancy and firmness may fairly expect to happen; and the act must be one which a prudent man would do, to avoid the danger.

Thirdly, the escape from the anticipated harm, by making the promise, must be suggested by some one other than the promiser himself, and the act must be the direct consequence of the suggestion.

292.   The effect of duress upon criminal liability, and upon civil liability independently of the agreement of the parties, has never, as far as I am aware, been discussed. Cases of this kind are of rare occurrence, and are frequently capable of being solved on other principles.

CHAPTER VII.

OWNERSHIP.

293. Although primary duties and obligations are not sufficiently expressed in law to enable us to discuss them, except in connection with liability, some of the matters connected with them, especially those which concern their loss and acquisition, have received some attention; and the principal of these I proceed to consider.

293 *a.* Ownership in its most general sense is a highly abstract term. It comprises the idea of a thing and a person, and expresses the condition of a person, in whom are united, to the exclusion of every one else, such rights over the thing as are available against the world at large. Such absolute ownership very rarely exists; and the term is often used to express the condition of a person, who unites in himself a portion, less than all, of these rights. Thus I purchase a watch, and thereby become the owner; perhaps in this case, the absolute owner. I pledge it with a pawnbroker, and thereby part with many of the rights which, while I retained them, would be called rights of ownership; but I should still be called the owner of the watch, and the pawnbroker would not. *Abstract meaning of ownership. As such rarely exists.*

294. No general rule exists for determining what severance of the rights over a thing will put an end to ownership; and English lawyers have been rather fanciful *Arbitrary application of the term.*

on this point.   Thus we are told that, if I lease land to
you for ninety-nine years if you should so long live, I still
remain owner of the land, and you do not become so; but
if I lease it to you for your life, which (as is very truly
said) is precisely the same thing, then you become owner,
and I cease to be so[1].

295.   So highly abstract a notion as ownership in its
absolute form is scarcely capable of discussion.   On the
other hand, modified forms of ownership are only capable
of being intelligibly discussed with reference to one or
other of its modifications; as for instance, with reference
to pledge or mortgage, the relation of landlord and
tenant, or the like.

Distinction
between
"ownership"
and "pro-
perty."

296.   What I have called 'ownership' is sometimes
called 'property.'   But the word 'property' also signifies
the thing owned; and it is inconvenient to call the thing,
and the right over it, by the same name.

Duration of
ownership.

297.   Not only are the rights which are summed up
in the term ownership frequently disunited, and distributed
amongst different persons, so that the rights of each are
restricted by the rights of the rest, but the time during
which these rights are to last is also capable of indefinite
restriction and expansion.   Any one of these rights, or any
aggregate of them, may last for a certain number of years,
for a man's life, or for ever.   Thus, if I am the owner of a
piece of land, I may grant a right of way (which is one of
the fragments of ownership very often found separated) over
it to you and your heirs for ever; I may grant the right to
hold the same piece of land for purposes of cultivation or,

---

[1] I never feel quite sure I have rightly understood what is
to be found in all English law books about the distinction
between 'chattels real' and 'chattels personal,' but this is how
I understand the propositions of the learned author to whom I
specially refer.   See Smith's Real and Personal Property, vol. i.
p. 142 (fourth ed.).

as it is usually called, a lease of it, to another for life ; and
the right to receive the rent and all my other rights, I may
mortgage to a third person for a term of years. And we
may here remark, in illustration of what has been said
above, that in common language, even after this, I should
still be called the owner ; probably because, though I have
parted with nearly all my rights, at least for a time, yet
I am the person from whom all the others derive their
rights, and my ownership would be restored, pro tanto,
as these rights respectively came to an end.

298. Ownership, or any of the various rights which
make up ownership, may be subject to conditions : that
is to say, may be made to commence or cease, upon the
ascertainment by our senses that a certain fact does or
does not exist. Thus, I may be the lessee of a piece of
land on condition of paying a certain fixed sum of money
annually to the crown ; or I may become the owner of
the estate which belongs to you, upon your declining to
take the name of a certain family.

Conditional ownership.

299. It is not part of my present plan to discuss the
notions which lie at the bottom of those rules which regulate the transfer of the ownership of property, whether *inter
vivos*, or by succession, testamentary, or intestate. I am
only about to refer to them, in order to mention, that many
modern ideas upon the subject of ownership have their
origin in the eager desire of owners of landed property to
direct the course of succession according to their liking.
To exercise and extend to the very utmost the power of
tying up the course of succession to land, has been the
steady object of owners of landed property in every country
of Europe ; and, at this moment, it largely occupies the
attention of landowners in India [1]. It has been the policy
of the ruling powers in different countries sometimes to

Persevering attempts to tie up succession to ownership.

[1] See *infra*, sect. 306, note.

increase these facilities, sometimes to diminish them.
They were nearly all swept away in France by the Revolution of 1792, and have only been very partially restored[1].
In England, though many attempts have been made to
restrict them, they exist in a form, and to an extent,
nowhere else ever known.

Furthered
by English
notions of
ownership.

300. Two peculiarities of the law of ownership in
England have specially tended to favour the exercise of this
power; and, as far as I am aware, there is nothing analogous to these in any other system of law, ancient or modern.

First, by
separation
of owner-
ship into
'estates.'

301. It has been usual, as already observed, to regard
ownership as capable of being limited in point of duration.
Two, three, four, or more persons may be the successive
owners of property. But in England this limitation of
ownership in point of duration has been dealt with in a
very peculiar way. If land in England be given to A,
and after his death to B, and after his death to C, and
after his death to D in perpetuity, these four persons are
not considered, as they would be anywhere else, to be
four successive owners, differing only in the date of the

---

[1] See Code Civil, Art. 896, and the observations of M. Troplong,
Droit Civil Expliqué, Donations entre Vifs et Testaments, vol. i. p.
138. M. Troplong's observations upon the effect, of what at the time
was considered a very extreme measure, are remarkable. Though
strongly repudiating all sympathy with the extreme Republican
School, he declares his conviction that the abolition of the old law
of substitution has been in the highest degree beneficial to France.
He says: 'Cette question ne divise plus les esprits. L'abolition des
substitutions a pu paraître un coup hardi à la génération qui n'en
avait pas fait l'épreuve; mais l'expérience d'un demi-siècle a
démontré à l'époque actuelle les immenses avantages d'un régime de
liberté qui laisse la propriété à son mouvement légitime, qui en fait un
gage sérieux pour le crédit, et un patrimoine assuré à chaque
membre de la famille. Les substitutions étaient un obstacle énorme
au développement de la richesse publique. Elles avaient, sans doute,
un certain avantage de conservation, mais elles préféraient une
immobilité stérile au movement fécond qui donne la vie aux
intérêts économiques.'

commencement and end of their ownership; each taking by *substitution*[1] their turn as it came, but having nothing till that came. The English lawyer views them in a far different and highly technical light. By an extremely bold effort of imagination, he treats the ownership in perpetuity as something he can presently deal with, and out of which he may carve (to use his own expression) any number of slices, and confer each slice upon a different person; who, though he may have to wait a long time for his enjoyment of the property, is nevertheless the present owner of his slice. English lawyers do not seem to consider this matter-of-fact mode of dealing with so highly abstract a notion as perpetual ownership, as anything peculiar; but it nevertheless is peculiar to English Law. Other nations share with us the idea that, as certain events arbitrarily chosen may happen, the ownership of land may pass from one person to another; and have invented contrivances, which are, for the most part, restrictions on alienation[2], to ensure that, when the event happens, the land shall so pass. But the notion of an 'estate,' as it is called, is, I think, unknown in any system which has not taken it directly from us. If I give my land to you for your life, I am not looked upon as having parted with it altogether for this indefinite period, at the end of which it will come back to me, or go to some other person. According to the language and ideas of English lawyers the land is partly yours, but still remains partly mine: and with what remains mine, I may deal.

302. It is also true that the result of both devices for

[1] This is a technical term of French Law; it was by means of substitutions that succession was tied up under the old French Law, and it was by the abolition of substitutions that the great change was effected; see Code Civil, Art. 896.

[2] The 'shifting use' of English real property law is very little more than a well-concealed device for preventing alienation.

controlling the succession to the ownership of land is very often the same. It might come pretty nearly to the same thing, whether I gave land to my eldest son for life, and after his death to his brother, or whether I substituted my younger son for my elder, on the death of the latter. But it does not follow from this, that the existence of two different machines does not widen the facilities for tying up succession. Nor is this the point to which I now wish to draw attention. What I wish to establish is, that the English idea of ownership as applied to land is peculiar [1].

303. A case has arisen in India which is remarkable as being one to which it was open to apply, either the English, or the more general notion; and the actual determination of it may have no little influence on the future development of law in that country. If a Hindoo dies leaving a widow, she takes his property, but her ownership terminates at her death. It was perfectly, therefore, in accordance with English ideas, though contrary to the general ideas of jurisprudence, to treat her—not as unlimited owner of the property for the limited time, the ownership shifting over at her death to the next taker—but as owner only of, what we should in England call, an estate for life; the next taker being at the same time present owner of the rest. But this is one of the instances in which English lawyers have escaped the error of transferring into a foreign system the ideas peculiar to their own. The widow in India, though her ownership lasts only for life, has (as the phrase is) the whole estate vested

---

[1] I confine my observations to land, although the ideas of English law relating to other species of property, the funds for instance, possess similar peculiarities; but I have selected land as the best for purposes of illustration. Nor do I wish to indicate it as my opinion that these ideas could be wholly swept away : though I cannot conceal my opinion that they might be advantageously simplified.

in her; and the next taker after the widow has, as he
would have in most countries under similar circumstances,
nothing, until his term comes by the death or other determination of the widow's ownership, when the whole shifts
over to him.

304.   Another peculiarity of the English Law relating   Secondly, by separation of legal and equitable ownership.
to land arises out of the very strange conflict between
Courts of Common Law and Courts of Chancery.   To
take a simple case.   If I give land to you in trust for
myself, in one set of courts I cease to be the owner, in the
other set of courts I continue to be so.   How this came
about is an inquiry which belongs to the history of
English Law, and need not be pursued.   It is only noticed
here as an idea of ownership by which the attempts at
simplifying the notions comprised under that term have
been eluded.   The Court of Chancery, had it confined
itself to compelling owners of property, either to fulfil
certain fiduciary relations, such as those of guardian and
ward, or to fulfil the wishes of persons from whose bounty
they had received the ownership, would have kept within
the limits of analogous institutions in other systems of
jurisprudence.   Had too this been done, not only in those
cases where there are special reasons for the exercise of
good faith, but in all cases alike, where the owner of
land had accepted the ownership, subject to a condition
to exercise his rights for the benefit of some other person,
and the ordinary remedies of law were insufficient to compel him to do so—this would have been a stretch perhaps
of the doctrines of equity, but would have been very likely
beneficial, and would have introduced no entirely new
principle.   But the English Court of Chancery has done a
great deal more than this.   It has created an entirely new
interest in land ; an interest as comprehensive, as general,
as beneficial, as transferable, as ownership itself—which *is*

ownership in fact, only the rights of the owner are somewhat clumsily exercised; and so it is frequently called. This equitable ownership, or use, or trust estate, or whatever other name we may give it, exists, however, only in that court which invented it. The Courts of Common Law take no notice of it. For this they have been sometimes blamed, and it has been said that it is to their action, and not to the action of Courts of Chancery, that the anomaly is due. It is not the least worth discussion which of these charges is correct; but if, as is possible, an attempt should be made in some succeeding generation to remedy this anomaly, it will be desirable to bear in mind, that simply to require a recognition of the equitable owner by Courts of Common Law, though it would no doubt effectually cause the anomaly complained of to disappear, would at the same time render it necessary to provide some new method of enforcing upon owners of property certain fiduciary and other obligations, such as are recognised in all modern systems of jurisprudence, but which, in common with the whole system of trusts, depend in England upon this anomalous double ownership.

No analogy to our equitable ownership in Roman Law.

305. The doctrine of the English Court of Chancery in respect of ownership has been compared to two entirely distinct institutions of the Roman Law; and if only the germ of it were to be there found, its existence in any modern system would be easily accounted for. But there is nothing like it. There is to be found in the Roman Law a body of rules supplementing the old stricter law, something like our system of equity. There are also to be found well recognised in the Roman Law certain relations of a special fiduciary character, which are governed by special rules framed with a view to their nature. Hence much that takes place in our Courts of Chancery, where similar fiduciary relations are specially

considered, has its analogy in Roman Law. But there is nothing in the Roman Law analogous to the relative position of the Common Law and Chancery owners of property. The point of contact has been supposed to be, where the prætor, exercising what may be called his equitable jurisdiction, enforced what was called a *fidei commissum.* But a moment's consideration of the Roman Law on this subject will shew that, so far from there being, as in England, any conflict of ownership in such a case, what the prætor did, was to compel the transfer of the ownership in accordance with the fiduciary request. The other institution of Roman Law which has been referred to as analogous to the Chancery ownership is what is called *usus;* and in former times (probably in reference to this supposed connection) what we now call *trusts* were then called *uses.* But the Roman *usus* was a wholly different and a far less comprehensive conception. When the Roman owner of a house granted the *usus* of it to another, there was nothing fiduciary in the matter; and the relation created was very like that of an ordinary tenant to his landlord. It was, as the name imports, a right to occupy and make use of the house. It was however a right over the thing available against all the world, and therefore a fragment of ownership : but the grantor remained owner, he did not even lose the possession, of the house. And the same was the case with the more extended right of usufruct. The grantee of the usufruct had not even the possession ; he had only the bare physical detention, which he held on behalf of the owner. And both these rights were classed amongst servitudes; with rights of way, rights to support, and so forth[1]. The leading features of

---

[1] The force of this distinction will appear more clearly from the Chapter on Possession.

the relationship between the Common Law and Chancery owner in England are wholly wanting—namely, trust and conflict. The rights of the grantee of the Roman use no doubt derogate from the absolute ownership, but the rights of the grantee and the rights which remain in the owner stand clearly separated, and each may use his rights for his own benefit. In England the Common Law rights of one owner and the Chancery rights of the other are constantly in conflict, and the Common Law owner would be restrained by the Court of Chancery, if he attempted to use a single right on his own behalf.

Why it is desirable to observe these peculiarities. 306. I have noticed these peculiarities of the English Law at some length, and have pointed out the fallacy of linking them with institutions of a wholly different character, chiefly because of the very peculiar position which English lawyers occupy, with reference to the law which they are called upon to administer. Englishmen are frequently transferred from the arena of the English courts, and the familiar practice of the English law of real property, to countries in which they have to apply systems of law, which are either altogether different from their own, or which are to a large extent incomplete. Under such circumstances it is certain that we shall be strongly tempted to transfer into the new system the ideas we take with us. Some such transfer may be in some cases forced upon us—in India it certainly has been so—as the only safe and practical method of filling up the huge gaps in the declared law of that country. But it is most important in all such cases, to distinguish between that which is in consonance with the ideas common to all systems of jurisprudence, and that which is anomalous and peculiar to our own. Ideas of the former kind it is sometimes not unsafe to transfer. But to transfer ideas of the latter kind is always very

dangerous. The imported principle does not easily fit
in with the institutions of the country into which it is introduced, and consequently its introduction is very likely
to throw the whole law of that country into confusion[1].

307. I have pointed out above that the several rights Co-owner-
over a thing which go to make up ownership may be ship.
parcelled out amongst a variety of persons, each holding
one or more of such rights ; in which case each of these
persons is in a certain sense in opposition to the rest;
inasmuch as the right of each one with reference to the
thing is necessarily limited and controlled by the rights
of all the others. I have also pointed out how rights
over a thing may be held for periods of limited duration,
and pass successively from one person to another[2]. I have
now to advert to a case in which the relation of several
persons to one thing, considered as the subject of ownership, assumes a very different aspect.

308. Every right, and therefore of course every right
comprised in ownership, may belong at the same time to

---

[1] The recent attempts to employ English conceptions of ownership
for the purpose of tying up the succession to property in Lower
Bengal, are probably intended to counteract the effects of the
impulse given by us to the counter notion of the right of absolute
alienation, in the absence of such restrictions. It is a curious history.
Owners of landed property in Bengal met the introduction of
English ideas as to the absolute right of alienation *inter vivos*
by demanding the right to make a will, declaring the course of
succession. This was again met by insisting that, if this were
allowed, the English restrictions on perpetuities must also prevail.
It may indeed be well doubted whether this method of proceeding
can be justified, either legally or politically. Perhaps a compromise
acceptable to the natives of India may be one day arrived at, by
putting some restrictions on the caprice or prodigality of a single
heir, without a wholesale introduction of our cumbrous English
law of real property.

[2] See supra, sections 293, 297.

M

several persons collectively, and we may therefore have several persons who are collectively owners of a thing, or who have collectively some right or other over the thing.

Differs from ownership of juristical person.

309. This co-ownership of several persons must not be confounded with the ownership of juristical persons; that is to say, of those aggregates of persons, such as a railway company or a municipal corporation, which are by a fiction of law considered as a person. In these the ownership is in the juristical person, and not in the natural persons who compose the fictitious juristical person at all: whereas in the case of co-ownership the ownership is in the several natural persons themselves.

Only one kind of co-owner-ship in English Law.

310. In all English treatises on law we find co-ownership divided into three kinds : — joint - tenancy, tenancy-in-common, and coparcenary. I cannot, however, discover any substantial difference between these species of ownership. It is true that the succession to the ownership differs in each of these cases, but the rights of the co-owners appear to me to be, as nearly as possible, the same[1].

Ownership of Indian joint family.

311. There is in India a very peculiar kind of co-ownership, the nature of which has never been exactly determined. I will not attempt to explain the whole law upon this point, but I will state the rule in a single case, the study of which is highly instructive. A Hindoo dies leaving three sons ; these three are, under the Hindoo law, co-owners of the property which belonged to the father. It is the nature of this co-ownership which it has been found difficult to determine.

Is co-owner-ship not cor-porate ownership?

I know but of two alternatives for the settlement of the question. Either the ownership is in the natural persons who compose the family, or it is in the family itself, which

---

[1] Compare the incidents of joint-tenancy with those of tenancy-in-common, as given by Blackstone, Commentaries, pp. 182, 194.

is then made a juristical person[1] capable of rights. The
latter view is one which would in no way conflict with
general notions of jurisprudence, and it is extremely
probable that such a notion may, at some time or
other, have prevailed in India. But no one asserts
it now; nor can it, as it appears to me, be reconciled with
the well-known maxim of the Hindoo Law, that ownership in the paternal estate is by birth, and not by partition[2]. This clearly points to the co-ownership of the
individuals who comprise the family, and not the ownership of the family itself, considered as a juristical person.
When, therefore, the Privy Council said, in a well-known
case[3], that according to the true notion of an undivided
family in Hindoo law, no individual member of that
family, whilst it remains undivided, can predicate of the
family property that he has a certain definite share, it
must be meant, that no member of the family can assert
of any part of the family property, that it belongs exclusively to himself. There are, however, some passages
in the same judgment, which would seem, at first sight, to
deny to members of a joint Hindoo family individual
ownership even of their shares. But this would involve
as a necessary consequence corporate ownership in the
family, considered as a juristical person, for there is no
other alternative. If the several members of the family
are not the owners of their shares, they are not owners
of anything; and if they are not owners of anything, then

[1] See section 123.

[2] Mitachshara, chap. i. sect. 1. par. 27. This, of course, is a
maxim in those schools only, which accept this commentary. But
it is in these very schools that individual ownership has been thought
to be denied. In the Bengal school individual ownership has not,
I think, ever been explicitly denied; and has been to some extent
recognised.

[3] See Moore's Indian Appeals, vol. xi. p. 88, where the case is
reported.

the *family* must be the owner; which, as I have already pointed out, is inconsistent with the text of the law and the views now prevalent in India.

312. And though there may be some slight difficulty about particular passages in this judgment, it is clear that the Privy Council did not intend to say, that a partition of ownership in a Hindoo family was a change from corporate to individual ownership; for the effect of partition is compared, by way of illustration, to a change from joint-tenancy to tenancy-in-common. Now, under the English law, a joint-tenant is not only the owner, but is in possession of his share. Littleton says that, if there be two joint owners, each is seised of the whole and of the half[1]; which clearly means, that he has access to and control over every part of the property, but in contemplation of law is only in possession of his share; a difference the full force of which will be explained hereafter[2]. And a little further on, he says that, if there be two joint-tenants, one hath by force of the jointure one moiety, and the other the other moiety[3].

There can hardly be any doubt, therefore, that, in modern times at any rate, the family property of Hindoos is owned by the members of the family individually in shares, and not by the family corporately.

313. The case is well worthy of attentive consideration. It is a difficult one, as are all cases, where we come across a form of ownership which differs from that to which we are by tradition accustomed. Yet it is only by comparing several forms of ownership that we can form an accurate conception of any one. Of course the actual solution of the question is, in India itself, of the highest importance on other grounds.

---

[1] Littleton, sect. 288.   [2] In the Chapter on Possession.

[3] Littleton, sect. 291.

CHAPTER VIII.

Possession.

314. The substance of the following chapter is taken from Savigny's well-known treatise on this subject [1]. Austin, in the Introduction to his Lectures on Jurisprudence, announced his intention of availing himself of Savigny's labours in his discussion of possession [2]; but he never accomplished this, because he never arrived so far in his intended course. Savigny's treatise is founded upon the Roman Law, and consists in a great measure of minute criticisms of the Latin texts, and an exhaustive inquiry into the actual views on possession held by the Roman lawyers. It is not these parts of Savigny's work which are useful for our present purpose. What I have borrowed is his analysis of the general legal conception of possession. This conception is universal: the rules of Roman Law, though they have been largely borrowed, and, I may add, largely misunderstood, are not so. We have, therefore, no occasion to trouble ourselves with ascertaining whether in any particular case our conclusions do, or do not agree with those of the Roman lawyers.

[1] The original work appeared in 1803. The later editions published during the author's lifetime were considerably altered by him. The last edition was published at Vienna in 1865, to which my references are made. It has been translated by Sir Erskine Perry.

[2] Outline of the Course of Lectures, vol. i. p. 55 (third ed.).

Physical idea of p s-session.

315. Possession originally expresses the simple notion of a physical capacity to deal with a thing as we like, to the exclusion of every one else. The primary and main object of ownership is the protection of this physical capacity ; and, as pointed out by Savigny [1], if this physical condition had alone to be considered, all that could be said upon possession from a juristical point of view, would be contained in the following sentences :—The owner of a thing has the right to possess it. Every one has the same right to whom the owner has given the possession. No one else has that right.

Legal idea of possession.

316. The legal notion of possession, however, is not confined to this simple physical condition. Possession is treated in law, not only as a fact, which is a consequence of the right of ownership, but as a right in itself. From possession, under certain conditions, important legal consequences are derived. Moreover, the possession with which the law thus deals, is not that simple physical condition which we have described above, and to which, for the sake of distinction, therefore, we may give the name detention. It is true that the physical element is never altogether lost sight of ; on the contrary, a physical element of some kind or other is essentially necessary to possession in its widest legal sense, as we shall see in the sequel. But the physical element greatly varies under rules prescribed by law.

317. So also, inasmuch as possession is a right in itself, as well as a fact, or condition, from which legal consequences are derived, rules are laid down by the law, as in other similar cases—in the case of ownership, for instance—which prescribe the mode in which it may be gained or lost.

[1] Sav. Poss. s. 1. p. 27.

318. There has been a good deal of controversy in Legal conse quences of possession. Germany upon the question—what are the legal con- sequences of possession? Savigny maintains[1] that the Roman Law (from which, no doubt, modern jurists mostly derive their ideas on the subject), attributed only two rights to possession; namely, the acquisition of ownership by possession (*usucapio*), and the protection of possession from disturbance (*interdictum*)[2]. Other lawyers would include, as legal consequences of possession, the acquisition of ownership by occupancy or delivery; the advantage which the person in possession has, in a contest as to ownership, that the burden of proof is thrown upon his adversary; the right to use force in defending posses- sion; the right of the possessor, merely as such, to use and enjoy (to some extent) the thing in possession; and some other advantages of a more intricate kind. This controversy is one which it is not necessary for us to pursue. Every known system of law attributes *some* legal consequences to possession; and even in cases in which it may be, strictly speaking, incorrect to attribute legal consequences to possession, as in the case of occupancy or tradition, the acquisition of possession may yet be an important element of inquiry, and the subject of legal regulation.

319. I will now proceed to consider what is the con- Physical ele- ment in the conception of posses- sion. ception of possession in a legal sense; and I will first examine the physical element which, as I have said, lies at the bottom of the conception of possession.

320[3]. It is very common to say that possession consists in the corporal seizure or apprehension of the thing pos- sessed by the possessor, and that, in all cases where this

---

[1] Sav. Poss. s. 2. p. 20.   [2] Ib. s. 3. p. 32.
[3] Ib. s. 14. p. 206 sq q.

corporal contact does not exist, there is not a real, but only a fictitious possession. And there has been derived from this a theory of symbolical possession, which Savigny considers to be not only erroneous, but to the last degree confusing, when we come to deal with practical questions, and which he has taken great pains to combat. The

Contact not necessary. truth is that, though we undoubtedly do possess most of the things with which we are in corporal contact, and though we come into corporal contact at some time or other with most of the things which we possess, corporal contact has nothing whatever to do with the matter. A man walking along the road with a bundle sits down to rest, and places his bundle on the ground at a short distance from him. No one thinks of doubting that the bundle remains in his exclusive possession, not symbolically or fictitiously, but really and actually; whereas the ground on which he sits, and with which he is, therefore, in corporal contact, is not in his possession at all. So, as Savigny puts it very forcibly, a man is bound hand and foot with cords—no one thinks of saying that he possesses the cords; it would be just as true to say that the cords possess him.

321[1]. Corporal contact, therefore, is not the physical element which is involved in the conception of possession. It is rather the possibility of dealing with a thing as we like, and of excluding others. If we consider the various modes in which possession is gained and lost we shall recognise this very clearly.

Acquisition of possession of land. 322[2]. Take, for instance, first the case of land. A man buys a piece of land. He pays the price, and both parties sign the contract of sale. The buyer goes to take possession. It is not necessary for him to come into physical contact with every part of the land by walking

[1] Sav. Poss. s. 14. p. 211.   [2] Ib. s. 15. p. 212 sqq.

all over it. He enters upon it and stands there ; the seller withdraws or signifies his assent ; and the buyer is at once in full possession. This is on the supposition that the claim to take possession is unopposed. If the seller is there and disputes the purchaser's right to take possession, however unjustly, or if a third person is there who disputes the right of both, all the walking upon the land in the world, until this opposition is overcome, will not give the buyer possession ; and for this reason—because the physical element which is necessary to put the buyer in possession is not corporal contact, but the physical power of dealing with the land exclusively as his own. In such a case there are but two modes in which he can obtain possession — either by inducing those who oppose him to yield, or by overcoming their opposition by force.

323. It is not necessary in order to obtain possession that the purchaser should step on to the land at all. If it is near at hand, and the seller points it out to the buyer, and shews that the possession is vacant, and signifies his desire to hand it over to the buyer, whilst the buyer signifies his desire to receive it, enough has been done to transfer the possession. The physical possibility of the buyer dealing with the thing exclusively as his own, which is all that is necessary, exists, whether he thinks proper to use it by stepping on to the land, or not.

324. We must be careful to distinguish between what is necessary to constitute ownership, and what is necessary to constitute possession. If the owner of land agrees to transfer his rights of ownership to another, that may be, and very frequently is, sufficient to transfer the ownership. But sometimes, in order to effect the transfer, it is necessary to observe certain solemnities. And it so happens that one of the solemnities which it is frequently necessary

Delivery of possession as a solemnity in the transfer of ownership.

to observe is, that the transferor should put the transferee in *possession*. In this case, therefore, the delivery of possession serves a double purpose; it is a performance of the solemnity which the law requires to constitute the transferee owner, and it is at the same time a proceeding which puts him in a position to exercise his rights as owner. This delivery, or tradition (as it was called), was a solemnity necessary to constitute ownership in all cases under the Roman Law; and it was also necessary to constitute ownership of land under English Law, in ancient times, but it is not so now [1]. Other solemnities have been substituted for this one, and in most cases it is sufficient to record the transaction in a document with certain ceremonies of signing, sealing, and so forth; whilst in other cases a twig or clod of earth is handed over. Blackstone in one passage [2] falls into the common error of supposing that solemnities of the latter kind are a symbolical delivery of possession. Their sole object (as he elsewhere rightly states) is to give notoriety to the transfer of ownership, by the performance of a ceremony which is at once significant and impressive. The possession is left untouched; and if the transferee wants to get possession, he will have to set about obtaining it, just as if no such ceremony had been performed.

Possession of land how retained.

325. If we consider what is necessary in order to retain possession, we shall find the same notion more strikingly exemplified. In order to retain possession, it is not necessary that the possessor should remain on, or

[1] The English name for it was seisin. The formality which replaced it was a most complicated one. And it is curious that the Act of Parliament by which the change was effected was intended for a widely different purpose, which it entirely failed to accomplish. But the legislature did not think it necessary to interfere with this unexpected result. See Williams' Real Property, chap. ix.

[2] Commentaries, vol. ii. p. 313.

even near the land. Possession having been once received, it is not necessary that the physical power of dealing with the land as he pleases should be retained by the
possessor at every moment of time. He will continue in
possession, if he can reproduce that physical power at any
moment he wishes it. A man who leaves his home, and
goes to follow his business in a neighbouring town, may
still retain possession of his family house and property.

326 [1]. An examination into the mode of acquiring the
possession of moveable things will lead us to the same
result. Possession of moveable things can undoubtedly be
taken, and very frequently is taken, by placing oneself in
corporal contact with them. I can take possession of
money by putting it into my pocket ; of a coat by putting
it on my back ; of a chair by sitting upon it. But this
contact is not necessary. I should take possession of the
money just as well, if it were placed on the table before
me ; of the coat, if it were placed in my wardrobe ; of
the chair, if it were placed in my house. In the same
way, if I purchase heavy goods lying at a public wharf,
I take possession of them by going to them with the
seller, and by his there signifying his intention to deliver
them, and by my signifying my intention to receive them.
So also, if I buy goods stored in a warehouse, possession is
given to me by handing over the keys. So too, timber
is delivered by the buyer marking the logs in the presence
of the seller ; not because the marking is a sort of apprehension, but because that is the intention of the parties.
The marking might take place without any change of possession ; as for instance, if the logs were marked to prevent their being changed, but were not to be delivered
till the price was paid [2].

327. In all these cases it is a great mistake to suppose

Acquisition of possession of move-ables.

---

[1] Sav. Poss. s. 16. p. 216.   [2] Ib. s. 16. p. 219.

that there is anything fictitious, or symbolical, or constructive in the acquisition of possession. Each case depends on the physical possibility of dealing with the thing as we like, and of excluding others. In all the cases above put, except two, the thing is actually present before us. But in one of these two, namely, that in which we say possession is taken by placing the thing in my house, we only apply to a particular case a well-known principle, which embodies the very idea we are now insisting on; namely, that a man has the actual custody of all that is in his house, by reason of the complete and exclusive dominion which he has over it[1]. The other of these two cases is that in which the keys of the warehouse, where the goods are stored, are handed over by the seller to the buyer. But there cannot be a more complete way than this, of giving to the buyer the power of dealing with the things sold exclusively as his own[2].

Possession of moveables how retained. 328. And, as in the case of immoveable things, so in the case of moveables, when possession of them has once been taken, it may be retained, so long as the power exists of reproducing the physical capacity of dealing with the thing, and of excluding others. Thus, if after handing over and receiving possession of goods at a public wharf both buyer and seller go away, the goods remain in possession of the buyer. Not so, however, if the goods are in the warehouse of a private person, unless the owner of the warehouse agrees to give the buyer the use of the warehouse as a place for keeping his goods.

Capture of wild animals. 329[3]. Instructive illustrations of the conception of possession may also be gained by a consideration of the possession of live animals. Those animals which ordinarily exist only in a domestic state, such as cows and horses, hardly differ from other moveable property. Animals,

[1] Sav. Poss. s. 17. p. 226.   [2] Ib. s. 16. p. 223.
[3] Ib. s. 31. p. 342.

on the other hand, which are in a wild state, are only
in our possession as long as they are so completely in
captivity, that we can immediately lay hold of them.   We
do not possess the fish in a river, even though the river, and
the exclusive right of fishing in it, belongs to us.   We do
not even possess the fish in a pond, if the pond be so large
that the fish can escape from us, when we go to take them.
But we do possess fish, when once they are placed in a stew
or other receptacle, so small that we can at any moment
go and take them out.   Animals that are born wild, but
have been tamed, are generally considered to be in the same
position as animals which are born tame, so long as they
do not escape if let to go loose.   A wild animal, that has
been wounded mortally by us, is not in our possession,
until we have laid hold of it ; for not only is the physical
control yet wanting, but a thousand things may happen
which will prevent us ever getting it.   Another larger
animal may seize it and carry it off; it may get into a
hole ; we may lose its track, and so forth [1].

[1] For the purpose of illustration, I refer here to the law relating to
the capture of wild animals as derived by continental lawyers from
the Roman Law.   This law has, in England, been very considerably
modified, by reason of the more exclusive privileges generally conceded to owners of land.   There is not the least difficulty in a man
having possession of that of which he is not the owner ; and it was
quite consistent with the idea which attaches to our word 'close,' to
treat the owner of enclosed land as in possession of all the game,
which at any time happens to be there.   It was, therefore, obviously
correct to decide (as has been decided) that when a trespasser kills
game on my land the game is mine.   See the case of Blades against
Higgs, reported in the Common Bench Reports, new series, vol. xx.
p. 214.   The idea analogous to that expressed by the word 'close'
hardly existed under the Roman Law, and I doubt if there is anything quite analogous to it on the continent.   But we find that
the French Law does not apply the restrictions as to killing
game to a person doing so 'dans ses possessions attenant à une
habitation et entourées d'une clôture continue faisant obstacle à

Loss of pos-
session of
moveables.

330.   The consideration of the modes in which possession is lost will make the result clearer still.   Every act
by which our physical control is completely destroyed puts
us out of possession.   It makes no difference, whether or
no the person who does the act himself gains possession
thereby, or indeed, whether or no any one does so.   Thus,
if I take anything belonging to you, and throw it into the
sea, you lose possession, though no one gains it.   We may
also lose possession of a thing, not only by the act of
another person in removing it, but simply because, under
the circumstances, we cannot any longer exercise that control.   As, for instance, if a tiny jewel drops from my hand
in passing through a dense forest, or a captured animal
of its own accord escapes back into the wild.   So also, if
we left a thing somewhere, but cannot recollect where, and
search for it in vain, we have lost possession of it.   There
is said to be an exception to this where the thing, though
it cannot be found, is still in the owner's house, or on his
adjoining premises ; as, for instance, if I drop a coin in my
garden, and cannot, on searching, find it, it is said that I
do not lose possession of it.   But there is a reason for this
which shews that it is no real exception.   Everything in
a man's house, and on his premises immediately adjoining,
is, on a principle already adverted to[1], and widely recognised by the law, considered to be in the immediate custody of the owner of the house and premises, by reason of
his exclusive control and dominion over it, and all persons
residing therein.

331.   On the other hand, a man does not lose posses-

toute communication avec les héritages voisins.' Loi du 3 Mai,
1844, sur la police de la chasse ; art. i. sect. 2.   This is probably
because the nature of the locality is inconsistent with the absence
of possession *as well as* ownership, which is assumed in the French
notions on the subject of game.

[1] Supra, sect. 32, ; Sav. Poss. s. 31. p. 340.

sion of a thing by leaving it in a place, which he knows,
and to which he can return. Thus, if I leave my hatchet
in a wood, intending to return the next day and continue
my work, I retain possession of the hatchet all the time.

332. The same general rule applies to the loss of im- Loss of possession of
moveables. The possession lasts so long as there is land.
physical control over them, and ceases when that physical
control ceases. I do not lose possession of my house by
filling it with my friends and servants, even if I should go
away, and leave them there. But should they, on my
return, refuse me admittance, declining upon some pretext
to acknowledge my rights as owner, then, until I have
ejected them, I have lost possession.

333[1]. There was a rule in the Roman Law that if, in Loss of possession by
my absence, a piece of land, which had hitherto been in my intrusion.
possession, was occupied by another, who would oppose
me if I attempted to return and exercise my rights over
the land, I did not thereby lose possession until I was
informed of the intrusion. Such a rule is clearly in conflict with the notion of possession, as it has been developed
above. The physical power of dealing with a thing as
we like being necessary, according to our conception, to
constitute possession in a legal sense, it follows that when
I have lost this, whether I know it or not, I have lost
possession. The question then is, whether we must, in
consequence of this rule, modify our general conception of
possession, with which it does not harmonize? Savigny
has examined this at great length, and has decided
that we ought not, but that it ought to be treated as an
exceptional case. It is in fact a fiction, introduced, as
fictions generally are, to avoid consequences that are considered to be inconvenient or unjust. The fiction is that
I remain in possession when I have really ceased to be so ;

<hr>

[1] Sav. Poss. s. 31. pp. 348, 353.

and it no more modifies the general notion of possession than the similar fiction on which was founded the old action of ejectment. It has never (as far as I am aware) been extended to moveables; and, of course, it can only be applied in those systems of law in which it has been expressly recognised.

Mental element in conception of possession.

334 [1]. The physical element, however, forms only one portion of the conception of possession. Besides this, there is what I may call a mental element. without which the physical relation will remain as a mere fact, having no legal consequences, and not in any way subject to special legal considerations. In order to constitute possession in a legal sense, there must exist, not only the physical power to deal with the thing as we like, and to exclude others, but also the determination to exercise that physical power on our own behalf.

Transfer of detention without possession.

335. This important feature in the legal conception of possession may be illustrated by the consideration of a simple case. A person has a valuable article of jewelry, which he wishes to send from London to his house in the country; and for that purpose he gives it to his servant with instructions to take it to his house, and there deliver it to his wife. The servant does not thereby gain possession of the jewelry, nor does the master lose it. True it is that the servant has the physical control over the jewelry; but, if he is obedient to his master's orders, he has no intention of exercising that control upon his own behalf. The master, on the other hand, by delivering the jewelry to his servant, does not for one moment lose possession of it, if his orders be carried out. Through his servant, who is obedient to his orders, he has the physical control which is necessary to possession; and he has also determined to exercise that physical control on his own behalf.

[1] Sav. Poss. s. 20. p. 246.

336. The position, that possession (in a legal sense) consists not only in the physical control, but also in the determination to exercise it on one's own behalf, is equally apparent, if we consider how possession is transferred. Suppose that you and I are living together in the same house ; that you are the owner, and that I am a lodger. And suppose that you, being in want of money, sell the house to me ; that you receive the money, and formally acknowledge me as the owner, agreeing to pay me a weekly sum for permission to continue to reside in the house. No external change whatever need have taken place in our relative position ; we may continue to live on precisely as before ; yet there can be no doubt, that I am now in possession of the house, and that you are not.

Transfer of possession by change of mind only.

337. In order to constitute possession (in a legal sense) it is not necessary, that the intention to possess should be constantly present to my mind. If I have once determined to exercise my physical control over a thing on my own behalf, and so completed my possession, it will be sufficient for the purpose of retaining possession, that I should, if I adverted to it, keep to that determination. Savigny seems to go further, and to think that, provided the physical control continues, the possession continues also until I have adverted to it and changed my determination [1]. Whether this is so or not ; whether it is necessary, in order to lose possession, that I should advert to it ; or whether it is sufficient that, if I adverted to it, I should determine not to exercise that physical control any longer, or at least not on my own behalf, we need not further discuss : because in this, as in every other case, where we have to inquire into the state of mind of a person, we can only judge of it from external circumstances : and the external circumstances from which we should infer

Intention to possess need not be always present.

[1] Sav. Poss. s. 32. p. 355.

N

that *after* advertence a change of determination had taken place, are precisely those which *upon* advertence would render a change of determination likely. For instance, we infer that the gold digger has abandoned his possession of the quartz from which he has extracted the gold, because we know that he could have no further use for it, and men do not generally care to keep what is useless ; and we should draw the same inference, whether an actual determination to abandon is necessary or not. In many such cases we affirm that the possession is gone, without troubling ourselves with the inquiry, when exactly it was parted with.

How change of mind ascertained.

338.   Questions however sometimes arise, which render it necessary to determine with exactness the point of time when possession is lost ; and if the physical control does not pass at once into any other hands, this is frequently a question of no little difficulty. If indeed the party in possession chooses publicly to declare his intention to abandon it, the difficulty is then solved. But in the absence of such a declaration, we have not only to infer the change of mind from the surrounding circumstances, but also the date of that change. For instance, if the person who has been in possession of a piece of land neglects to cultivate it, or make any other use of it for some years, we may pretty safely infer that he has abandoned it. But if it is necessary to determine exactly when he abandoned it, we can hardly tell. He may have omitted to cultivate, in the first instance, from want of means, and only have abandoned his possession, when he finally discovered that to procure such means was hopeless : or from the experience of previous years he may have concluded, that cultivation at present prices was unprofitable ; but may not then have abandoned all hope of a better market. Thus, the date at which his determination to possess finally changed,

may have been considerably later than the first season for cultivation which he allowed to pass. In such a case, however, in the absence of all evidence to the contrary, it would be the usual rule to take the date of the first indication of an intention to abandon, that is, of the first omission to cultivate, as the date of that determination, leaving it to those interested to establish any other date, if they could.

339[1]. That a person can be in possession of a thing by his representative has never been doubted. But there has not been a complete agreement amongst jurists as to the nature of that possession. It has been frequently treated as a fictitious possession; but against this Savigny argues; and, it appears to me, successfully. Possession through representative

340. The error of treating possession through a representative as fictitious or constructive possession only, is a branch of the error noted above, which treats corporal contact as necessary to true possession. All that is necessary to my possession being the power to resume physical control, and the determination to exercise that control on my own behalf, it is clear that I possess the money in the pocket of my servant, or the farm in the hands of my bailiff, just as much as the rings on my finger, or the furniture in the house of which I live. is real possession.

341. This, however, presumes a representative who is Representative must assent.

---

[1] Sav. Poss. s. 26. p. 304. The idea of possession through another person varies somewhat with the relation between the parties. It is strongest (if I may use the expression) where the relation is that of master and slave; less strong where the relation is that of master and servant; but nevertheless stronger here than where the relation is that of ordinary principal and agent. The difference between theft by a servant and criminal misappropriation in the Indian Penal Code depends upon this variation. See ss. 381 and 405.

N 2

obedient to my commands. In other words, whilst in
order to constitute possession of a thing through my
representative. I must determine to exercise control over
it on my own behalf, the representative must also determine to allow me to exercise that control. As soon as
my representative determines to assume control on his
own behalf, or to submit to the control of another than
myself, my possession is gone. If there be any cases in
which this rule does not apply, they are exceptions, which
the law has introduced to obviate the effects of fraud, or
for some similar purpose : as in the case already discussed,
where some one has intruded upon the property of an
absent owner[1].

Subsequent
assent of
principal is
sufficient.

342. It is not necessary, in order that the principal may
get into possession, that he should have had his attention
turned to the fact, that his representative has brought the
thing under his control. It will be sufficient, that the
representative has this control ; that he means to exercise
it, not for himself, but for his principal ; and that in
so doing, he acts within the scope of the authority conferred upon him. Probably also English lawyers would
consider that, even if without my authority you assumed
control over a thing on my behalf, and I subsequently
ratified your act, I was in exactly the same position as
if the act had been done originally by my order.

Possession
of infants
and
lunatics.

343[2]. It is desirable here to point out how the doctrines
of representative possession are applied to such persons
as infants and lunatics, whom the law considers as labouring under incapacity. The case of these persons appears
at first sight to present considerable difficulties. It may
be said that, as possession in the legal sense comprises a
determination of the will, it follows that persons whom
the law considers as incapable of making such determina-

---

[1] Supra, sect. 333.   [2] Sav. Poss. s. 21. p. 248.

tion—such as children under a certain age and lunatics—
are incapable of acquiring possession; that, however
completely they may have obtained physical control over
a thing, they can have no possession in a legal sense;
that it is (as the Roman lawyers expressively said) as if
one were to put a thing into the hand of a person asleep [1].
Nor can they acquire possession through the act of a
representative; for the assent of the lunatic or infant
as principal would still be necessary to complete it, and
this the infant or lunatic is equally incompetent to give.

344.   To solve this difficulty, we must remember that
the only representative of an infant is his parent or
guardian, and that the only representative of a lunatic is
his committee. Now the relation of parent or guardian to
the infant, and the relation of committee to the lunatic who
is intrusted to his care, is not the simple and ordinary
relation of principal and representative—it is a very
special one; and the primary feature of it is, that the
representative here supplies the mental deficiency of the
person whom he represents. His determination on behalf
of his incapacitated principal has the same result, as the
determination of a principal of full capacity on behalf of
himself. Hence it follows, that if the guardian, for
instance, acquires the physical control over a thing, and
determines to exercise that physical control on behalf of
his ward, though it might be a straining of language to
say that the ward was in possession, yet between the
guardian and the ward, who are in a manner identified,
there is one complete person who is in complete possession :
which possession has precisely the same results for the
benefit of the infant as the possession of a fully competent
person. So too, where the ward himself obtains the
physical control over the thing, the guardian can supply

[1] Dig. bk. 41. tit. 2. sect. 1. par. 3.

what is necessary to complete the possession. For the
ward is under the control of the guardian, so that the
guardian can determine, that the control which his ward
has obtained shall be exercised by the ward on his own
behalf; and thus the possession is complete.

345. It is no doubt curious to find ideas presented in
this somewhat inverted order—to find the representative
acquiescing in the act of the principal, instead of the
principal acquiescing in the act of the representative.
And difficulties naturally arise out of this inversion in
some cases. But many have been cut short by simply
solving them in favour of the disabled persons.

Conditions
necessary for
representa-
tive posses-
sion.
346. Reverting to the main subject of consideration,
we see that, in order to constitute possession in a legal
sense through a representative, three conditions must be
fulfilled :—first, the representative must have the physical
control over the thing; secondly, the representative must
determine that this physical control shall be exercised on
behalf of his principal; thirdly, the principal must assent
to its being so exercised.

347. If either the representative has not the physical
control over the thing, or if the principal does not assent
to that physical control being exercised on his behalf, then
the possession is gone. So too, if the representative
changes his determination to hold the thing for his
principal, and determines to hold it for himself, or for
another, then, properly speaking, the possession is gone. But
here again the law sometimes steps in to prevent the consequences of fraud. For instance, if the thing were land,
and if the representative were simply to change his determination, from a determination to hold the land on behalf
of his principal, to a determination to hold it on behalf of
himself, I think that in every system of law the possession
of the principal would be treated as uninterrupted—at least,

until the denial of the principal's right, or some unequi-
vocal act inconsistent with that right had been brought to
the knowledge of the principal. Such a case would be
very closely analogous to that mentioned above ; namely,
where a man's land is taken possession of by a stranger in
his absence, in which case he does not lose possession, till
he becomes aware of the intrusion[1].

348.   Indeed the law of England as to the possession
of land through a representative goes further. It is
almost impossible for you, if you have received land from
me, upon the understanding that you are to hold it on my
behalf, to change this into a possession on behalf of yourself, and so to oust me without my consent. No declaration
that you could make—no act, however inconsistent with
my possession, could have that effect. So long as you
held the land, the law insists that I am in possession,
and not you.

349.   I am not aware that this exception has been extended to moveables, and therefore, if my representative
determines to exercise his control over them either on
behalf of himself, or of another person, my possession is at
an end ; but the fraudulent character of this act often prevents the legal consequences of possession taking effect.

350 [2].   Derivative possession is the possession which Derivative
one person has of the property of another. The physical possession.
control of a representative is sometimes called his possession ; though, as we have seen, the legal possession in this
case is in the principal. But derivative possession is true
legal possession ; the holder of the thing having the physical
control over it coupled with the determination to exercise
that physical control on behalf of himself.

---

[1] Supra, sect. 333.   [2] Sav. Poss. sect. 23. p. 282.

Distinction between it and representative possession.

351. Hence, between the bare detention of a representative, which is not possession in a legal sense at all, and derivative possession, which is true legal possession, though detached from ownership, there can be no confusion. But there are many well-known legal relations, in which the transfer to one man of the physical control over the property of another forms an essential feature; and it is frequently a question to be determined, whether or no, subsequently to this transfer of the physical control, the possession is in the owner through the transferee as his representative, or whether the transferee holds it derivatively on behalf of himself.

In what cases the possession is transferred.

352. The relations in reference to which this question arises are very numerous; but it most frequently occurs in reference to the relation of principal and agent, of lender and borrower, of letter and hirer, of pledgor and pledgee, or of bailor and bailee.

353. These are relations which constantly arise out of the commonest transactions in daily life; and they are of course subject to express stipulation, as well upon the question of possession as upon any other; but such express stipulation is very rare. And the difficulty is to determine, in the absence of express stipulation, in whom the possession remains.

Under the Roman Law.

354. The Roman lawyers would seem to have proceeded upon the principle, that, where an owner transfers to another the physical control over a thing without the ownership, the transferee should hold the thing as a representative, and that the possession should remain in the owner, in all cases; unless it was necessary for the enjoyment of the other rights which the transferee was to have, that he should have the right of possession also.

355. Nevertheless there has been very considerable contention, even under the Roman Law, in reference to

some of the relations enumerated above, as to where the possession is, after the physical control is transferred. Savigny thinks that under the Roman Law in the case of the agent, the borrower, the hirer, and the bailee, the possession is never transferred; but that in the case of the pledgee it is. And he makes no distinction between land and moveables [1].

356. The English Law would, I think, generally coincide with this; but in one case, that of letting and hiring land, it is very difficult to seize the position taken by our law, because it has remedied special inconveniences by provisions which are hardly consistent with each other. Inasmuch as the tenant of land has in every case an action for any disturbance of his physical control over the land which he holds, not only against strangers, but against his own landlord; seeing too, that in case of loss he recovers the enjoyment of his physical control by a judgment precisely similar in form to the judgment, by which the owner himself recovers; and that the landlord is not nominally, either plaintiff, or defendant, in any action relating to possession, whilst his land is let to a tenant; it would seem as if it were impossible to deny that the tenant has, in contemplation of law, the possession of the land which he holds under his tenancy. Nevertheless this is not so. The view of the English Law was from the first, and still is, that the occupier of land for purposes of cultivation has no interest in, and therefore, *a fortiori,* if he accepts that position, no possession, of the land which he occupies. In this view the tenant is treated merely as a sort of bailiff for the owner, paying the owner a fixed sum out of the profits, and retaining the remainder as his remuneration.

Possession of land by tenants under the English Law.

[1] Sav. Poss. sec. 23, passim.

There is nothing exceptional or peculiar in this view. A similar view has been taken of the position of the *colonus* in Rome, of the *pachter* in Germany, and, I believe, of the *bailleur* in France: and when it was adopted into the English Law, it was probably universal in similar cases throughout Europe. But when the law gave to the tenant rights wholly foreign to the bare relation of bailiff and employer, one might expect to find that the rule, as to which of these parties was in possession, would have been reconsidered. But this was not done. Moreover the notion, that the tenant takes no interest in the land which he occupies, and only represents his landlord, who remains in possession through his tenant (which was reasonable enough when applied to mere cultivating tenancies), has been extended to all cases of lessor and lessee without distinction—to cases where the rights of the owner have been surrendered to the tenant, so completely and for so long a period, that the latter is not only the occupier, but, for the time, almost the owner. Thus suppose, in order to make the matter clearer, that I let my land to you to cultivate at a fixed rent, there is no reason why you should not be considered to hold the land merely as my representative, cultivating it under a contract with me, and having no other rights than such as arise directly out of the contract. But the law has given the cultivating tenant a better position than this, and has conferred upon him rights and remedies which belong properly to possession, and not to contract. This being done it would seem natural to treat his position in reference to the land as thereby changed; in fact to treat him as in possession. But so far from this, if I grant land to you for a term of years, however long, and whether for cultivation or for any other purpose, you take, as grantee, no interest in the land whatever; and

taking no interest in the land, you can only have *detention*
of it, and not *possession*, under the grant. You cannot
even have derivative possession of it; and you must,
therefore, hold it only as my representative, and I must
remain in possession.

357.   These anomalous views upon the subject of the
relation between the occupier of the land and the owner
have caused a good deal of trouble in India. It so happens
that, though the variations in the relation between the
owner of the land and the cultivators of it are almost
infinite, the external features of that relation very rarely
differ.· We almost always find a cultivator in occupation,
making a fixed payment, or handing over some share in
the produce, to the owner. Our early Indian adminis-
trators (as persons would naturally do, who had never
become acquainted with any but one system) took for
granted, that the relation which these external features
represented in India, was the same as that to which we
are most accustomed at home; and transferred to zemindar
and ryot the notions applied by us to landed proprietors
and yearly tenants holding without a lease. This was
highly advantageous to the zemindar, who possibly was
up to that time only a farmer of the revenue, and had no
interest in the land at all. But it would have been
ruinous to the ryot, if it had been pressed against him,
as it placed him entirely at the mercy of the zemindar,
who could, consequently, raise his rent, or eject him at
any moment.

Fortunately several causes combined to prevent the
zemindar taking full advantage of his new position.
But some legislative protection of the ryot has been found
necessary, and the contrivance hit upon is to give the
ryot, under certain circumstances, what is called a 'right
of occupancy,' not at a fixed rent, but at a rent to be

*Possession
of land by
tenants in
India.*

assessed between the parties by a court of law. There
has been scarcely any attempt to ascertain precisely to
what class of rights this 'right of occupancy' belongs ; but,
as there seems to be, on the one hand, a decided inclination to treat the ryot, not as in possession of the land on
his own behalf, but as representative of his landlord, whilst
on the other hand his right is clearly one which is available against all the world, and not merely by way of contract against his landlord (*in rem* and not *in personam*),
it follows that the right must be one in the nature of
a servitude in the general sense of that term [1]; and it is
not altogether unlike that servitude which was known as
superficies in the Roman Law, but it has a more extended
application [2].

Quasi-pos-
session of
incorporeal
things.

358. The term possession, as we have hitherto explained it, clearly assumes some tangible existing thing,
over which the party in possession may exercise his
physical control : but the Roman lawyers extended the
idea of possession to abstractions; to things which are not
perceptible to the senses ; to incorporeal things, as they
are usually called by lawyers.

359. Possession, in a legal sense, as distinguished from
the mere physical control or detention, plainly does not
rest upon a notion, exclusively applicable to things corporeal. The notion upon which the legal idea of
possession rests, is that of making the simple exercise of
this physical control a subject for legal consideration and
protection, apart from ownership. But the simple exercise

---

[1] See infra, sect. 367.

[2] For an explanation of the nature of *superficies* see Smith's
Dictionary of Antiquities *sub voce*. I may observe generally, that
nearly all the expressions of Roman Law which occur in the text
will be found ably explained in this Dictionary.

of any right may, it is obvious, be so considered and pro
tected.

360. We must not conclude from this, that all that we To what
have said about possession may be applied, without dis- things ap-
plicable.
crimination, to the exercise and enjoyment of any rights
whatever. Many of the rules which govern the question
of possession are founded on the existence of something
which may be seen, felt, and handled, and it is only by
a metaphor that these rules can be extended to a right
which may be enjoyed. This is an easy metaphor when
confined within certain limits ; as, for example, when we
speak of a person who enjoys the use of a pathway, or
a watercourse running over the land of another, as being
in possession of the way, or of the watercourse. But
it would be at the least a bold metaphor to speak of a
doctor in large practice as in possession (in a legal sense)
of his practice.

361. The Roman lawyers contented themselves with
extending the legal idea of possession to those rights
which they denominated servitudes—a class of rights
similar to, but more extensive than, that class of rights
which we call easements. And they constructed for
the protection of the enjoyment of rights of this class
rules closely analogous to those for the protection of the
physical control over things corporeal. Modern lawyers
have attempted to give to the idea of possession a much
wider extension ; and this extension with us is somewhat
indefinite. Thus by statute the possession of an advowson
is expressly protected as opposed to the title of it : so
also a person collecting tolls has been treated as in legal
possession of the right to take tolls : and it has been even
suggested to treat a person collecting the interest of a debt
as in possession of the debt.

362. Whether or no such an extension of the idea of

possession is useful, this is not the place to consider. It is certain that the extension, if made at all, should be made with some circumspection. Care must be taken in each new application, not only that the nature of the subject is such that the idea of possession is capable of being analogically applied to it, but also that it is one to which the legal consequences of possession are suitable. To apply those consequences to the exercise of all rights, without discrimination, would produce the greatest confusion.

363.   To whatever extent the idea of possession has been carried, the discussion of it has remained within the limits assigned by the Roman lawyers, namely, the possession of things corporeal, and of servitudes. All, therefore, that we can say further on this subject, must be in connection with the latter class of rights, which we shall hereafter consider [1].

Only one person in possession at a time.

364.   It is a fundamental principle which is obscured by language in ordinary use, but which must never be lost sight of, that only one person can be in possession of the same thing at the same time. This principle is easily deduced from what has been above stated as to the legal notion of possession. Possession, in a legal sense, is the determination to exercise physical control over a thing on one's own behalf, coupled with the capacity of doing so ; and is, therefore, of necessity exclusive.

365.   This principle has, however, been obscured by the double meaning of the term possession. Possession sometimes means the physical control simply ; the proper word for which is detention. And of course, one person may have the detention and another may have the possession in the legal sense of the term. Thus the money which is in

[1] See infra, sect. 376.

the hands of my servant is under his immediate control, and in popular language is in his possession; but in a legal sense, inasmuch as that control will be exercised on my behalf exclusively, it is in my possession, and not in his.

366. A more difficult case is that of co-ownership. But, as I have already had occasion to state, the English Law has expressed itself on this subject by a phrase, which recognises in a very remarkable manner the distinction between possession, in the sense of simple detention, and possession in a legal sense; and by so doing exactly clears away, so far as co-owners are concerned, any difficulty as to the proposition which we are now considering. The rule of English Law, laid down by Littleton, and adopted by every succeeding lawyer up to the present time, is, that ·if there be two co-owners, each is in possession of the whole and of the half. As I said above[1] (and it will be clearer now), what this must mean is, that whereas each owner has access to, and control over every part of the property, and so may be said to have possession in the sense of detention of the whole, yet he exercises that control, not on behalf of himself alone, but partly on behalf of himself, in respect of his own share, and partly as representative of his co-owner, in respect of his co-owner's share. In contemplation of law, therefore, he is only in possession of his own share. However many co-owners there may be, each will in contemplation of law be exactly in the same position; that is to say, each will be in possession of his share. It will be remembered, that I have stated some reasons for the application of similar ideas to family ownership in India[2]. Of course where several persons are united into one juristical person there is no difficulty.

Possession co-owners.

---

[1] Supra, sect. 312.　　　　　[2] Supra, sect. 311.

CHAPTER IX.

SERVITUDES OR EASEMENTS.

Servitudes, how related to ownership.

367. Servitudes belong to that class of rights which are *in rem* and *in re :* in other words, they are rights over a thing, which are available against the world at large, and not against any particular person. They are also, in the neat and expressive language of the Roman Law, rights *in re alienâ*—rights over a thing which is owned by another. They are rights closely analogous to ownership, but less in extent ; and they may be sometimes conveniently viewed as fragments of ownership, which is then considered as the sum of all those rights over a thing, which are available against persons generally.

Real and personal servitudes.

368. The Roman lawyers, and most European lawyers following their example, have divided servitudes into real and personal. This distinction does not in any way correspond with the English distinction of property generally into real and personal. Real servitudes was the name given to those rights, which a man had over one thing by reason of his ownership of another. Personal servitudes was the name given to those rights, which a man had over a thing independently of his ownership of anything else. Thus the right of the owner of Blackacre, as such, to walk across his neighbour's close Whiteacre, would, in the language of the Roman Law, be called a real servitude. But the right

of a lodger to occupy an apartment in another man's house, would, by a Roman or continental lawyer, be considered as a personal servitude. This distinction corresponds to the general one made by English lawyers between rights appendant and rights in gross.

369. The rights generally comprised by both ancient and modern lawyers, under the term servitudes, real and personal, are far more numerous than those which English lawyers comprise under the term easements. None of those servitudes, which are generally deemed to be personal, and only some of those servitudes, which are generally deemed to be real, are rights to which an English lawyer would give the name of easements.

Easements a kind of servitudes.

370. On the other hand, there is a doubt, whether all the rights to which we give the name of easements, and which, in general jurisprudence, would fall under the class of real servitudes, must, under the English Law, be real also ; or, to use an English phrase, whether the rights which we call easements must be all appendant, and not in gross. Some persons think, that it would be impossible under the English Law to create any right of the nature of an easement in gross ; and that if I granted to you a right of way over my field, that would only give you a right *in personam*, and not an easement. No doubt this is the true test : a right *in personam*, created by contract, to do something on the land of another, is not an easement at all. An easement belongs to that class of rights which, like ownership, are available (*in rem*) against the world at large [1].

Whether all easements are real ?

371. Adopting the language of the Roman Law, English lawyers call the land to which the easement is attached the dominant land, and the land over which it is exercised, the servient land : the owner of the dominant

Dominant and servient.

[1] See Gale on Easements, p. 13 (fourth edition).

O

land they call the dominant owner, and the owner of the servient land they call the servient owner.

Enumeration of easements. 372.   The rights over things to which English lawyers have applied the name of easements are—rights of way over the land of another ; rights to fetch water from a spring or stream on the land of another ; rights to convey water or any other substance on to your neighbour's land ; rights to the support of something affixed to your own land by your neighbour's land, or by something affixed to his land; rights to receive light, air, or water uninterrupted and undeteriorated by anything done on your neighbour's land.

The selection is an arbitrary one. 373.   This enumeration is, possibly, not perfect in expression ; for the catalogue of easements is perhaps not quite settled.   Anyhow there is an obvious error in supposing it to be otherwise than merely arbitrary.   There is no reason in the nature of the rights themselves, why a right to take water from a spring on your neighbour's land should be reckoned as an easement, but a right to take coal from a mine there should not.   It has been said that the distinction is, that the first is for convenience only, whilst the latter is for profit.   But this, besides being a very slender distinction, is not always observed.   The right to take water is just as much an easement, if the water be made into beer, and sold by the person who takes it, as if it be used by himself for domestic purposes. Sometimes the distinction is put in another way.   Thus it is said, that the mutual right of support, which adjoining owners of land have against each other, where there has been no building, is an ordinary or natural right of property (i. e. ownership), and not an easement ; and in like manner it is said, that the right to receive a flow of water in its natural stream is an ordinary or natural right of property (i. e. ownership), and not an easement [1].

[1] Gale on Easements, p. 21 (fourth edition).

But all the acknowledged easements of English Law are rights of ownership, in the same sense precisely that rights of natural support, and rights to water in its natural course, are so. All are rights of ownership in this sense only—that they are rights over a specific thing, available against the world at large. The force of the distinction, therefore, lies in the epithet 'natural' or 'ordinary,' which I take to mean pretty nearly the same thing; and to express that the rights in question are so common, that their existence is always assumed, without resort to the complicated rules which I shall hereafter discuss. But if this be the right interpretation of the distinction (and the terms are so vague and obscure, that I cannot be quite sure of it), then it has nothing whatever to do with the nature of the rights, but only with their mode of acquisition.

374. The truth is, that the reason why certain rights came to be specially considered under the name of easements, is a mere reason ·of convenience, and not a legal reason at all. It arose from the fact that the rights, which are usually considered under that name, are those which regulate the enjoyment of their respective properties by contiguous owners, on points of great importance, upon which they are very likely to come into conflict: they are rights which relate to getting rid of that which is noxious; to procuring a plentiful supply of that which is useful; to free ingress and egress; and to the commodious exercise of trade. It was perceived by the judges, who created this branch of law, that some of these rights could be conveniently governed by a single set of rules; and in framing these rules, it was of course desirable to call by one name all the rights to which they applied. If any rights of the same kind have not been called easements, and so excluded from the operation of these rules, it has

been simply because it was not considered desirable to bring such rights within their operation.

Acquisition of easements by prescription.

375. All the special rules upon the subject of easements have reference to this single question—how they may be acquired or lost upon a principle which, speaking generally, I may call prescription. I shall, in the next chapter, explain the conception of prescription in English Law, and shall shew how it is based upon possession, or rather, if we are speaking of things not corporeally existent, upon quasi-possession; the general nature of which I have already discussed.

What constitutes possession of an easement.

376. I shall now confine myself to the consideration, preliminary to the discussion of the rules of prescription as applied to easements, of what constitutes the quasi-possession of an easement. It may be truly said that no subject has proved a greater stumblingblock to jurists of all countries, than the acquisition of easements by prescription; and nearly all the difficulties upon this matter may be traced to an imperfect conception of the possession on which prescription is based. Fortunately the subject has been fully investigated by Savigny, and I have borrowed the results of his investigation. For although Savigny professes to give only such conclusions as are founded upon the Roman Law, they are substantially the same as those at which English lawyers have long been struggling to arrive; and partially have arrived; though sometimes by a method admitted to be clumsy [1], and nearly always by a route which is not the most direct.

Analogy to possession of corporeal things.

377 [2]. The legal conception of the quasi-possession of

[1] First Report of Real Property Commissioners, p. 51.

[2] What follows, to the end of the chapter, is chiefly a paraphrase of parts of section 46 of the Treatise on Possession. But in order to make it more easy of comprehension, I have occasionally amplified Savigny's very condensed expressions, and inserted two or three illustrations.

an incorporeal thing, such as an easement, is analogous in
all respects to' the conception of the possession of a corporeal thing; of which conception, as above stated[1], it is an
extension. Thus, in order that there may be quasi-possession of an easement, it is not necessary that there should
be actual enjoyment of it, any more than it is necessary
that there should be actual contact, in order to constitute
possession of a thing corporeally existent. The physical
possibility of exercising or enjoying the easement, coupled
with the determination to exercise and enjoy it on one's
own behalf, constitutes quasi-possession, just as a similar
combination of physical and mental elements constitutes
possession of land or goods. Neither the physical possibility of enjoyment, nor the actual enjoyment, will alone
constitute quasi-possession. I may walk across your-land
whenever I like to pay you a visit, or transact business
with you at your house, but I am still not in quasi-possession of any easement in the nature of a way across your
land. In walking across your land I am only using the
means, which all owners of houses provide for their
friends and neighbours, of obtaining ready access to
them as occasion may require : should you lock the
gate, I should have nothing to complain of, and could
not force my way in. To use the exact expression of
Savigny, to constitute quasi-possession of an easement, it
is not sufficient that the exercise or enjoyment of it should
be merely *de facto*, or accidental, it must be as of right
(*tanquam suo jure*); and there must be not only the permission, but the *submission* (*patientia*) of the person upon
whose land the easement is exercised or enjoyed. So, on
the other hand, if my neighbour grants me a way across
his field, and consequently removes from his gate a lock
which has hitherto prevented my using it, and informs me

---

[1] Supra, sect. 358.

that the road is at my service, I am just as completely in possession of the way by such a ceremony, as if, in assertion of my right, I actually walked along the road in question.

Positive and negative easements.

378.   In the case of positive easements, that is to say, easements which consist in doing something upon your neighbour's land, there is not much difficulty in determining, whether or no the circumstances constitute quasi-possession of them ; and the distinction above pointed out between the mere *de facto* exercise or enjoyment, and exercise or enjoyment as of right, has always been recognised with tolerable clearness.   But the quasi-possession of negative easements, that is, of easements which consist in your neighbour abstaining from doing something on his land—of which the easement not to build so as to obstruct the passage of light and air is the most frequent example—is far more difficult to comprehend, and has not been so well understood.   Savigny has discussed the quasi-possession of negative easements very fully, and he points out, first, that we must carefully distinguish between acquiring the right itself, and acquiring the mere quasi-possession of the easement, which may be without the right ; just as we may acquire possession of land without acquiring the right to possession, or ownership.   For acquiring the right a simple grant is sufficient : but suppose two strangers to be adjoining owners, how does one of them get into quasi-possession of negative easements over the land of the other?   That is the question to be solved.

Enjoyment as 'of right.'

379.   One case of acquisition (he says) of the possession of this kind of easement is undisputed ; namely, when the act, which is opposed to the servitude, is actually attempted by the owner of the servient land, but prevented ; whether by the simple protest of the owner of the dominant land,

by force, or by the decree of a court of justice. As, for
instance, if I claim as an easement the uninterrupted
flow of a stream issuing from a spring in your land, I
should clearly be in possession of it, if, upon your damming
up the stream before it left your land, I complained to
you, and you thereupon re-opened it ; or if I myself cut the
dam, which act you did not, resent ; or if I obtained an
order of court, that it should be reopened. Where no
such actual attempt to do the act, which is opposed to the
easement, is made and prevented, some persons have
maintained that, in order to put the owner of the
dominant land in possession of the easement, a pretence
must be made by the owner of the servient land of doing
the act opposed to the easement—as, for instance, a pretence of damming up the stream by throwing in a few
shovelfuls of earth—to be followed by formal opposition on
the part of the dominant owner, and that again by a pre-
tended submission on the part of the servient owner.
Savigny protests strongly, as he always does, against
this sort of symbolical action, which he considers as
unsuitable to the idea of possession, as it is undoubtedly
unknown in practice. Others hold an exactly opposite
opinion, which Savigny himself at one time shared ; main-
taining, that the simple omission by the servient owner to
do any act opposed to the enjoyment of the easement, puts
the dominant owner in possession of it. But this leads
at once to the conclusion, which Savigny, with good
reason, declares to be nothing less than monstrous, that
every landowner is in legal possession, and entitled to all
the advantages which result from that possession, of
numberless easements, as against all his neighbours ; so
that, for instance, the moment a man builds a house, he
is, not of course entitled to, but in possession of, and (as it
were) on the road to acquire by enjoyment, an easement

which prevents all his neighbours from building within a certain distance of him. The error of the latter opinion consists in this: that it loses sight of that which is so important, when we are considering what constitutes quasi-possession in a legal sense ; namely, that it is founded, not upon every enjoyment or exercise of the easement, but only upon an enjoyment or exercise of it *as of right ;* not upon the mere inaction of the other party, but on his submission (*patientia*) to necessity. Anything which establishes, that the exercise or enjoyment is of this character, and not merely *de facto* or accidental, is sufficient to establish quasi-possession in a legal sense. This is clear enough in the undisputed case mentioned above, where there has been an actual attempt to do the act opposed to the easement, followed by a protest submitted to or enforced. So, where the right itself has been granted, no formal or symbolical induction into the exercise or enjoyment of easement is necessary. The exercise or enjoyment of the easement and the passiveness of the other party are now, not merely *de facto* or accidental, but directly referable to the right, which has been acquired by grant.

CHAPTER X.

Prescription and Limitation.

380.   Having in a former chapter considered the nature *Possession, how pro-* of possession in a legal sense, we have now to discuss *tected by prescription* one of its principal consequences.   As I have pointed *and limita-tion.* out, what gives to the topic of possession its greatest importance is that, apart from ownership, it is itself a right which is protected by the law.   What I have now to consider are those rules of law, by which that protection is carried to the extent of recognising the person in possession, by reason simply of his possession, as himself the owner, or, at any rate, of refusing to recognise any other claim to the ownership.

381.   This protection, in one form or the other, is *Two forms of protection.* extended to long possession by every system of law with which we are acquainted.   Sometimes it is laid down, plainly and simply, that a person, who has been for a certain time in possession, shall be considered as owner. Sometimes, without professing in express terms to recognise the person in possession as owner, all means of asserting his ownership are taken away from any other claimant, who has been for a certain time out of possession.   In the Roman Law, the English Law, and systems derived from the English, both forms of protection are in use ; and are sometimes, as will be seen, rather curiously combined.

382. It is a remarkable instance of the shifting use of language that the word 'prescription' has been used, sometimes exclusively in reference to one of these distinct forms; sometimes exclusively in reference to the other; sometimes in reference to both, without any distinction. Thus the Roman lawyers expressed by the term prescription the defence, which a person who had been a certain time in possession could set up, when a claim of ownership was made against him—that he had been so long in possession, and ought not to be disturbed. Lord Coke [1], on the other hand, defines prescription as the acquisition of title by length of time and enjoyment. The authors of the French Code use very similar language to that of Lord Coke in their definition of prescription [2]; and French lawyers do not recognise the distinction between barring the remedy and transferring the right, which our law so carefully preserves [3]. I shall distinguish these two kinds of protection, which the law extends to possession, by the terms 'prescription' and 'limitation;' using the term prescription, not in the sense of the Roman lawyers, but in the sense which Lord Coke has given to it. It is true that Blackstone (and in this respect he is followed by later writers) gives to the word prescription a narrower signification, which will be explained presently [4]; but I think it better to use an old

[1] Coke upon Littleton, p. 113, folio *b.* The Latin name for what Lord Coke describes as prescription was *usucapio.* The distinction between barring the remedy and transferring the ownership was, however, abolished by Justinian. See Book II. tit. 6, of the Institutes. Savigny points out, that it would have been more correct thenceforward to drop the term prescription, and to call it all usucaption. Sav. Poss. sect. 2.

[2] Code Civil, sect. 2219.

[3] See Pothier, Traité de la Prescription, chapitre préliminaire. See also infra, sect. 393.   [4] Infra, sect. 384.

word, in the sense attributed to it by Lord Coke and most
continental writers, than in deference to Blackstone's
authority, to invent a new one.

383. The English law relating to limitation and prescription presents some peculiar features, mostly traceable to its historical development. The rules on the
subject are partly the expressions of the legislature, and
partly the growth of judicial decision. The earlier legislative provisions relate almost entirely to the ownership
of land. They have been carefully collected in the First
Report of the Real Property Commissioners. Some of
these provisions, after a certain length of possession, merely
bar the remedy of the owner, and are, therefore, rules of
limitation; but others, under similar circumstances, transfer
the ownership, and are, therefore, rules of prescription.
So that, when Blackstone asserts that prescription in
English law does not apply to land [1], this is not true of
prescription in the sense which Lord Coke attributes to
the word, and in which I use it.

Early English law of prescription and limitation as applied to ownership of land.

383 *a*. It is as well to note here one feature of the
English law relating to the acquisition of ownership by
prescription, which distinguishes it from almost every
other system, both ancient and modern. The Roman
Law, and the numerous foreign systems founded upon it,
require, as a general rule, that the possession by which
a person is to acquire ownership should have been founded
on a 'just title;' which I think an English lawyer would
express by saying, that it must have been obtained under
a colour of right. Upon this general rule the Roman
Law and the other analogous systems have then proceeded
to graft numerous exceptions. Our law, on the other
hand, does not start with any distinction between possession acquired under colour of right, and possession

---

[1] Commentaries, vol. ii. p. 264.

acquired by a trespass; in some cases, however, as for instance where the possession has been acquired by fraud, we find exceptions.

As applied to rights over land other than ownership.

384. No rules, either of prescription or of limitation, having been at first laid down by the legislature, for the protection of the possession, or rather the quasi-possession, of rights over land other than ownership—such, for instance, as easements, rights of common, and the like—the judges, justifying themselves by the analogy of the two cases, adopted rules for the protection of the possession of such rights, similar to those which the legislature had adopted for the protection of the possession of the land

Time immemorial.

itself. The first rule so adopted was, that an indefeasible title to such rights should be gained by a possession of them (that is, a quasi-possession), which had lasted so long that its origin could not be traced; or, as it was expressed, which had lasted from time immemorial. This, of course, was a rule of prescription; and it is this alone which Blackstone consents to recognise as prescription in English law [1]; though why he should limit the use of that word to the acquisition of rights over land other than ownership does not appear. That the ownership of land, under the old law at any rate, could be acquired by lapse of time, cannot be denied.

Arbitrary restriction to reign of Richard I.

384 a. The next step taken by judges was somewhat bolder, when they held (still following the analogy of the legislative provisions as to ownership) that time immemorial should be reckoned to commence from the first year of the reign of Richard the First. The result of this was to establish, with reference to rights over land other than ownership, a definite but constantly increasing period of prescription. As time went on, this period got to be

Twenty years' enjoyment.

very long, and an expedient was resorted to for shortening

[1] Commentaries, vol. ii. p. 264.

it, which could never have been thought of, but for the peculiar relation which subsists between judge and jury in England. Still following in the steps of the legislature, which had adopted a period of twenty years as the basis of some of its provisions, the judges got into the habit, when it was shewn that the enjoyment of a right of this kind had lasted twenty years, of advising juries to presume that it had been enjoyed from time immemorial; and they at last came to insist on this in such strong terms, that it is very difficult to distinguish their advice from a direction in point of law, that twenty years' enjoyment was sufficient to constitute a title[1]. Upon such matters juries generally conform pretty readily to the advice which comes to them from the Bench, and the expedient, though open to very grave objections, and far from being entirely successful, has been more so than might have been expected.

[1] Nothing can be more difficult than to say, whether those remarks which judges have usually made to juries upon such topics, are directions as to the law, or advice to them as to how they ought to deal with questions within their own province, and therefore, in common language, questions of fact. I have adverted below to the radical distinction between a rule of prescription and the presumption of a title (sect. 417); but English judges have, in their struggle to obtain satisfactory results, been obliged, not only to confound this distinction, but also to confound the distinction between presumptions, which the law requires to be made, and presumptions, which experience teaches us ought to be made. I doubt if it would be possible to give a stronger instance of legal contortion than that state of the law, under which a jury were, and to some extent still are, required to find that to be true, which is well known to themselves, to the judge, and to the counsel, to be untrue (see First Report of Real Property Commissioners, p. 51); which allows their verdict to be set aside as *against the evidence*, if they should not do as they are required (see Gale on Easements, p. 149, fourth ed.); but which provides no better means for securing the ultimate object, than to ask another jury to become parties to a similar proceeding.

385. In the meantime, for various reasons, the rules laid down by the legislature relating to the protection of the possession of the land itself against a claim of ownership, had become almost entirely obsolete. But the judges have never ventured to lay down on their own authority any new rules, either of prescription or limitation, relating to the ownership of land. When dealing with long possession, as against claims of ownership which had been long dormant, they have contented themselves with supplementing the existing legislative rules upon the subject, by impressing upon juries, but rather less imperatively than in the case of rights other than ownership, the duty of presuming particular facts in favour of the title of the person in possession. How such presumptions differ from rules of prescription or limitation, I shall have occasion hereafter to explain [1].

386. All the rules both of prescription and limitation, as well those which relate to the ownership of land, as those which relate to rights over land other than ownership, were reconsidered about forty years ago; and the result of this reconsideration was the passing of two statutes, the 2 and 3 William IV. ch. lxxi. and the 3 and 4 William IV. ch. xxvii. [2] The first of these statutes contains provisions as to the effect of possession, or quasi-possession, upon rights over land other than ownership; the second contains provisions as to the effect of possession on the ownership itself. The wording of both statutes has been the subject of much criticism. It deserves careful notice; for whilst these two statutes are the basis of the present English law of prescription and limitation, the language in which their provisions are expressed, and the conceptions of the law which they disclose, have also largely influenced the analogous law in all the great

---

[1] Infra, sect. 417.　　　　[2] See App. B.

dependencies of England ; whether that law has been expressly created by local legislatures, or has been generated in the course of judicial decision by local courts.

387.   The Prescription Act, as the Act of 2 and 3 William IV. is usually called, and as its name implies, directly provides for the acquisition of the right by the possession or enjoyment of it.   I shall have, hereafter, to make some observations on the wording of these provisions; I now only refer to their general character.   On the other hand, the Act of 3 and 4 William IV. which relates to ownership, and provides that after a person has been out of possession of land for twenty years, he shall not be able to resort to the usual procedure to establish his ownership and regain possession, is generally classed as a statute of limitation.   But this statute contains a further provision, which, if it does not justify us at once in taking it out of the category of rules of limitation, and inserting it amongst those of prescription, at least gives it a special place somewhere between the two.   Besides barring the remedy, the statute expressly declares that the *right and title* of the person, who has been for the given period out of possession, shall be extinguished.

388.   In order, however, to arrive at a conclusion as to the true nature of this statute, we must contrast with this a third feature in it, which, like that first noticed, belongs rather to a rule of limitation than to a rule of prescription. Nothing is anywhere said in this statute about how long the party, who seeks to protect himself by it, must have been in possession ; all that is necessary both to bar the remedy and to extinguish the title of a claimant is, that he should have been for a certain specified time *out* of possession ; and the party in possession will get the benefit of the statute, however short a time he has been *in*.   Now, in rules of prescription, we generally find that, in order to

[margin note:] Prescription Act.

[margin note:] Whether 3 & 4 Wm. IV. c. xxvii. is a rule of limitation or prescription.

gain a title, the party claiming it must either himself have been long in possession, or have succeeded to others who have been so, and with whom, either as heir, or purchaser, or devisee, or in some other way, he is closely connected. A succession of mere strangers could not generally tack their periods of possession one to another.

389. I may also point out one more peculiarity in the statute, which would seem to indicate that the frame of it had not been very clearly settled before it was drawn : a circumstance which perhaps accounts for its ambiguous character. The statute, as I have said, bars after a certain period the remedy of the claimant ; and it also simultaneously extinguishes his ownership. But it was not necessary to have both these provisions; the latter renders the former altogether superfluous.

Tendency of decisions.

390. These peculiarities have naturally led to very grave doubts upon the construction of the statute. Where, by lapse of time and want of possession, the ownership of the original owner is extinct, a question is very frequently raised, whether this is replaced by the ownership of the person who is then in possession. There seems to have been an inclination to take a middle course, and to recognise the ownership of the possessor, where his possession has lasted twenty years ; and also where a continuous twenty years' possession can be made up of the possession of the party actually in, and the possession of his predecessors, whom he has succeeded as heir, or purchaser, or devisee, or the like ; but to refuse it to the last of a series of persons, strangers to each other, though the total period of their possession may be so long, that the title of any other owner is extinguished. It is obvious that such a distinction is not altogether at variance with the current rules of prescription, which, as I have already pointed out, do generally

require a certain duration of possession, but under certain
circumstances will connect successive periods. Still there
is nothing in the statute itself which justifies the distinction, and it leaves the absurd and mischievous result
that, in cases where the successive periods cannot be
added together, the land is without an owner. And there
is some indication that the courts will yet refuse to
recognise any such distinction, and that they will treat
the ownership in all cases where the act applies, as being
transferred to the party in possession [1].

391. I may here also observe, that the analogous provisions made by the Indian legislature are in form rules
of limitation : they merely bar the remedy after the
claimant has been a certain number of years out of possession ; and they do not contain any provision for extinguishing the title of the owner after that period has
elapsed. It has, nevertheless, been the practice in India
to consider, that the result of these provisions is to transfer
the ownership to the party in possession ; and this view
has been confirmed by a decision of the Privy Council [2].
It cannot be doubted that this is a bolder step than is
required to put a similar construction on the English
statute, which, besides barring the remedy, extinguishes
the title ; and it would, therefore, be somewhat strange
if the English statute should not be also construed as
transferring the ownership. It may be true that the
courts in India felt very strongly the inconvenience which
would result from that anomalous condition, in which the
possessor has all the rights of an owner except the title,
and there are claimants to the title, who can neither

*Interpre-
tation of
analogous
provisions in
India.*

[1] See the case of Asher against Whitelock, reported in the Law
Reports, Queen's Bench, vol. i. p. 1; and Dixon against Gayfere, in
Beavan's Reports, vol. xvii. p. 421.
[2] See the case reported in Moore's Indian Appeals, vol. ii. p. 345.

exercise or recover any of the rights of ownership: but similar considerations are not altogether inapplicable to the question in England also.

Transfer of ownership of moveables to party in possession.

392. The rules of English Law which relate to the protection of the possession of moveables are always in form rules of limitation. After a period, generally very much shorter than in the case of land, the person in possession is protected against any claim set up as owner. I do not think, however, that it has ever been doubted that the ownership is transferred to the person in possession, after the possession has lasted so long that the claim of any other owner is barred.

Prescription and limitation protect possession.

393. Rules of limitation and prescription are always founded on possession. Lord Coke's definition of prescription (to which I have already referred[1]) is, that it is the acquisition of title, under the authority of law, by user and time. Pothier[2] defines prescription as the means by which a man acquires the ownership of a thing, through the peaceable and uninterrupted possession of it for a period of time determined by the law. The word employed by Lord Coke, which I have translated by 'user,' is *usus:* and I have no doubt he means to express by it the same thing as the French lawyers express by possession. *Usus* is a technical term of the Roman Law, from which Lord Coke borrowed it. As such it had two perfectly distinct meanings. It signified the mere use or enjoyment of a thing by permission or agreement of the owner, as the use of an apartment in another person's house; and I have before adverted[3] to the connection which has been supposed to exist between *usus* in this sense, and the use which is the foundation of a peculiar

---

[1] Supra, sect. 382.

[2] Traité de la Préscription, chapitre préliminaire.

[3] Supra, sect. 305.

doctrine of Courts of Chancery in England as to the ownership of property. But *usus* had another signification in the Roman Law; it signified specially that kind of enjoyment which by (what we call) prescription leads to ownership. It is in this sense that it is employed in the Twelve Tables, and in the compound word *usucapio*[1].

394. Rules of limitation are equally founded on possession; only instead of being based, as rules of prescription generally are, on the duration of the retention of possession by one party, they are based upon the duration of the loss of it by the other. Though the mode in which the period is calculated is sometimes rather complicated, these rules generally amount to a declaration, that the claimant shall have no action or suit to recover the land, but within so many years of the time when he was last in possession.

395. When we speak of the loss of possession subjecting us to the penalty, or the gain of possession procuring for us the benefit of rules of limitation or prescription, it is not the mere physical detention of which we speak, but possession in the legal sense; namely, the physical control over the thing, coupled with the determination to exercise it on one's own behalf. He who holds a thing as representative of another, whether as servant or agent, or in any other capacity, does not thereby acquire the benefit of limitation, or of prescription, on his own behalf: whilst, on the other hand, the principal, who can hold possession, in the legal sense, through his representative, may thereby acquire that benefit. Moreover, rules of limitation and prescription have never been extended to that kind of possession which we have

The possession which is protected is not detention, but possession in a legal sense,

and which is not derivative.

---

[1] '*Usus auctoritas fundi biennium cæterarum rerum annuus usus esto.*' The phrases *usu capere* and *possessione capere* were equivalent. See Smith's Dict. of Antiquities, art. *Usucapio*.

called derivative; where, though a man has the physical control over a thing, and determines to exercise that physical control on his own behalf, and is, therefore, in possession, yet he does not possess the thing as owner, but acknowledges some one else as owner; as in the case of the pledgee or tenant in possession.

396. Most systems of law expressly acknowledge these requirements. Thus Pothier [1] lays it down that possession is necessary to prescription, and that it must be possession as *owner*, adopting the phraseology of the Roman Law. This excludes both representative and derivative possession. It is perhaps to be regretted that this simple and expressive language was not adopted by our own legislature, when summing up the law in the two statutes I have mentioned; as we should have been thereby saved a long and somewhat troublesome investigation into the meaning of these statutes, in order to establish, that the rules of limitation and prescription now existing under them embrace these general principles, which a very few words would clearly have expressed. But practically we have been brought to the same result. It is true that the 3 and 4 William IV. c. xxvii. in its main provision says nothing about possession [2]. No person, it says, shall bring an action to recover any land, but within twenty years after the right to bring such action first accrued. But subsequently the time when the right to bring the action accrues is explained to mean, the time when the person claiming the land was dispossessed, or discontinued his possession. Now that the statute does not here speak of mere physical detention is shewn by this; that no one ever thought of applying it to the case in which the physical detention alone is parted with; as, for instance, when a thing is given into the hands of a servant or agent.

[1] Traité de la Préscription, s. 27.   [2] See Appendix B.

Though the rules which govern the acquiring and retaining possession by a principal through a representative
have not been recognised expressly in this statute,
they have been always acted upon in applying it.
So too the statute is never applied to cases where,
though, the possession is undoubtedly parted with by
the owner, and gained by some one else, the possession
gained is derivative possession only. Thus no one can
deny that the pledgor, when he hands over the thing
pledged to the pledgee, is thereby dispossessed. He loses
thereby, not only the bare detention, but the possession
in the legal sense ; for the pledgee both holds the thing
under his physical control, and holds it not *for*, but
against the owner. Yet because he holds not as owner,
but all the while recognising the pledgor as owner, he
has not the benefit of prescription in any system of jurisprudence. And accordingly the English Law has not
applied to the pledgor the penalty which this statute
imposes on loss of possession. Such cases would fall
within the literal definition of the commencement of the
period of limitation contained in the statute. The
pledgor is dispossessed or has discontinued his possession.
But both cases of derivative possession, and also cases
where the physical possession only is transferred, are
equally excluded by the assumption, which obviously
overrides the whole statute, that there has been a complete dispossession by a person, who does not acknowledge
the other's rights, but denies them ; and not only denies
them, but interferes with them in such a way as to amount
to a breach of the law, for which an action would lie.
But between the owner and the derivative or representative possessor there is no breach of the law, and,
therefore, no right of action.

397. The general principles adopted by English Connection
between

lawyers with regard to the acquisition of rights over land other than ownership, and which are, therefore, only sus- ceptible of possession in a metaphorical sense, have, like most of the rules upon the same subject which prevail upon the continent, been in some sort derived from the Roman Law. It has indeed been said, that the law of England 'as cited by Lord Coke from Bracton, exactly agrees with the Civil Law[1],' by which is probably meant the Roman Law of the time of Justinian. But to this I am unable altogether to assent. I doubt whether the present law of England on this point can be identified with that laid down by Bracton; or that laid down by Bracton with what is called the Civil Law. I must first remark that Lord Coke, in the passage referred to, applies to the acquisition of things incorporeal words which Bracton expressly limits to the discussion of the acquisition of things corporeal; the acquisition of rights over things incorporeal being reserved by Bracton for the following chapter, which contains nothing directly bearing upon the subject of prescription[2]. Bracton, indeed, as far as I can discover, nowhere treats directly of the acquisition by prescription of rights other than ownership,

---

[1] Gale on Easements, p. 122.

[2] Coke upon Littleton, fol. 113 a. The passage of Bracton to which Lord Coke refers is in book ii. chap. xxii. fol. 51 b. The words are, '*Dictum est in praecedentibus, qualiter rerum corporalium dominia ex titulo et justâ causâ acquirendi transferuntur per tradi- tionem. Nunc autem dicendum qualiter transferuntur sine titulo et traditione per usucaptionem scilicet per longam, continuam, et paci- ficam possessionem, ex diuturno tempore et sine traditione.*' The acqui- sition of things incorporeal commences (as he tells us) in chapter xxiii. I have not overlooked the passage at the end of chapter xxii., where Bracton undoubtedly speaks of easements, but only of their *posses- sion*, which he certainly does *not* say will confer a title, and rather implies the contrary ('*ita quod taliter utens sine brevi et judicio ejici non poterit*').

except in the single case of common of pasture ; to which
passage Lord Coke also refers, but which he does not
correctly quote [1]. Moreover, neither as regards corporeal
things, nor as regards incorporeal things (so far as he treats
of them), would it be safe to affirm that Bracton's rules of
prescription are identical, either with the strict Roman
Law, or any modification of it, which may at any time
have been known as Civil Law. As regards corporeal
things, Bracton ignores the distinction, so important in
the Roman Law, and never lost sight of by the com-
mentators upon it, between possession which is founded
on a just title and possession which is not ; contenting
himself with the far less comprehensive requirements,
that the possession must be continuous and peaceful [2].
As regards the acquisition of incorporeal things, the rules
of Roman Law varied so greatly at different times, and
so greatly also in reference to different kinds of rights,
that any general statement of identity would be most
hazardous. Upon the cardinal point just referred to, I
very much doubt whether here again Bracton did not
exactly reverse the Roman Law. I doubt whether he
was prepared to admit the acquisition by prescription of
incorporeal things in any case without just title [3]. At

[1] Bracton, book iv. chap. xxxviii. fol. 222 b.

[2] Ib., book ii. chap. xxii. fol. 51 b. See the passage quoted above.
He says expressly that ownership may be acquired *sine titulo et
traditione,* which he opposes to *ex titulo et justâ causâ.*

[3] I do not state this positively ; but it is remarkable that in the
passage above referred to, where he speaks of the acquisition of the
right of common of pasture he says, '*item [acquiritur] ex longo
usu sine constitutione* [not *sine titulo] cum pacificâ possessione* [not
*per pacificam possessionem] continuâ et non interruptâ, ex scientiâ
negligentiâ et patientiâ dominorum, non dico ballivorum, quia
pro traditione accipiuntur.*' I take Bracton's meaning to be this :—
'Common of pasture is acquired without any express intention to
transfer it (see Dirksen, Manuale Latinitatis, s.v.) by reason of long

any rate he is not explicit on the point: whereas the
Roman Law did (as an exceptional case) admit such
acquisition in respect of certain special easements [1];
and the modern English law admits it as to all. It is,
therefore, incorrect, as it seems to me, to identify the
English law of prescription with the rules laid down by
Bracton, or the rules laid down by Bracton with those of
the Roman or Civil Law.

True point of contact. 398.   The true point of contact between the English
and the Roman Law in the matter of the acquisition by
prescription of rights over things other than ownership,
seems to be that exceptional rule of the latter which has
been just now referred to.   I think that, if we couple the
general conception of possession under the Roman Law,
as extended by analogy to things incorporeal, with the
rules laid down in the eighth book of the Digest as to the
acquisition of a right to fetch water (which probably also
applied to certain kinds of rights of way), we shall find
that this combination is pretty nearly identical with the
law, which we apply to the acquisition by prescription
of easements in general, and of other rights of a similar
nature, such as rights of common, and the like.   Though,
therefore, there are still marked contrasts between the
English and Roman Law, which must not be overlooked; and though we have applied to a whole class of
rights over land the law which Roman lawyers only applied to one or two particular kinds of those rights, and
not to the rest, the doctrines of one system are in a certain
sense traceable to the other.

enjoyment coupled with quiet possession continuous and uninterrupted, on account of the knowledge, negligence and endurance of
the owners—not of the bailiffs, because these things stand in the
place of delivery.'   (See Croke's Reports in the time of James the
First, p. 142.)

[1] Digest, book viii. art. 5. sect. 10.

399.   If this be the true point of connection between
the English and the Roman system it is obvious that we
must be extremely careful in the use we make of the
latter. The two systems are not generally identical; but,
on the contrary, that which is the rule in the one is only
exceptional in the other. We are not therefore at liberty
to extract from the Roman Law its general rules of prescription, and to transfer them to our own; though, from
its being founded on the same general conceptions as our
own, and those conceptions being expressed with remarkable clearness, we may find the study of it a most useful
exercise.

400.   The quasi-possession or, as it is sometimes called
simply, the possession, or, as it is at other times called by
way of better distinction, the enjoyment of a right, must,
in order to secure the benefit of prescription, be such as I
have described above [1], when speaking of the extension to
incorporeal things of the legal conception of possession.
I have there shewn, in reference to easements, that to constitute possession of them in a legal sense the enjoyment
must be as of right [2]; and the same is true of the possession
of all rights over things which are owned by another to
which prescription is applicable. No mere accidental, or
de facto enjoyment or exercise of the right will put me in
possession, unless the enjoyment is as of my own right;
or, as it is generally shortly expressed, unless it is as of
right. And here it is very remarkable that whilst, in the
Prescription Act, just as in the Limitation Act, there is
evinced no desire to adopt in its general wording the
strict and accurate technical language of the Roman Law,
one of its expressions should be identically that which
Savigny, against considerable opposition and after a complete revolution in his own opinions, has fixed upon as

What en-joyment of a right necessary for prescrip-tion.

[1] Supra, sect. 358.   [2] Supra, sect. 376.

the special characteristic of that kind of enjoyment of a right which leads to its acquisition [1]. Lord Tenterden (who is generally supposed to have drawn the Prescription Act) says the enjoyment, in order to be effectual, must be 'as of right.' Savigny says that it must be 'as of *his* (the claimant's) right [2].' But I do not doubt that the two expressions are identical, and that Lord Tenterden or his predecessors (for I think the term had been used before), as well as Savigny, have borrowed in this instance directly from the Roman Law.

Derivative possession not sufficient.

401. Again, as a person who holds derivative possession of land is excluded from the benefit of prescription, so also is the person who holds derivative quasi-possession of an easement, and for the same reason ; namely, that the very relation under which he holds excludes the possibility of any other than a limited right. Thus, if the owner of Whiteacre grants to the owner of Blackacre a right of way for a fixed period of twenty years, the owner of Blackacre by using the way takes full quasi-possession of it, and enjoys it for the time being as of right. He can during the twenty years assert his right against the grantor, and under most systems of jurisprudence (perhaps also under our own) against all the world besides [3].

---

[1] I have not been able to refer to the first two editions of Savigny's treatise, but he states in a note contained in the subsequent editions, that he was at first one of those who thought that the mere inaction of the servient owner put the dominant owner in possession, in a legal sense, of any negative servitude, which he *de facto* enjoyed. See Sav. Poss. sect. 46. p. 492.

[2] '*Tanquam sui juris.*' In section 2 of the Act the words are 'by a person claiming right thereto :' in section 5 the words are 'as of right.' But Lord Wensleydale treats the latter expression as conveying the true meaning of the legislature. See the case of Bright against Walker ; Crompton, Meeson and Roscoe's Reports, vol. i. p. 219 ; Gale on Easements, p. 128. See Appendix B.

[3] See supra, sect. 370.

But he cannot claim the benefit of prescription, because his possession, though as of right, is like that of the pledgee, derivative. This is a wholly different reason from that which prevents a person, who exercises or enjoys an easement merely under a permission which may be at any moment withdrawn, from gaining a right by prescription. Such a person is not in quasi-possession of an easement in a legal sense at all. The tradesman who daily for twenty years opens my gate and walks up to my door is never in possession of an easement in the nature of a way. The grantee of the way for the term of twenty years is in possession of it, and as of right, but only derivatively so. Both, therefore, are excluded from prescription, but for entirely different reasons. And I think, therefore, that if, in a well-known case[1], Lord Wensleydale means to treat the exclusion of prescription in the case of the licensee, and of the grantee, as two applications of the same principle, he is not quite accurate in his reasoning, though he is undoubtedly right in his conclusions.

402. The same judgment illustrates another error in the reasoning by which it has been attempted to support conclusions which are correct. The statute of William the Fourth requires, in order that a person may procure the benefit of prescription, that he should have enjoyed the easement claiming right thereto. I have already pointed out[2] the very important signification which attaches to these words, and the purpose which they serve, of distinguishing the possession of a right which has legal consequences from the mere *de facto* and accidental enjoyment. But besides this, it has been tried to make them serve a totally different, and I may almost say, a contrary purpose.

Secret and violent enjoyment.

---

[1] The case of Bright *v.* Walker, reported in the first volume of Crompton, Meeson and Roscoe's Reports, p. 219; Gale on Easements, p. 128.   [2] Supra, sections 379, 400.

To explain what this purpose is, I must go back for a moment to the Roman Law. I have already had occasion to point out[1] that our law of prescription, as applied to the acquisition of rights over land other than ownership, is similar, not to the Roman Law generally, but to that law as it is applied exceptionally to one or two easements; our law giving in all cases, as the Roman Law did in the exceptional cases, the benefit of prescription, whether the enjoyment is founded on a 'just title' or not. But the Roman lawyers did not, even in these exceptional cases, allow the right to be gained where the enjoyment had been *vi* or *clam*, or *precario*. Now I will not stop to inquire, whether the usual English paraphrase of these Latin expressions is correct. The Latin terms are highly technical, and it would probably be difficult to find any exact English equivalent for them. It is sufficient for our present purpose to observe that English lawyers had, prior to the Prescription Act, established three analogous limitations, by requiring that the enjoyment of the right, in order to secure the benefit of prescription, must be peaceable, open, and not permissive. Now it has been quite rightly argued that the expression 'as of right' or 'claiming right,' in the statute, preserves one of these limitations, namely, that which excludes enjoyment which is merely permissive. But there has been an attempt to make these same words serve the additional purpose of preserving the other two limitations also, and of excluding from the benefit of prescription the enjoyment which is violent or which is clandestine. This would only lead to great confusion. We must never forget Savigny's caution not to confound the acquirement of the title to the right with the acquirement of the possession of it[2]; and I think this caution is forgotten

---

[1] Supra, sect. 398.   [2] Sav. Poss. sect. 46. p. 492.

when we find these words 'as of right' interpreted,
as Lord Wensleydale seems desirous to interpret them, as
if they meant 'rightfully'[1]. I do not think it has ever
been doubted that positive easements, a footpath for instance, may commence in the English, as in this particular case in the Roman Law, by an act which is a
pure trespass; and that the enjoyment of the footpath
may continue to be a trespass until by prescription it has
grown into a right. It would have been impossible to
apply the statute to half the cases to which it has been
applied, if such a trespasser could not in the view of the
English Law enjoy the easement as of right. To exchange the necessary and (if I may use the expression)
scientific interpretation of the phrase 'as of right' for that
which Lord Wensleydale suggests, would throw the law
in the greatest possible confusion; and it is a sufficient
answer to the attempt to use language for one purpose,
that it has already been appropriated to another, and an
inconsistent one.

403. The truth is, that the rule of English Law, which *Not ex-
excludes from the benefit of prescription that enjoyment cluded by
the statute.*
of an easement which is clandestine, or violent, is a provision of positive law, copied by us from the Roman Law,
and based upon reasons of convenience, precisely analogous
to those which exclude prescription in some cases of trust
or fraud. It was necessary originally to introduce these
exceptions; and necessary to preserve them, though the
statute did not expressly do so. But they cannot be
extracted from the words 'as of right,' which are appropriated to a different purpose.

404. The position which is necessary in order to give *The term
'adverse.'*
one party the benefit of rules of limitation and prescription

[1] See the case in Crompton, Meeson and Roscoe's Reports, vol. i.
p. 219; Gale on Easements, p. 128.

against another, is sometimes described as *adverse;* and there can be no doubt that the word admirably describes this position. Unfortunately the phrase 'adverse possession,' prior to the passing of the statutes of William the Fourth, had acquired a special technical meaning so complicated and obscure, that the ablest lawyers declared the doctrine of adverse possession, as it then existed, to be hopelessly unintelligible[1] ; and one of the main objects of one of these statutes was to sweep away this unintelligible doctrine. But the general requirement that one party should hold adversely to the other is still, as we have seen, preserved ; and restoring the term 'adverse' to its natural sense, it may still, if the abolished doctrine is kept entirely out of sight, be useful to express this relation.

Exceptions to English Law.

Light and air.

405. I may further illustrate the general truth of the principles above stated by referring to the cases in which they have been really, or apparently departed from. The most noticeable of these cases is the provision in the Prescription Act, which gives to the mere *de facto* and accidental enjoyment of light for twenty years the same benefit, which in other cases is only conferred upon enjoyment as of right. We have seen how nearly the desire to render the enjoyment of light under similar circumstances continuous and secure, had perverted the interpretation of the Roman Law on the general question of acquisition of negative servitudes[2]. The obvious cause of the proneness to error on this point is, that the ordinary law of prescription is not suited to the circumstances of that particular easement ; questions as to which generally arise where habitations are closely packed, and where the respective parties stand to each other in special and

---

[1] Lord Mansfield said of it, ' the more we read the more we shall be confounded.' See Smith's Leading Cases, fifth ed., vol. ii. p. 578.

[2] Supra, sections 379 and 400.

exceptional relations. This has led to a rule of law on the subject in England which is now acknowledged to be special and anomalous [1]. Most European countries have dealt with the subject in a similarly exceptional manner, only this has been done avowedly; whilst we have caused a good deal of confusion by so long a struggle to meet the difficulty by the application of general principles.

406. So where land is given in pledge, and the pledgee takes possession, by the English statute the ownership of the pledgor is in some cases [2] extinguished, and he can take no proceedings to recover the land of which he has given up possession. Now the pledgee's possession being derivative, it ought never, according to the principles above stated, to operate in his favour. But it may have ceased to be so. If the pledgor has not manifested for a very long period any intention to redeem the land, it is not unreasonable to presume that the pledgee has taken to the land in lieu of the debt; that he has ceased to hold derivatively, and has determined to hold on his own behalf. We know that a derivative possessor cannot always do this; he cannot change at will the character of his possession, from derivative possession to possession on his own behalf as owner. But this is a special protection given to persons who part with the possession of their property to others, retaining the ownership: and there is ample reason for not extending this protection to cases, where persons are so inactive in regard to their own interests as in the case under consideration.

Pledgee of land in possession.

[1] The distinctly anomalous character of the English Law upon this point was, I believe, first pointed out by Mr. Justice Willes, in the case of Webb against Bird, where the owner of a windmill claimed, as an easement appurtenant to his mill, the free and uninterrupted passage of air. It is reported in the tenth volume of the Common Bench Reports, new series; see pp. 284, 285.

[2] See 3 and 4 William IV. chap. xxvii. section 28, and Appendix B.

407. This provision must not be confounded with another method of arriving at a very similar result; namely, by presuming the assent of the pledgor to the transfer of the land in lieu of the debt. By the place which this provision occupies in the English Law, that is to say in a statute relating to prescription, its true character is clearly determined.

Tenancies at will and where payment of rent has ceased.

408. So in the provisions[1] as to what are called tenancies at will and tenancies from year to year, where there is no payment of rent, or it has ceased. The result of these provisions is, that a period of dispossession which bars the remedy and extinguishes the title, commences at the end of the first year of the tenancy, or if rent be paid, at the last time when the rent was received. Now the possession of a tenant in such a case would be at least derivative, and probably representative; and therefore, it is contrary to the rules we have laid down, that the statute should, in any case, operate for his benefit. And we know how jealously the English Law in most cases applies to tenants the rule, that neither a representative nor derivative possessor can change possession on behalf of his principal, into possession on his own behalf. But again, this rule is itself only a qualification of a more general principle: and what the provision under consideration really does, is to refuse the benefit of this qualification to the landlord, who has allowed a tenant to hold for twenty years, without any agreement fixing the termination of his tenancy, without collecting any rent, and without taking any sort of acknowledgment of his title. In such cases a tenant is allowed to assert that his possession during this period has been not derivative, but adverse.

409. Substantially the same principles are recognised

[1] See 3 and 4 William IV. chap. xxvii. sections 7 and 8. Appendix B.

in the Indian statutes. The period which brings the
statute into operation is generally measured from a date
which is described as that 'when the cause of action arose[1].'
No suit can generally be brought to recover any property
but within so many years after that date. No further
technical definition of this date is given, as in the English
statute, but it is obvious that the cases in which the statute
affects *ownership* are those in which there has been, or
might be a dispute as to *possession*; and the position of
hostility thus implied requires that the party in possession
should hold, not for, but against the other; should hold
also as owner, and not derivatively; not consistently with
the ownership of the other, but adversely. And, as already
pointed out, if a person has been in possession, thus adversely, of land or moveables for the necessary period, and
the means of recovering them by any other person are taken
away, it is considered in India, though not so expressed
in the law, that the ownership follows the possession.

410. No special rules relating to the acquisition by
prescription of rights over land other than ownership have
been laid down in India. But it seems to be understood,
that some kinds of easements at any rate may be so
acquired. The rules relating thereto will have to be
evolved by the process of judicial decision; and possibly
this is a subject in which most difficulties, except in the
case of light and air in crowded cities, might be solved by
the application of principles, which are so general as to be
suited to any system of jurisprudence.

411. I have taken for analysis and discussion only the
most salient of the principles which lawyers of the English
school adopt with reference to limitation and prescription
as applied to ownership, and rights over things which are

[1] See Act xiv. of 1859, sect. 1.

Q

fragments of ownership. It is exceedingly important that the student should thoroughly grasp and comprehend these principles ; and it is impossible that he should do so without understanding something of their relation to closely related principles adopted in other systems. I have therefore contrasted the rules adopted in England and India with those of the Roman lawyers, and those current on the continent of Europe: and, notwithstanding important differences of detail, I think on the whole we have here brought before us a very striking example of the vitality and generality of a certain class of legal ideas.

Prescription and limitation as applied to other rights.

412. It is, of course, not only to ownership of a thing, and the several rights over a thing which may be detached from ownership, that the rules of prescription and limitation are applied ; and I have only selected these applications of them for discussion, because of their importance. Rights available against the world at large, but which, not being rights over particular things, are not ownership or fragments of ownership ; rights also which are merely *in personam*, such as obligations which arise out of contract or rights of action, may be acquired or lost by lapse of time.

413. I follow the ordinary use of language, when I say that rights may be gained or lost by lapse of time, but it must be borne in mind how far that expression is correct. Of course what creates or destroys the right is the sovereign authority alone, which is the source of all rights as well as of all obligations : and lapse of time, combined with other circumstances, is only a frequent occasion for the exercise of this authority. For instance, when a man gains by prescription the right to take toll from all persons passing over a certain bridge, what really happens is that, after he has collected toll for a certain number of years, the courts of law, exercising delegated sovereign authority, will recognise his right to do so. But generally, other circumstances must combine. He must have collected

the toll as of right. It must not be on a bridge which forms part of the street of a town. If it is in a public thoroughfare the claimant must shew that he has always kept the bridge in repair; or whatever else may be the restrictions which the sovereign authority thinks fit to impose on the acquisition of the right. When, therefore, we say rights are gained or lost by lapse of time, we only use a convenient and compendious expression which fixes our attention on that part of the matter which we wish to bring into prominence.

414. A large class of rights which are invariably ex- Limitation tinguished by lapse of time, and sometimes by the lapse of rights of action. of a very short time, are rights of action. I have already[1] discussed the effect of extinguishing the right of action, or barring the remedy, as it is called, when the right which the right of action is intended to protect, is ownership; and I have shewn that it is in some cases a question, whether the protected right ceases to exist, when the protecting right is taken away. A similar question may be raised when the protected right is of any other nature. And this question has sometimes an important practical result. For, in the first place, a right of action is not always the only mode of protecting a right : sometimes a person who has a right may, by his own act, without the assistance of a court of law, recover satisfaction for a violation of it; as for instance, in the case above put, of a right to collect toll, what is called a distress might be levied for unpaid tolls. So when a man loses by lapse of time his right of action to recover a debt, the English Law has drawn important consequences from the view sometimes taken that the debt is only barred, and not extinguished.

415. We very often see it stated somewhat loosely

---

[1] Supra, sects. 317 sqq.

Incorrect-
ness of the
maxim that
prescript on
presumes a
grant.
that prescription, or the acquisition of a right by lapse
of time, always presumes a grant [1]. This is one of those
plausible ambiguities which not unfrequently occur in
English Law, and are apparently intended to render its
doctrines more acceptable. It might mean that prescription has no application, except in cases where the party
who uses it to protect himself has a title from the supposed last owner, but which, in consequence of some defect,
cannot be established. This, or something nearly approaching to this, is the general view of the Roman Law,
and of the French Law, which was taken from it [2]; though
even in these two instances it only applies to the ordinary
periods of prescription : for here also, if the possession has
lasted thirty or forty years, even though it originated in a
trespass, it may secure the benefit of possession. But there is
nothing like this in English Law. Our law does not recognise the rule which requires a 'just title' as a foundation
of prescription, and therefore, if this is what the phrase
in question is intended to assert, it is incorrect.

416. On the other hand, the assertion that prescription always presumes a grant may mean that, under
the given circumstances, the law, in spite of everything,
presumes a grant. Of course, if persons armed with the
necessary authority lay down such a proposition, it cannot
be contradicted. All one can say is, that whilst the assertion
in its first and milder sense has no application to English
Law, this interpretation of it gives to prescription a colour
of arbitrary violence which does not at all belong to it.
There is no advantage in the law forcing us to presume
that which never existed. A legal fiction is at best a
clumsy contrivance, but it sometimes has the advantage of

[1] See for instance Broom and Hadley's Commentaries, vol. ii.
p. 420. Blackstone, in the corresponding passage, seems to imply the
same thing.   [2] See supra, sect. 383 *a.*

marking out the exact limits of the consequences which may be derived from the assumption : and if any consequences were dependent on whether the right originated in a grant or trespass, there might be some use in this fiction. But as far as I am aware there are none; and the fiction, if it exists, is absolutely gratuitous.

417.   The use of a phrase so ambiguous is particularly mischievous in the present case, because it confounds the distinction to which I have before adverted, between the acquisition of right, under a rule of law, by prescription, and the inference of right, as a fact, by evidence[1]. This confusion is very noticeable in the contrivance (rightly characterised as 'clumsy'[2]) of presuming that a grant which is well known never to have existed, has been accidentally lost. A single illustration will shew the importance of keeping this distinction clear. Protestation by the owner of the servient tenement ought to have precisely an opposite effect, according as the owner of the dominant tenement relies on prescription proper, or attempts to induce the jury to infer a lost grant from the actual enjoyment. A clear and distinct protest excludes acquiescence on the part of the servient owner, which acquiescence is so often relied on as supporting the notion of a grant. Whereas a protest by the same person, standing alone and not followed by any attempts at interruption, strengthens rather than otherwise the position of a person who has enjoyed an easement, and who relies on prescription ; because it shews that he holds the easement, not by a mere licence, nor in any way derivatively from the other, but adversely and as of right ; and it thus contributes to establish that adverse possession which, as we have seen, is necessary in order that prescription may take effect.

Mischievous effect of phrase.

[1] Supra, sect. 385.
[2] See the First Report of the Real Property Commissioners, p. 51.

CHAPTER XI.

SANCTIONS AND REMEDIES.

Relation
between
sanctions
and rights.
418. I have hitherto considered law, and the duties, obligations, and liability which arise out of law, only from one point of view—as the machinery by which a political society is governed. It is true that I have adverted to the division of duties and obligations into those which are absolute and those which are relative ; and I have spoken of the right which corresponds to the relative duty or obligation : but I was desirous not to complicate further a discussion already sufficiently complex, by remarking then upon another distinct order of ideas which these terms connote.

Laws are not
made for the
benefit of in-
dividuals
but of
society at
large.
419. As a general principle the point of view above taken is the only true one in this sense—namely, that it is the only one which justifies the existence of laws at all. No one creates or enforces duties and obligations now-a-days for the benefit of individuals, or classes of individuals, but for the benefit of the community at large. If any modern law has the aspect of conferring new advantages on one class of society alone, we may be sure that it has been adopted only on account of the indirect advantages which it is alleged will be derived from it by the remainder.

This is not
historically
true.
420. Of course when I assert this, I do not mean to say that a conviction of their utility was the original moving cause of the introduction of all, or even of any very

large proportion of existing laws ; for many of them came
into existence long before any such ideas as those to which
I now advert were started in the countries where they
now prevail. Nor do I doubt that there are everywhere
to be found persons who, in their own minds, are persuaded that they have an hereditary and indefeasible right
to certain privileges, an interference with which considerations of utility would have little weight in justifying.
But no one avows this ; and we need only look to the
debates of legislative bodies, or to the published declarations of the rulers in every state, to see that the only
principle on which they pretend to govern, the only ground
on which they expect that their subjects will consent to
obey—in other words, the only means by which a political
society can in modern times be kept together—is that the
object of government should be, or at least should profess
to be, the happiness and prosperity of the people at large.

421.   In this respect there is no distinction between
those duties and obligations which are relative and those
which are absolute.   The law of ownership, for example,
which comprises a great variety of relative duties and obligations, is supposed to exist as completely for the benefit of
society at large, as the law of treason, or the bribery laws.
The law of ownership is said to encourage industry and
commerce, to promote an increase in the production of the
necessaries and luxuries of life and in their distribution,
and so forth.   If it could be shewn not to possess these
advantages it would gradually disappear, or be modified.
Nobody really doubts this, or denies it : only whilst some
men are prone from time to time to renew the test of
utility, and to try this as well as other institutions by this
standard with great care, other men are, or profess to be,
so convinced of its excellence, that they are impatient of
any inquiry about the matter.

It is true now
of all laws,
whether
they create
absolute or
relative
duties.

422.   It may possibly be suggested that this is hardly in accordance with what we see around us, or that it is at any rate too widely stated.   For while it is true that some breaches of the law of ownership are considered as offences against society at large, others evidently are not so.   For instance, if a man steals or mischievously destroys my property, he may be prosecuted and punished in the Queen's name at the public expense ; but if a man injures my property by negligence, no one dreams of treating this as a matter of public concern ; I am left to proceed against him or not as I like ; and if I do proceed against him, it is not to punish him, but to recover compensation for the injury which I have sustained.   I must take the whole trouble and risk of this upon myself, and if I am satisfied, there is an end of the matter.

423.   There is, no doubt, this apparent inconsistency between the proceedings of courts of civil and courts of criminal jurisdiction.   Whilst in criminal courts we see plainly before us the breach of the law followed by its appropriate *punishment*, which deters others from breaking the law by warning them that they too will incur the like consequences—which, in other words, operates as a sanction ; in civil courts we find that the only thing thought of is *redress*, and there is apparently nothing which is intended to operate as a sanction at all.

424.   I do not think however it will be difficult, without going minutely into an historical inquiry as to the origin of legal tribunals, to discover whence this apparent divergence between the functions of civil and criminal courts arose ; and hence to infer that it is only apparent, and that the real functions of all courts are the same—namely, the enforcement of obedience to the commands of the sovereign authority.

425.   Prior to any distinction between criminal and

civil procedure, prior even to legal procedure of any kind, there seems to have arisen everywhere the notion of retaliation; that is, of inflicting an evil upon the wrong-doer exactly in proportion to the wrong he has inflicted upon you. 'Breach for breach; eye for eye, tooth for tooth,' says the Mosaic Law[1]. '*Si quis membrum rupit aut os fregit talione proximus cognatus ulciscatur,*' says the Law of the Twelve Tables[2]. And the earliest customs of all Teutonic nations were based on similar principles. This is obviously punishment, and not redress; it is the direct application of a sanction; and would operate precisely in the manner which Austin considers a sanction to operate in enforcing an obligation in modern jurisprudence[3].

426. Retaliation, however, though it is punishment and not redress, was undoubtedly looked upon as some *satisfaction* to the party injured, and this may very likely have suggested, when a fixed money payment was substituted for the *talio*, or equivalent injury inflicted on the wrong-doer, that the money should be paid to the sufferer. This obviously answered all the purposes of a sanction: loss of money being an evil which persons are generally anxious to avoid, and not the less so because it is paid to a particular person, and not, as money payments used directly as sanctions now generally are, into the public treasury.

Substitution for it of a money payment.

427. There is still a considerable step, no doubt, from this to our modern ideas of compensation. Thus, under the laws of Alfred, for the loss of a forefinger the compensation was fixed at fifteen shillings in all cases. In a suit

Modern ideas of compensation.

[1] See Leviticus xxiv. 20.

[2] See the article *Talio* in Smith's Dictionary of Greek and Roman Antiquities.

[3] See *supra*, section 148.

against a modern railway company for a similar injury, it would vary in every case according to the pecuniary loss which the sufferer might be supposed to have incurred in consequence. And there is no doubt the ideas of compensation have made a prodigious advance, even within the last few years[1]; but still no one, I think, would doubt that they have grown gradually out of the ' were' and ' bot' of the Anglo-Saxon law, just as the ' were' or ' bot' itself grew out of the 'feud[2].'

Specific enforcement of duties : and obligations.

428.   But there is another point of view in which it is necessary to consider the action of legal tribunals in enforcing the law, which will be best brought out by

---

[1] See the general view of the subject of damages in the treatise on that subject by Mr. Sedgwick, where the authorities are collected with much industry and research. The earliest declaration of the rule, that the damages are to be measured by the injury sustained, is quoted from Lord Holt (see p. 29). But I think the notion of calculating the compensation for a personal injury upon an estimate of what money the sufferer, but for the injury, might have earned, is of still later origin. It may possibly be doubted whether these notions about compensation will be very long lived. The cases in which damages are most liberally awarded are those where the defendant is a large public company. But a company has it in its power to exclude its liability in almost all cases by express stipulation, or by raising its prices to cast back the burden, in a great measure, upon the general body of its customers. At present the doctrine seems to affect even international relations. The Americans claimed 2,000,000*l*. sterling, on account of damages sustained by private persons by reason of our alleged breach of neutrality. The Germans have obtained compensation on an equally large scale for what they assume to be a wrong done to themselves by the French nation in declaring war. Claims not less extensive have been made before, by the strong hand; but I think that it is new to place such claims on a quasi-legal ground.

[2] See Kemble's Anglo-Saxons, book i. chap. x., and the Laws of Alfred, 43, 44. ' Bot' is the name given to the compensation ordered to be paid in case of a wound ; which when life was taken was called ' were.' The right of private warfare to revenge an injury was called 'feud.'

an illustration. If a wound be inflicted, or valuable property be damaged, a great, possibly an irreparable injury
has been inflicted, but the circumstances which give rise
to such a breach of the law are generally transient; there
is not generally a probability that the wrong will be
repeated; and the sanction which is applied either in
the shape of inflicting punishment, or compelling such
redress as is possible, is left to have its general effect
in deterring the wrong-doer from any further injury. On
the other hand, if I wrongfully keep my neighbour out of
possession of his property, the damage as yet done may
be very slight; but if I retain the property, asserting that
it is mine, this is equivalent to a declaration of intention
on my part to continue the wrong, and law would be
incomplete unless provision were made for taking some
special measures for preventing me from so acting.

429. The mode of dealing with the very large class
of cases from which I have selected this as an example, is simple enough. Wherever I am kept out of
possession of a specific thing which I have a right to
possess, the obvious course is to turn the wrong-doer, by
force if necessary, out of possession, and put me in. This
(if I may use the expression) is more than redress; it
puts me in actual enjoyment of my right. And though
from the habit of obedience to the law which generally
prevails amongst men, a resort to such extreme measures
is rarely necessary, it is this which is contemplated under
our law in all cases as the ultimate result, where the
injury in question is the wrongful detention of land.
Forcible transfer of the possession of things other than
land has not been thought necessary under our law, but
this is only upon an assumption which is in the present
day hardly in accordance with the facts; and which, were
extreme measures frequently necessary, would undoubtedly

be rectified. This assumption is that the limit of the injury
is, except in very rare cases, the present money value of
the article detained, and which may therefore be covered
by compensation.

430. Obligations, the performance of which is thus
secured, are said to be specifically enforced ; and there are
many others which may be so dealt with besides those of
the class above mentioned. Where there is a dispute about
the title, whether to land or moveables, which are at the
moment not in the possession of either party, but of a third
person holding as the representative of, or derivatively from,
the true owner, the right of the true owner may often be
specifically enforced by declaring it, and requiring this third
person (who generally, not being interested in the dispute,
will be ready to obey) to acknowledge the right of ownership as declared[1]. So also a very large number of obligations
are either primarily to pay money, or are such that a breach
of them results in an obligation to pay money ; and all obligations to pay money are in their nature capable of being
specifically enforced, by seizing the property of the debtor,
if he has any, selling it, and handing the proceeds over to
the creditor ; which is invariably done, should the debtor
delay or refuse to pay the money, after he has been
ordered by a court of law to do so. So again, through
the power which every court has over duties and obligations of every kind, rights may be transferred from one
person to another, and where the obligation which it is
desired to enforce is to make this transfer, this can be

---

[1] It is sometimes said that, when an officer of a court executes a
conveyance in the name of another person who has been ordered to
convey, but who refuses to do so, the obligation to convey is thereby
specifically enforced. But this, I think, is hardly correct. The
order of the court is amply sufficient to pass the ownership without
any conveyance ; and the document executed by the officer is only
convenient evidence of title.

done, whether the party obliged to make it consents or no, and, therefore, without resort to the pressure of a sanction. Thus if I owe you money which I am ready to pay, and you owe the same sum to a third person, the court can secure the performance of your obligation by simply annulling these two obligations and creating a new one of the same kind between me and your creditor; or, as the transaction is generally, though I think not quite so correctly described, by simply transferring the debt.

431.   Probably also the idea of rendering further breaches of the law to a great extent physically impossible, is to some extent involved in transportation, and in the modern practice of substituting long terms of imprisonment, with comparatively mild treatment, for shorter and sharper suffering.

432.   The more direct enforcement of duties and obligations, so far as matters of civil procedure are concerned, is, like the procuring of compensation, left entirely to the control of the party injured, and there are many circumstances which combine to render this mode of proceeding effectual. There is no better way of securing obedience to the law than to give to private individuals an interest in enforcing it.   That interest is given at once in all cases of relative duty or obligation, by giving to the party who has the right corresponding thereto means, either of enforcing the right, or of obtaining redress when the right is infringed. He at once becomes, not only the public prosecutor, but takes upon himself the whole trouble, risk, and expense of prosecution.   And this method is found so effectual, that so far as concerns all those violations of right which come within the denomination of civil injuries, the State is able to relieve itself entirely of the trouble of enforcing obedience to the law, beyond appointing proper officers to perform the duties of the Civil Courts.

Why the methods of civil procedure are effectual.

433. The injury to the individual, therefore, though it is never the cause of the action of a Court of Law, is the occasion of it. And in matters of civil procedure and a few other cases it is not only the occasion of the action, but the exact measure of it. The whole ostensible object of the proceedings from beginning to end in those cases is not punishment, but redress, and they are fashioned upon the hypothesis that redress alone is the object.

Secondary aspect of right as foundation of claim for redress.

434. From this point of view, therefore, to have a right expresses, not merely the condition of a person towards whom a duty or obligation has to be performed, as it would if violations of that duty or obligation were only punished and not redressed; but it expresses the condition of a person who can put in motion the whole machinery of Courts of Law to obtain a private object. If, for instance, injuries to property were followed only by a fine payable to the Crown, or imprisonment, the compound right which we call ownership would still exist, but it would have no legal importance independently of the duties and obligations to which it corresponds: but when the owner of the property injured is also enabled to claim compensation for the injury, the right assumes a new and important aspect. It is no longer the mere correlative of the primary duties and obligations commanding us to abstain from acts injurious to the property of others; it has, as the foundation of a claim for redress, an altogether independent existence correlative to an obligation to make amends on the part of the delinquent[1].

---

[1] It is, I apprehend, this combination of a public with a private object which determines the apportionment of costs in civil proceedings. They are borne partly by the public, for the same reason that costs in criminal proceedings are so borne entirely. But I do not see exactly on what principle Bentham (vol. ii. p. 112) would require the government to take upon itself the whole burden of costs in civil proceedings. If so, all notion of giving redress would have to

435. It is obvious enough that none of the conse- Imperfect
laws.
quences of a breach of the law will render it certain that
the command which contains the law will be obeyed.   If
we punish the wrong-doer, or compel him to make redress,
we only warn him in a significant manner against a repetition of the wrong.   If by a transfer of rights we fulfil an
obligation, or by the use of physical force we render a
man powerless to repeat an injury, we have only rendered
ourselves secure in an individual case ; and we must trust
to the example to deter others from doing the like.   Nothing, therefore, can be more inappropriate than the expression by which some laws are distinguished as perfect,
and others as imperfect.   All laws are imperfect, in the
sense that we cannot be sure that they will be obeyed
by those on whom they are imposed.   On the other
hand, a law which has no sanction of any kind, either
legal or moral, if that is what is meant, is a thing
that I confess myself unable to conceive.   Again, a
moral law, or a law accompanied by a sanction which
is not enforced by a legal tribunal (which is also sometimes said to be what the term is intended to express),
is no more imperfect than one which is so enforced.   If
we consider the very rare cases in which the sanctions set
by the law, or legal sanctions, come into competition with
the sanctions of so-called imperfect obligations, which are
the sanctions set by society, and which are commonly
called moral sanctions ; that is, if we look to cases where
the conduct required of us by the law conflicts with that
which is expected of us by our neighbours, it would be
obviously untrue to imply that the moral sanctions were,

be abandoned, for it is not a duty incumbent upon a government to
procure redress for individuals ; no government has ever assumed
any such function ; and to charge upon the public the duty of per-
forming it could hardly be justified.

as compared with the legal ones, imperfect. There are
many men who, upon deliberate choice, in order to gain
the approbation of those with whom they are accustomed
to associate, would rather leave unpaid their debts to a
tradesman than their wagers on a horse race. But this is
in reality a wholly distorted view of the subject ; the sanctions set by law do for the most part not conflict, but concur
with, moral sanctions, and every political society depends
for its existence in a great measure upon this concurrence. It is this concurrence which has enabled the law to
impose sanctions which are sometimes so light as scarcely to
be perceptible. Nothing, indeed, can be more striking than
to contrast the habit of obedience to law which prevails in
most countries with the slightness of legal sanctions, that
is, with the smallness both in quantity and intensity of the
suffering which the law inflicts in cases of disobedience [1].

436. I have in an earlier chapter [2] stated generally the
nature of a sanction, and the mode in which it operates.
As I have said, I did not then advert to the indirect mode
in which the law is enforced through the interests of individuals, from a desire not further to complicate a discussion
already sufficiently complex. I can now discuss the nature
of a sanction somewhat more in detail, and, by so doing,
the truth of some of the observations I have just now
made will become clearer.

Inter-
mediate and
ultimate
sanctions.

437. Sanctions are divided into the two following
kinds. Frequently, indeed most frequently, disobedience
to the law is only followed in the first instance by the
imposition of a fresh obligation. I have disobeyed the
law by smoking in a railway carriage, by driving carelessly in the street, or by not fulfilling my contract ; the
result in each case is that I am ordered to pay a sum of

[1] Infra, sect. 441.   [2] Supra, sect. 148.

money. The obligation to pay the money is a secondary or sanctioning one, inasmuch as it exists for the sake of enforcing a primary obligation. But it is only an obligation, and requires therefore a further sanction to enforce it if it be disobeyed.

438. Sanctions which consist merely of an obligation, that is, which merely command a man to do something, with the prospect of incurring certain further consequences if he do not, I will call *intermediate* sanctions. Sanctions which consist not of an obligation, but of some other evil which it is supposed the party would be desirous to avoid, I will call *ultimate* sanctions.

439. The ultimate sanctions of all primary duties and obligations, whether the breach of them be what is usually called a civil injury, or what is usually called a crime, are the same. They are of three kinds—bodily pain including death, imprisonment, and forfeiture. This division of sanctions is not scientifically correct; for imprisonment is itself a kind of bodily pain, and also an instrument for inflicting it: though it is generally something more; loss of liberty being regarded by most men as an evil, independently of any bodily suffering. The division is, however, convenient. Forfeiture is of two kinds; it may consist in the simple annulment of all or some of those rights which the party has, or it may consist in depriving him of all or some of those rights which are in their nature transferable, and transferring them to another. Whether the right be simply annulled, or transferred to another, the sanction consists in the forfeiture only.

440. The application of sanctions has varied considerably at different times, but there is a good deal of similarity in the views which prevail at present in regard to them in most civilised countries, especially in courts of civil procedure. These courts, shaping their proceedings,

Application of sanctions by courts of civil procedure.

R

as they ostensibly do, for the sole purpose of giving
redress to the party injured, always select that form of
sanction which will best accomplish that purpose : sometimes they order the party delinquent to make compensation in money ; sometimes, where the wrong done is
keeping the rightful claimant out of possession, they
restore the possession, using force if necessary for the purpose ; sometimes they proceed by way of restitution ; that
is to say, creating, destroying, or transferring rights,
duties, and obligations, for the purpose of putting the
parties as nearly as possible in the same position as if the
wrong had not been done.   In the two first of these cases,
keeping only the sanction in view, and disregarding the
remedy, we should find that the order of the court results
in the imposition of an obligation, that is, the application
of an intermediate sanction, or in forfeiture, that is, the
application of an ultimate sanction.   The process of restitution consists partly of the imposition of an ultimate
sanction in the shape of forfeiture, and partly of the
specific enforcement of obligations.

Courts of civil procedure never in the first instance
apply the ultimate sanction of imprisonment, and they
have no power to inflict bodily pain in any other form
than that of simple detention.   Even this power has
recently been very largely curtailed in England by what
is called the abolition of imprisonment for debt[1].

Slightness of
sanctions
actually in
use.

441.   I have already said that the only sanction of
many duties and obligations is the liability to make
amends for the damage caused to an individual by their

---

[1] See the statute 32 and 33 Victoria, chap. lxii, by which the
imprisonment for debt in purely civil matters is wholly done away
with, except in cases where the court, being satisfied that the debtor
has means to pay, makes a special order for payment, which the
debtor disobeys.

breach ; and in a very large number of such cases the only
form in which compensation can be given is by an order for
the payment of a sum of money by the delinquent to the
party injured.   But since the passing of the last-mentioned
act, no person, except in very special cases, can be arrested
or imprisoned for making default in the payment of a sum
of money.   For all this class of cases, therefore, the only
ultimate sanction is forfeiture.   Moreover, forfeiture,
when resorted to as an ultimate sanction of an order to
pay money by way of compensation, has always been confined by us to the forfeiture of such rights as may be
seized and sold, so as to produce the money and satisfy
this secondary obligation.   And it is not an unimportant
reflection that we thus arrive at an ultimate sanction of
a very limited kind; and one which entirely depends
on the possession by the delinquent of rights of that
nature.

442. When the breach of the primary duty or obligation is the subject of criminal procedure[1], and is called a
crime, or an offence, it is customary to apply the ultimate
sanction at once, by ordering the guilty person to suffer
death, or imprisonment, either alone or accompanied by
some kind of physical inconvenience, such as whipping or

Application of sanctions in criminal courts.

---

[1] It would seem to be the tendency of modern legislation to
enlarge considerably the field of crime, and to mitigate punishment,
that is to say, to increase the direct application of ultimate sanctions, and to diminish their intensity.   On the other hand, whilst,
as I have already observed, our ideas on the subject of compensation for injuries have been rapidly developed, yet, in the absence of
certain characteristics, which are also generally the characteristics
of crime, such as fraud, intentional injury, and the like, the ultimate
sanction of imprisonment has, in civil matters, almost disappeared.
It is perhaps not very easy to decide to what this is tending.
Probably to some readjustment of the respective domains of civil
and criminal law.

hard labour. Sometimes, however, an alternative is still left of escaping from the ultimate sanction by the payment of a sum of money, which is then usually called a fine; and in cases which are of a mixed character, neither decidedly civil nor decidedly criminal, such as have been before referred to[1], a fine is generally imposed as an alternative intermediate sanction.

In India. 443. In India sanctions are substantially the same as in England, except that imprisonment for debt still exists; but under conditions which make it so onerous to the creditor, that it is very little resorted to.

In other countries. 444. The courts of civil procedure in America and in France also proceed upon principles almost precisely the same. And in both countries, in that very large class of cases where the proceedings result in an order for the payment of money by way of compensation, it has been found possible to dispense with the ultimate sanction of imprisonment, and to rely entirely on the apparently slender sanction of forfeiture[2].

[1] Supra, sect. 187.

[2] See Powell's Analysis of American Law, Philadelphia, 1870, Book iii. chap. ix. sect. 3, and the Loi de 22 Juin, 1870, in the Collection des Lois, vol. lxvii. p. 165, where there is a very interesting account of the discussions which preceded the abolition of imprisonment for debt in France.

CHAPTER XII.

PROCEDURE.

445. Procedure is the term used to express the action of courts of law. Courts of law are persons or bodies of persons delegated by the sovereign authority to perform the function of enforcing the duties and obligations which have been created tacitly, or expressly, by this authority in the form of law.

Procedure is the action of the courts of law.

446. I have already pointed out how this function generally divides itself into the several parts of ascertaining the precise nature of the duties and obligations which have been imposed by the sovereign authority; of further ascertaining which of these have been broken; and of applying the sanction appropriate to the breach. I have further pointed out that though this penal function is the only one for which courts of law exist, they do in fact perform it in some cases by ostensibly exercising a function which is merely remedial; the court taking action ostensibly, not for the purpose of punishing disobedience to the law, but for the purpose of giving redress[1].

Parts of the proceeding. Penal or remedial.

447. This cardinal difference between the ostensible functions of courts of law corresponds generally, but not exactly, with the distinction of courts into courts of civil and courts of criminal procedure. Though the ultimate object of all courts is the same, the civil court generally

Civil and criminal courts.

---

[1] See Chapters v. and xi.

professes only to give redress, and the criminal court only
to inflict punishment.

448. The general scheme of procedure in each court
also corresponds with the general object which each professes to pursue. In the civil court the person who makes
the complaint is the party who has suffered by the breach
of the law. He is responsible for the conduct of the proceedings, and in a great measure for the expenses of them,
inasmuch as they are treated as though they were carried
on entirely for his benefit. He may abandon them at any
moment, or he may settle the dispute privately, if he thinks
fit. On the other hand, in the criminal court, though it
has been the custom in England hitherto to trust the conduct of prosecutions to some extent to private individuals,
the prosecutor is in no way responsible for, nor has he any
control over the proceedings.

Suits will not gene- rally lie for mere decla- rations with- out wrong.

449. It is a general rule that courts of law will not
move unless some duty or obligation is broken. Very
often parties assert rights which they do not as yet exercise, or repudiate obligations which they are not at the
moment called upon to perform. And so disputes arise
without any wrong having actually taken place : and very
often parties are desirous, from reasons of convenience, to
come into court and get their rights declared at once
without waiting for the expected breach. No doubt
there are very often strong reasons of convenience in
favour of such a course. The intention to do an act would,
in a vast majority of cases, be abandoned, if it was known
to be illegal; or, what comes to the same thing, if it was
known that a court of law would treat it as illegal. The
consideration which counterbalances these reasons of convenience is, that thereby too much opportunity would be
given to persons of litigious character to bring useless and
vexatious suits against their neighbours, whereby the

number of suits would be greatly multiplied. And since
the burden and expense of litigation always falls to some
extent on the public at large, this burden and expense
cannot be increased solely with reference to considerations
of private convenience. The rule, therefore, is generally
adhered to, that there must be some actual wrong done
before the court will set itself in motion. An exception
is, however, generally made, where there is a reasonable
and well-grounded expectation that a breach of duty or
obligation will be committed, and that no proper redress
can be had, if it does take place. There is, indeed, one
class of cases in England in which parties are allowed to
come and ask simply for the opinion of the court upon their
rights and duties : but that is confined to trustees, who,
by a peculiarity of our law, may always practically cast
upon the court the duty which has been undertaken by
themselves. This being so, it is more economical to allow
them to consult the court, as it were, and to require the
court to give them its advice ; for a refusal might only
result in a far greater burden.

450. The respective schemes of procedure are fashioned
according to these views. In all courts the party who seeks
to set the court in motion has, except in very special cases
such as are mentioned above, to make a statement which,
whether it be called a complaint, an indictment, a charge,
a demand, a bill of complaint, a plaint, or a declaration,
is in fact an assertion that a wrong has been committed;
including also generally, in the civil courts, a claim for
redress. This is invariable : and there is also invariably
a defined mode of bringing before the court the person
whose conduct is complained of, in order that his answer
may be heard. But there is a good deal of variety, and
some peculiarity in the modes of doing this. Sometimes the
party against whom the complaint is made is summoned ;

Commence-ment of pro-ceedings.

that is, he receives a notice that his attendance is required
in court; sometimes he is arrested and brought there;
sometimes he is required actually to appear in court;
sometimes only to put in his answer or defence. Moreover
the practice varies as to the exact time of making the
statement of the particular wrong complained of. Sometimes it is made simultaneously with the first summons to
come into court and answer it. Sometimes the summons
into court takes place first, and the complaint is made
afterwards. And these varieties are to be found not only
in different countries, but in the same. For some crimes,
both in England and India, a party may be arrested and
brought into court; in others the proceedings can only
commence by a summons, followed by a warrant in case
Appearance. of non-appearance. In England, in the Common Law
Courts of civil procedure, the theory is, that nothing can
be done in the first instance beyond bringing the party complained against into court, and that no further proceedings
are possible, until this has been accomplished. And though
the rigour of this rule is now relaxed, it is still so much re-
spected, that the appearance (as it is called) of the defendant
is always feigned to have taken place, even when the proceedings go on without it. When both parties have appeared,
or are supposed to have appeared, then each makes his respective statements, answering and replying to each other
till both sides have nothing more to say. In the Court of
Chancery, on the other hand, the plaintiff commences proceedings by stating what he has to complain of, and delivering a copy of the statement to the defendant; at the
same time requiring him to appear and answer it. And the
rule requiring the defendant to appear before the case can
proceed further then applies, as in the Common Law Courts,
but is avoided by the same fiction. The curiously indirect
methods which were at one time in use both in Courts of

Common Law and Courts of Chancery, to compel a defendant to take the step of appearing in court, and some
expressions which are used regarding it, seem to point to
something voluntary in the submission of the defendant to
the jurisdiction of the court. This is analogous to what
has been pointed out by Sir Henry Maine in what he
considers the most ancient judicial proceeding known
to us—the *legis actio sacramenti* of the Romans, where the
form of the proceeding appears to treat the judge, rather
as a private arbitrator chosen by the parties, than as a
public officer of justice. But in modern times this appearance of voluntary submission has no significance[1].

451. It is impossible here to do more, than to point
out the leading characteristics of the procedure, by which
the complaint of one side and the defence of the other are
submitted to the judgment of the tribunal. The rules
upon this subject, called by us the rules of pleading, are
generally elaborate, and very often highly artificial, and
even capricious; but I will notice one or two leading distinctions of principle in the practice which has prevailed
in different courts respecting it.

452. In every dispute the two principal questions to Pleadings.
Issues of
be determined are, (1) what are the duties and obligations law and fact,
in civil cases.
which exist between the parties? (2) have they or any of
them been broken? The first of these questions depends
ultimately of course upon the law, but proximately it may
depend on whether certain events have happened, on the
happening of which duties and obligations will arise; such,
for instance, as whether a contract has been made; or a
will executed; or a marriage solemnized. The second
depends on whether certain events have happened. Hence
in every case which comes into court the questions to be

---

[1] See Maine's Ancient Law (first ed.), p. 375.

determined resolve themselves into questions of law and questions of fact ; and it is the object of the rules of pleading in English courts, and analogous rules in all other courts, to put into a more or less precise form the various questions of law and fact which have to be determined.

453. The difficulty of understanding the procedure in the English Courts of Common Law arises from the very wide difference which prevails between the theory and the practice based upon it. Theoretically the parties to a suit at common law are required to work out the questions of law and questions of fact into distinct issues, as they are called; and though at the present day this is but imperfectly done, yet, as these questions have to be decided by different tribunals—issues of law by the court and issues of fact by the jury—one would suppose that to whatever extent this has not been done before, the deficiency must necessarily be supplied at the hearing. The judge, one would think, would have first to completely separate, and then to decide the questions of law ; after which he would ask the jury to give their opinion on the facts. To a very considerable extent this is done. But then it is only done in a verbal address to the jury of which there is no regular record ; the observations on the facts are so mingled with the directions on the law, that it is sometimes very difficult to distinguish them ; and what is more important still, there is no regular mode of ascertaining, whether or no the jury accept the law as the judge lays it down ; because the ordinary form of finding is, not on specific questions exclusively of fact, but for the plaintiff, or for the defendant, in general terms[1]. Indeed, were it

---

[1] The jury cannot be compelled to find particular facts, or even to find the affirmative, or negative, on particular issues, though they are generally willing to do so, if requested. But it has been always recognised as their undoubted privilege to decline finding any other

considered necessary to keep the functions of the court and the jury as completely severed in practice as they are in theory, the proceedings at a trial at Nisi Prius would undergo a very considerable change. I even think it very doubtful whether with such a severance of functions the jury system could be as successfully worked as it is at present. The present success of that system depends almost entirely on the friendly co-operation and mutual good understanding between the court and the jury, which have been, in England, so happily established : and these it would be extremely difficult to preserve, together with such discussions as to their respective duties, as would be necessary to keep each within the strict limits of its own particular functions.

454. I have already adverted [1] to a similar indistinctness in the line drawn between law and fact in the proceedings subsequent to the verdict of the jury, when the tribunal, whilst professing to keep within the province of pure law, really enters into considerations which it seems impossible to call legal : as, for instance, whether a verdict is against the weight of the evidence. And though a legal form is given to another frequent consideration, namely, whether there is any evidence to support the verdict, yet I think it is impossible to doubt that under this form what is really very often considered is, whether the jury have drawn the right inference from the facts laid before them.

455. In criminal cases no attempt is made to separate the questions of law and fact prior to the hearing ; and though the functions of judge and jury are in criminal cases theoretically separated, there is still the same absence of all security that this separation should be practically

In criminal cases.

than a general verdict, and they have been known to exercise it. See a case reported in the third volume of Adolphus and Ellis' Reports, p. 506.　　　　[1] Supra, sect. 242.

observed; and the result in a criminal trial, even more than in a civil one, is in reality arrived at rather by a co-operation of judge and jury throughout the trial, than by the simultaneous exercise of two entirely independent functions.

In Courts of Chancery. 456. The proceedings in the Courts of Chancery are a good deal simpler. There it is not necessary to separate the issues of law and fact. The parties are not required to make this separation at any stage of the pleadings antecedent to the hearing, and there is nothing in the nature of the proceedings at the hearing which renders it then necessary, inasmuch as the presiding judges decide both law and fact simultaneously. And in practice the separation is only so far made, as is found to be convenient for understanding the case, and so far as the judges may make it, when in conformity with the tradition of the courts, they disclose to the litigants their reasons in detail for coming to a conclusion.

In India and other countries. 456 a. The provision of the Indian Code of Civil Procedure on this subject is a very peculiar and stringent one. It requires that the judge should settle the questions of law and fact upon which the parties are at issue in every case before the hearing commences. The French Code requires no settlement of issues, but there are very strict rules which require that the judgment should contain a specific statement of the points of law and of fact which have arisen, with the determination of each. The requirements of the Italian Code, and I believe also of the Spanish Law, are similar. Of all these methods, that provided for by the Indian Code is the most laborious and complete [1]. It contemplates that every possible issue which can arise should be raised prospectively; a much greater burden than is thrown upon

---

[1] See the Code of Civil Procedure, s. 141.

a judge by the French Code, who has only to declare
what issues have actually come into dispute; and in fact
this duty has been found so onerous that the courts in
India have almost universally neglected it. Upon a review
of the various methods of procedure adopted in different
countries in civil cases, a commission which recently sat to
consider the subject appears to have come to the conclusion,
that it may be safely left to the discretion of the court how
far, and when, and with what precision the issues shall be
ascertained; and that so far as this has to be done, it
should be done, if possible, by agreement of the parties[1].
But the report is silent upon the question of separating
the findings on these several issues, so that it may be
inferred that the practice of not doing so, as it at present
exists in England, is not disapproved.

457.   Another great point of difference in the practice
of various courts is, as to the responsibility which the
parties take upon themselves in making the statements
which embody the complaint upon one side and the defence
upon the other.   In the Court of Chancery the plaintiff
is not bound to swear to the truth of the bill, but the
defendant must swear that his answer is true to the best of
his knowledge and belief.   In the Criminal Courts, the
practice only concerns the accuser, for he alone makes
a formal statement; and as to that it varies.   In Courts
of Common Law, no oath or other pledge of veracity is
required from either plaintiff or defendant, when making
his preliminary statement; and as such statements are, in
these courts, made in a very technical form, they can very
often be repudiated, if it suits the purpose of the person
making them to do so.   In India, the parties to civil suits
verify the truth of their statements, and the law says that
they may be punished if that verification is false; but as

Verification of statements.

---

[1] See the Report of the Judicature Commission, p. 12.

they are to state not only what they know, but what they
are informed, and what they expect to be able to prove,
without distinction, this is no great security. Probably
the best thing that can be done is to call upon the parties
to state their case fully ; to allow them to put what they
have to say into any form they like, and to treat what is
so said as one would treat any other deliberate assertion,
that is to say, as one from which it is almost impossible
for them, without full explanation, very greatly to depart.

Decree often only declaratory in form.   458. When the case has been heard and the decision
given, the result, so far as the judgment is not merely decla-
ratory, is to impose either an ultimate or intermediate sanction.   In civil cases this will generally be an intermediate
sanction only, and, for the reasons explained above, generally
in the form of an order to make compensation or restitution.   But though the courts lay down as a general rule
that they will not move unless there has been some
wrong committed, the real object of many suits is not
to compel redress, either in the shape of compensation
or of restitution.   The real dispute is as to the rights
of the respective parties, and having once procured a
declaration on this point, it is generally well known to all
concerned in the litigation that every one will do what is
required, either from motives of honesty, or because the
means of compulsion are now so proximate and certain that
it is useless further to resist. For this reason we constantly
find that the result of litigation is a mere declaration.

Restitution.   459. Again, wherever it is possible, the Court of
Chancery, which alone has power to do so, gives redress
by way of restitution rather than by way of compensation.
Now the principle of restitution is to assume by a fiction
that the wrong done can be undone, and as far as possible
to treat the rights, duties, and obligations of all parties as
being at that moment, and as if they had been all along,

such as they would have been, had nothing taken place to
interfere with them. Thus, when a sale of property is set
aside on account of fraud, every effort is made to put the
parties precisely in the same position as if the fraud had
not taken place. The fraudulent conveyance is declared
void. The property is treated as never having ceased to
belong to the party who was induced by the fraud to part
with it. All the profits are declared to belong to him,
and so forth. The court only resorts to a money payment by way of compensation when it is compelled to do
so. But it would not always be easy to say whether, in
very strictness, the court, in making a decree of this kind,
was depriving the defendant of a right, or merely declaring
the existing rights of the plaintiff; that is to say, whether
it was applying an ultimate sanction, or not applying a
sanction at all. Nor is there any reason in practice for
distinguishing between the performance of these operations. On the contrary, it rather serves as a guide to the
measure of relief, to keep up the idea (even though it be
fictitious) that the rights of the parties are only being
declared. We have, therefore, another reason why in
form, at any rate, the final decree in a suit is often
only declaratory.

APPENDIX A.

THE following are the sections of the Indian Penal Code which define the crime of murder. It is the most elaborate attempt to define a crime which I have ever seen; but I think it has failed; and that the cause of the failure was the want of a proper preliminary investigation into the meaning of the terms in which it is expressed.

Section 299. Whoever causes death by doing an act—
    a. with the intention of causing death, or,
    b. with the intention of causing such bodily injury as is likely to cause death, or,
    c. with the knowledge that he is likely by such act to cause death,
commits the offence of culpable homicide.

Section 300. Except in the cases hereafter excepted, culpable homicide is murder—
    α. if the act by which the death is caused is done with the intention of causing death, or,
    β. if it is done with the intention of causing such bodily injury as the offender knows to be likely to cause the death of the person to whom the harm is caused, or,
    γ. if it is done with the intention of causing bodily injury to any person, and the bodily injury intended to be inflicted is sufficient in the ordinary course of nature to cause death, or,
    δ. if the person committing the act knows that it is so imminently dangerous that it must in all probability cause death, or such bodily injury as

s

is likely to cause death, and commits such act
without excuse for incurring the risk of causing
death or such injury as aforesaid.

The definition of murder is, therefore, arrived at by
combining *a*, *b*, and *c*, with *a*, *β*, *γ*, and *δ*; giving in all
twelve combinations, and as many definitions of murder.
But, as might be supposed, there are not as many different
kinds of murder. I think all are comprised in the three
following definitions :—

Def. 1. Whoever causes death by doing an act with the
intention of causing death commits the offence of murder.

Def. 2. Whoever causes death by doing an act with
the intention of causing such bodily injury as is likely to
cause death commits the offence of murder.

Def. 3. Whoever causes death by doing an act which
he knows to be so imminently dangerous that it must in all
probability cause death, or such bodily injury as is likely
to cause death, and commits such act without excuse for
incurring the risk of causing death or such injury as aforesaid, commits the offence of murder.

Probably the distinction which the authors of the Code
desired to draw between *knowledge* and *intention* is this:—
they would say a man intended consequences which he
expected and desired, either as an end, or as means; and
that he knew of consequences, which he expected, but
which he did not desire. In this they differ from Austin,
who, as has been seen, calls all three states of mind by the
name of intention. The difficulty, however, remains that
unless we give to the word 'knowledge,' in section 299.
another and a very different signification, cases of rash or
heedless killing are wholly unprovided for by the Code.
Some amendments of this portion of the Code are, I
believe, under consideration.

APPENDIX B.

For convenience of reference, I have inserted here those sections or portions of sections of the Prescription Act and the Limitation Act to which I have most frequently referred, omitting for the sake of brevity everything else.

2 and 3 William IV, chap. lxxi.

Section 2.   No claim which may be lawfully made at the common law, by custom, prescription, or grant, to any way or other easement, or to any watercourse, or the use of any water, to be enjoyed or derived upon, over, or from any land, when such way or other matter as herein last before mentioned shall have been actually enjoyed by any person claiming right thereto, without interruption, for the full period of twenty years, shall be defeated or destroyed by showing only that such way or other matter was first enjoyed at any time prior to such period of twenty years, but nevertheless, such claim may be defeated in any other way by which the same is now liable to be defeated ; and when such way or other matter as herein last before mentioned shall have been so enjoyed as aforesaid for the full period of forty years, the right thereto shall be deemed absolute and indefeasible, unless it shall appear that the same was enjoyed by some consent or agreement expressly given or made for that purpose by deed or writing.

Section 3.   When the access and use of light to and for any dwelling-house, workshop, or other building shall have been actually enjoyed therewith for the full period of twenty years without interruption, the right thereto shall be deemed absolute and indefeasible, any local usage or custom to the contrary notwithstanding, unless it shall appear that the same was enjoyed by some consent or agreement expressly made or given for the purpose by deed or writing.

Section 5. In all actions upon the case and other pleadings, wherein the party claiming may now by law allege his right generally, without averring the existence of such right from time immemorial, such general allegation shall still be deemed sufficient, and if the same shall be denied, all and every the matters in this Act mentioned and provided, which shall be applicable to the case, shall be admissible in evidence to restrain or rebut such allegation; and in all pleadings to actions of trespass, and in all other pleadings wherein before the passing of this Act it would have been necessary to have alleged the right to have existed from time immemorial, it shall be sufficient to allege the enjoyment thereof as of right by the occupier of the tenement in respect whereof the same is claimed for and during such of the periods mentioned in this Act as may be applicable to the case, and without claiming in the name or right of the owner of the fee, as is now usually done.

3 *and* 4 *William IV, chap. xxvii.*

Section 2. No person shall bring an action to recover any land but within twenty years next after the time at which the right to bring such action shall have first accrued to some person through whom he claims ; or if such right shall not have accrued to any person through whom he claims, then within twenty years next after the time at which the right to bring such action shall have first accrued to the person making or bringing the same.

Section 3. In the construction of this Act the right to

bring an action to recover any land shall be deemed to
have first accrued at such time as hereinafter is mentioned;
(that is to say) when the person claiming such land, or
some person through whom he claims, shall, in respect of
the estate or interest claimed, have been in possession or
receipt of the profits of such land, and shall while entitled
thereto, have been dispossessed, or have discontinued such
possession or receipt, then such right shall be deemed to
have first accrued at the time of such dispossession or dis-
continuance of possession, or at the last time at which
such profits were so received.

Section 7. When any person shall be in possession or
in receipt of the profits of any land, as tenant at will, the
right of the person entitled subject thereto, or of the person
through whom he claims, to bring an action to recover such
land, shall be deemed to have first accrued either at the
determination of such tenancy, or at the expiration of one
year next after the commencement of such tenancy, at
which time such tenancy shall be deemed to have determined ; provided always that no mortgagee or cestuique
trust shall be deemed to be a tenant at will, within the
meaning of this clause, to his mortgagee or trustee.

Section 8. When any person shall be in possession or
in receipt of the profits of any land, as tenant from year
to year or other period, without any lease in writing, the
right of the person entitled subject thereto, or of the
person through whom he claims, to bring an action to
recover such land, shall be deemed to have first accrued
at the determination of the first of such years or other
periods, or at the last time when any rent payable in
respect of such tenancy shall have been received (which
shall last happen).

Section 28. When a mortgagee shall have obtained
the possession or receipt of the profits of any land com-

prised in his mortgage, the mortgagor or any person claiming through him shall not bring a suit to redeem the mortgage but within twenty years next after the time at which the mortgagee obtained such possession or receipt, unless in the meantime an acknowledgment of the title of the mortgagor or of his right of redemption shall have been given to the mortgagor or other person claiming his estate, or to the agent of such mortgagor or person, in writing signed by the mortgagee, or the person claiming through him ; and in such case no such suit shall be brought but within twenty years next after the time at which such acknowledgment, or the last of such acknowledgments, if more than one, was given.

INDEX.

Fact and law, theoretical distinction between, not always observed, 242, 453.

Feræ Naturæ, possession of animals, 329.

Feud, 427.

Forfeiture, as a sanction, 439.

France, constitutions of 1848 and 1851, 24*n*.

Fraud, as a criterion of liability, 233.

— what it means, 233.

— distinction between believing and knowing, 233.

— includes mendacity, 234.

Fraudulent representation, 234. See Fraud.

Free government, meaning of expression, 17.

French code, scanty expression of, as to primary duties, 155.

— definition of contract in, 168 *n*, 170.

— definition of delict in, 182.

— definition of prescription in, 382.

French law, separation of law and fact by judges under, 59, 456 *a*.

— of substitution. 301 *n*.

— rule requiring just title for prescription in, 383 *a*.

— application of sanctions under, 444.

Futwa Alumgiri, an authoritative commentary on law, 63.

Game laws, notions on which they are founded in England, 329 *n*.

Government, is head of political society, 8.

— free and despotic, difference between, 17.

— not a difference of power, 17.

— origin of, 32. See Political Society.

— the avowed object of, is utility, 37, 419.

— of England is supreme in colonies, 45.

Grant, presumption of, not necessary in prescription, 415.

Guardian, possession of, on behalf of his ward, 343.

Guilty mind, not necessary to constitute crime, 189.

Hedaya, an authoritative commentary on law, 63.

Heedlessness, state of mind described by, 210, 214.

Hindoo family, co-ownership of, 311, 366.

— widow, interest of, how considered, 303

Hobbes, views of, as to origin of political society, 36 *n*.

House of Lords, judicial authority of, 54.

Ignorance, as a ground of non-liability, 254.

— difference between mistake and, 254.

— not a defect of the will, 257.

— Blackstone's explanation, 257.

— will not excuse an act otherwise unlawful, 259.

— in cases of contract, 260.

— no excuse if result of carelessness, 264.

— classification of cases, 265.

— unsettled state of the law, 265 *a*.

— cases where it is mutual, 265 *a*.

— where it is on one side only, 267.

— of law and of fact, rule as to, 270.

— Blackstone's explanation, 271.

— Austin's observations thereon, 271.

— rule too sweeping, 276.

— Roman law on this subject, 278.

Imperfect law, inappropriateness of expression, 435.

Imprisonment for debt, abolition of, 441, 443, 444.

India, delegation of legislative authority in, 45.

— attempts to tie up ownership in, 299, 306 *n*.

T

November, 1871.

BOOKS

PRINTED AT

THE CLARENDON PRESS, OXFORD,

AND PUBLISHED FOR THE UNIVERSITY BY

MACMILLAN AND CO.,

16, BEDFORD STREET, COVENT GARDEN, LONDON.

Many Books in this Catalogue have lately been much reduced in Price.

LEXICONS, GRAMMARS, &c.

A Greek-English Lexicon, by Henry George Liddell, D.D., and Robert Scott, D.D. *Sixth Edition, Revised and Augmented.* 1870. 4to. *cloth,* 1l. 16s.

A Greek-English Lexicon, abridged from the above, chiefly for the use of Schools. *Fourteenth Edition. Carefully Revised throughout.* 1871. square 12mo. *cloth,* 7s. 6d.

A copious Greek-English Vocabulary, compiled from the best authorities. 1850. 24mo. *bound,* 3s.

Graecae Grammaticae Rudimenta in usum Scholarum. Auctore Carolo Wordsworth, D.C.L. *Seventeenth Edition,* 1870. 12mo. *bound,* 4s.

A Greek Primer, in English, for the use of beginners. By the Right Rev. Charles Wordsworth, D.C.L., Bishop of St. Andrews. *Second Edition.* Extra fcap. 8vo. *cloth,* 1s. 6d.

A Practical Introduction to Greek Accentuation, by H. W. Chandler, M.A. 1862. 8vo. *cloth,* 10s. 6d.

Etymologicon Magnum. Ad Codd. MSS. recensuit et notis variorum instruxit Thomas Gaisford, S.T.P. 1848. fol. *cloth,* 1l. 12s.

Suidae Lexicon. Ad Codd. MSS. recensuit Thomas Gaisford, S.T.P. Tomi III. 1834. fol. *cloth. Price reduced from 3l. 12s. to 2l. 2s.*

Scheller's Lexicon of the Latin Tongue, with the German explanations translated into English by J. E. Riddle, M.A. 1835. fol. *cloth*, 1*l.* 1*s.*

Scriptores Rei Metricae. Edidit Thomas Gaisford, S.T.P. Tomi III. 8vo. *cloth.* *Price reduced from* 1*l.* 10*s. to* 15*s.*

Sold separately:
Hephaestion, Terentianus Maurus, Proclus, cum annotationibus, etc. Tomi II. 1855. 8vo. *cloth.* *Price reduced from* 1*l.* 5*s. to* 10*s.*
Scriptores Latini. 1837. 8vo. *cloth,* 5*s.*

Thesaurus Syriacus : collegerunt Quatremère, Bernstein, Lorsbach, Arnoldi, Field: edidit R. Payne Smith, S.T.P.R.
Fasciculus I. 1868. sm. fol. 1*l.* 1*s.*
Fasciculus II. 1871. sm. fol. 1*l.* 1*s.*

Lexicon Aegyptiaco-Latinum ex veteribus Linguae Aegyptiacae Monumentis, etc., cum Indice Vocum Latinarum ab H. Tattam, A.M. 1835. 8vo. *cloth.* *Price reduced from* 1*l.* 10*s.* 6*d. to* 15*s.*

A Practical Grammar of the Sanskrit Language, arranged with reference to the Classical Languages of Europe, for the use of English Students, by Monier Williams, M.A. *Third Edition,* 1864. 8vo. *cloth,* 15*s.*

Nalopákhyánam. Story of Nala, an Episode of the Mahá-Bhárata: the Sanskrit text, with a copious Vocabulary, Grammatical Analysis, and Introduction, by Monier Williams. M.A. The Metrical Translation by the Very Rev. H. H. Milman, D.D. 1860. 8vo. *cloth,* 15*s.*

A Sanskrit-English Dictionary, by Monier Williams, M.A., Boden Professor of Sanskrit. *Nearly Ready.*

An Anglo-Saxon Dictionary, by Joseph Bosworth, D.D., Professor of Anglo-Saxon, Oxford. *New edition.* *Preparing.*

An Icelandic-English Dictionary. By the late R. Cleasby. Enlarged and completed by G. Vigfússon.
Parts I and II. 1869-71. 4to. 1*l.* 1*s.* each.

A Handbook of the Chinese Language. Parts I and II, Grammar and Chrestomathy. By James Summers. 1863. 8vo. *half bound,* 1*l.* 8*s.*

Cornish Drama (The Ancient). Edited and translated by E. Norris, Esq., with a Sketch of Cornish Grammar, an Ancient Cornish Vocabulary, etc. 2 vols. 1859. 8vo. *cloth* 1*l.* 1*s.*
The Sketch of Cornish Grammar separately, *stitched,* 2*s.* 6*d.*

GREEK AND LATIN CLASSICS.

Aeschylus: Tragoediae et Fragmenta, ex recensione Guil. Dindorfii. *Second Edition*, 1851. 8vo. *cloth*, 5s. 6d.

Aeschylus: Annotationes Guil. Dindorfii. Partes II. 1841. 8vo. *cloth*, 10s.

Aeschylus: Scholia Graeca, ex Codicibus aucta et emendata a Guil. Dindorfio. 1851. 8vo. *cloth*, 5s.

Sophocles: Tragoediae et Fragmenta, ex recensione et cum commentariis Guil. Dindorfii. *Third Edition*, 2 vols. 1860. fcap. 8vo. *cloth*, 1l. 1s.

Each Play separately, *limp*, 2s. 6d.

The Text alone, printed on writing paper, with large margin, royal 16mo. *cloth*, 8s.

The Text alone, square 16mo. *cloth*, 3s. 6d.

Each Play separately, *limp*, 6d.

Sophocles: Tragoediae et Fragmenta cum Annotatt. Guil. Dindorfii. Tomi II. 1849. 8vo. *cloth*, 10s.

The Text, Vol. I. 5s. 6d. The Notes, Vol. II. 4s. 6d.

Sophocles: Scholia Graeca:

Vol. I. ed. P. Elmsley, A.M. 1825. 8vo. *cloth*, 4s. 6d.
Vol. II. ed. Guil. Dindorfius. 1852. 8vo. *cloth*, 4s. 6d.

Euripides: Tragoediae et Fragmenta, ex recensione Guil. Dindorfii. Tomi II. 1834. 8vo. *cloth*, 10s.

Euripides: Annotationes Guil. Dindorfii. Partes II. 1840. *cloth*, 10s.

Euripides: Scholia Graeca, ex Codicibus aucta et emendata a Guil. Dindorfio. Tomi IV. 1863. 8vo. *cloth*, 1l. 16s.

Euripides: Alcestis, ex recensione Guil. Dindorfii. 1834. 8vo. *sewed*, 2s. 6d.

Aristophanes: Comoediae et Fragmenta, ex recensione Guil. Dindorfii. Tomi II. 1835. 8vo. *cloth*, 11s.

Aristophanes: Annotationes Guil. Dindorfii. Partes II. 1837. 8vo. *cloth*, 11s.

Aristophanes: Scholia Graeca, ex Codicibus aucta et emendata a Guil. Dindorfio. Partes III. 1839. 8vo. *cloth*, 1l.

Aristophanem, Index in: J. Caravellae. 1822. 8vo. *cloth*, 3s.

B 2

Metra Aeschyli Sophoclis Euripidis et Aristophanis. Descripta a Guil. Dindorfio. Accedit Chronologia Scenica. 1842. 8vo. *cloth*, 5s.

Anecdota Graeca Oxoniensia. Edidit J. A. Cramer, S.T.P. Tomi IV. 1834-1837. 8vo. *cloth*, 1*l*. 2s.

Anecdota Graeca e Codd. MSS. Bibliothecae Regiae Parisiensis. Edidit J. A. Cramer, S.T.P. Tomi IV. 1839-1841. 8vo. *cloth*, 1*l*. 2s.

Apsinis et Longini Rhetorica. E Codicibus MSS. recensuit Joh. Bakius. 1849. 8vo. *cloth*, 3s.

Aristoteles; ex recensione Immanuelis Bekkeri. Accedunt Indices Sylburgiani. Tomi XI. 1837. 8vo. *cloth*, 2*l*. 10s.

Each volume separately, 5s. 6d.

Catulli Veronensis Liber. Recognovit, apparatum criticum prolegomena appendices addidit, Robinson Ellis, A.M. 1867. 8vo. *cloth*, 16s.

Choerobosci Dictata in Theodosii Canones, necnon Epimerismi in Psalmos. E Codicibus MSS. edidit Thomas Gaisford, S.T.P. Tomi III. 1842. 8vo. *cloth*, 15s.

Demosthenes: ex recensione Guil. Dindorfii. Tomi I. II. III. IV. 1846. 8vo. *cloth*. *Price reduced from* 2*l*. 2s. *to* 1*l*. 1s.

Demosthenes: Tomi V. VI. VII. Annotationes Interpretum. 1849. 8vo. *cloth*. *Price reduced from* 1*l*. 16s. *to* 15s.

Demosthenes: Tomi VIII. IX. Scholia. 1851. 8vo. *cloth*. *Price reduced from* 15s. *to* 10s.

Harpocrationis Lexicon, ex recensione G. Dindorfii. Tomi II. 1854. 8vo. *cloth*. *Price reduced from* 1*l*. 1s. *to* 10s. 6d.

Herculanensium Voluminum Partes II. 1824, 1825. 8vo. *cloth*. *Price reduced from* 1*l*. 5s. *to* 10s.

Homerus: Ilias, cum brevi Annotatione C. G. Heynii. Accedunt Scholia minora. Tomi II. 1834. 8vo. *cloth*, 15s.

Homerus: Ilias, ex rec. Guil. Dindorfii. 1856. 8vo. *cloth*, 5s. 6d.

Homerus: Odyssea, ex rec. Guil. Dindorfii. 1855. 8vo. *cloth*, 5s. 6d.

Homerus: Scholia Graeca in Odysseam. Edidit Guil. Dindorfius. Tomi II. 1855. 8vo. *cloth*, 15s. 6d.

Homerum, Index in: Seberi. 1780. 8vo. *cloth*, 6s. 6d.

Oratores Attici ex recensione Bekkeri:
  I. Antiphon, Andocides, et Lysias. 1822. 8vo. *cloth*, 7s.
  II. Isocrates. 1822. 8vo. *cloth*, 7s.
  III. Isaeus, Aeschines, Lycurgus, Dinarchus, etc. 1823. 8vo. *cloth*, 7s.

Scholia Graeca in Aeschinem et Isocratem. Edidit G. Dindorfius. 1852. 8vo. *cloth*, 4s.

Paroemiographi Graeci, quorum pars nunc primum ex Codd. MSS. vulgatur. Edidit T. Gaisford, S.T.P. 1836. 8vo. *cloth*, 5s. 6d.

Plato: The Apology, with a revised Text and English Notes, and a Digest of Platonic Idioms, by James Riddell, M.A. 1867. 8vo. *cloth*, 8s. 6d.

Plato: Philebus, with a revised Text and English Notes, by Edward Poste, M.A. 1860. 8vo. *cloth*, 7s. 6d.

Plato: Sophistes and Politicus, with a revised Text and English Notes, by L. Campbell, M.A. 1866. 8vo. *cloth*, 18s.

Plato: Theaetetus, with a revised Text and English Notes, by L. Campbell, M.A. 1861. 8vo. *cloth*, 9s.

Plato: The Dialogues, translated into English, with Analyses and Introductions, by B. Jowett, M.A., Master of Balliol College and Regius Professor of Greek. 4 vols. 1871. 8vo. *cloth*, 3l. 6s.

Plato: The Republic, with a revised Text and English Notes, by B. Jowett, M.A., Master of Balliol College and Regius Professor of Greek. Demy 8vo. *Preparing.*

Plotinus. Edidit F. Creuzer. Tomi III. 1835. 4to. *cloth*, 1l. 8s.

Stobaei Florilegium. Ad MSS. fidem emendavit et supplevit T. Gaisford, S.T.P. Tomi IV. 1822. 8vo. *cloth*, 1l.

Stobaei Eclogarum Physicarum et Ethicarum libri duo. Accedit Hieroclis Commentarius in aurea carmina Pythagoreorum. Ad MSS. Codd. recensuit T. Gaisford, S.T.P. Tomi II. 1850. 8vo. *cloth*, 11s.

Xenophon: Historia Graeca, ex recensione et cum annotationibus L. Dindorfii. *Second Edition,* 1852. 8vo. *cloth*, 10s. 6d.

Xenophon: Expeditio Cyri, ex rec. et cum annotatt. L. Dindorfii. *Second Edition,* 1855. 8vo. *cloth*, 10s. 6d.

Xenophon: Institutio Cyri, ex rec. et cum annotatt. L. Dindorfii. 1857. 8vo. *cloth*, 10s. 6d.

Xenophon: Memorabilia Socratis, ex rec. et cum annotatt. L. Dindorfii. 1862. 8vo. *cloth*, 7s. 6d.

Xenophon: Opuscula Politica Equestria et Venatica cum Arriani Libello de Venatione, ex rec. et cum annotatt. L. Dindorfii. 1866. 8vo. *cloth*, 10s. 6d.

THE HOLY SCRIPTURES, &c.

The Holy Bible in the earliest English Versions, made from the Latin Vulgate by John Wycliffe and his followers: edited by the Rev. J. Forshall and Sir F. Madden. 4 vols. 1850. royal 4to. *cloth*. *Price reduced from 5l. 15s. 6d. to 3l. 3s.*

The Holy Bible: an exact reprint, page for page, of the Authorized Version published in the year 1611. Demy 4to. *half bound*, 1l. 1s.

Vetus Testamentum Graece cum Variis Lectionibus. Editionem a R. Holmes, S.T.P. inchoatam continuavit J. Parsons, S.T.B. Tomi V. 1798-1827. folio, *in sheets. Price reduced from* 10l. *to* 7l.

Vetus Testamentum Graece secundum exemplar Vaticanum Romae editum. Accedit potior varietas Codicis Alexandrini. Tomi III. 1848. 12mo. *cloth*, 14s.

Origenis Hexaplorum quae supersunt; sive, Veterum Interpretum Graecorum in totum Vetus Testamentum Fragmenta. Edidit Fridericus Field, A.M.

Tom. II. Fasc. I-III. 1867-1870. 4to. 2l. 9s.

Tom. I. Fasc. I. 1871. 4to. 16s. *Just Published.*

Pentateuchus Hebraeo-Samaritanus Charactere Hebraeo-Chaldaico. Edidit B. Blayney. 1790. 8vo. *cloth*, 3s.

Libri Psalmorum Versio antiqua Latina, cum Paraphrasi Anglo-Saxonica. Edidit B. Thorpe, F.A S. 1835. 8vo. *cloth*, 10s. 6d.

Libri Psalmorum Versio antiqua Gallica e Cod. MS. in Bibl. Bodleiana adservato, una cum Versione Metrica aliisque Monumentis pervetustis. Nunc primum descripsit et edidit Franciscus Michel, Phil. Doct. 1860. 8vo. *cloth*, 10s. 6d.

Libri Prophetarum Majorum, cum Lamentationibus Jeremiae, in Dialecto Linguae Aegyptiacae Memphitica seu Coptica. Edidit cum Versione Latina H. Tattam, S.T.P. Tomi II. 1852. 8vo. *cloth*, 17s.

Libri duodecim Prophetarum Minorum in Ling. Aegypt. vulgo Coptica. Edidit H. Tattam, A.M. 1836. 8vo. *cloth*, 8s. 6d.

Novum Testamentum Graece. Antiquissimorum Codicum
Textus in ordine parallelo dispositi. Accedit collatio Codicis Sinaitici.
Edidit E. H. Hansell, S.T.B. Tomi III. 1864. 8vo. *half morocco,*
2l. 12s. 6d.

Novum Testamentum Graece. Accedunt parallela S. Scrip-
turae loca, necnon vetus capitulorum notatio et canones Eusebii. Edidit
Carolus Lloyd, S.T.P.R., necnon Episcopus Oxoniensis. 1869. 18mo.
cloth, 3s.

The same on writing paper, with large margin, small 4to.
cloth, 10s. 6d.

Novum Testamentum Graece juxta Exemplar Millianum.
1868. 18mo. *cloth.* 2s. 6d.

The same on writing paper, with large margin, small 4to.
cloth, 6s. 6d.

Evangelia Sacra Graecae. *The Text of Mill.* 1870. fcap. 8vo.
limp, 1s. 6d.

The New Testament in Greek and English, on opposite
pages, arranged and edited by E. Cardwell, D.D. 2 vols. 1837. crown
8vo. *cloth,* 6s.

Novi Testamenti Versio Syriaca Philoxeniana. Edidit Jos.
White, S.T.P. Tomi IV. 1778-1803. 4to. *cloth,* 1l. 8s.

Novum Testamentum Coptice, cura D. Wilkins. 1716. 4to.
cloth, 12s. 6d.

Appendix ad edit. N. T. Gr. e Cod. MS. Alexandrino a C. G.
Woide descripti. Subjicitur Codicis Vaticani collatio. 1799. fol. 2l. 2s.

Evangeliorum Versio Gothica, cum Interpr. et Annott. E.
Benzelii. Edidit, et Gram. Goth. praemisit, E. Lye, A.M. 1759. 4to.
cloth, 12s. 6d.

Diatessaron ; sive Historia Jesu Christi ex ipsis Evangelistarum
verbis apte dispositis confecta. Ed. J. White. 1856. 12mo. *cloth,* 3s. 6d.

Canon Muratorianus. The earliest Catalogue of the Books of
the New Testament. Edited with Notes and a Facsimile of the MS. in
the Ambrosian Library at Milan, by S. P. Tregelles, LL.D. 1868. 4to.
cloth, 10s. 6d.

The Five Books of Maccabees, in English, with Notes and
Illustrations by Henry Cotton, D.C.L. 1833. 8vo. *cloth,* 10s. 6d.

The Ormulum, now first edited from the original Manuscript
in the Bodleian Library (Anglo-Saxon and English), by R. M. White,
D.D. 2 vols. 1852. 8vo. *cloth,* 1l. 1s.

Horae Hebraicae et Talmudicae, a J. Lightfoot. *A new
edition,* by R. Gandell, M.A. 4 vols. 1859. 8vo. *cloth. Price reduced
from* 2l. 2s. *to* 1l. 1s.

FATHERS OF THE CHURCH, &c.

Catenae Graecorum Patrum in Novum Testamentum. Edidit J. A. Cramer, S.T.P. Tomi VIII. 1838–1844. 8vo. *cloth*, 2*l.* 4*s.*

Clementis Alexandrini Opera, ex recensione Guil. Dindorfii. Tomi IV. 1869. 8vo. *cloth*, 3*l.*

Cyrilli Archiepiscopi Alexandrini in XII Prophetas. Edidit P. E. Pusey, A.M. Tomi II. 1868. 8vo. *cloth*, 2*l.* 2*s.*

Cyrilli Archiepiscopi Alexandrini in S. Joannis Evangelium. Accedunt in D. Pauli Epistolas quasdam fragmenta quae supersunt, necnon fragmenta alia. Edidit P. E. Pusey, A.M. Tomi III. *In the Press.*

Cyrilli Archiepiscopi Alexandrini Commentarii in Lucae Evangelium quae supersunt Syriace. E MSS. apud Mus. Britan. edidit R. Payne Smith, A.M. 1858. 4to. *cloth*, 1*l.* 2*s.*

The same, translated by R. Payne Smith, M.A. 2 vols. 1859. 8vo. *cloth*, 14*s.*

Ephraemi Syri, Rabulae Episcopi Edesseni, Balaci, aliorumque, Opera Selecta. E Codd. Syriacis MSS. in Museo Britannico et Bibliotheca Bodleiana asservatis primus edidit J. J. Overbeck. 1865. 8vo. *cloth*, 1*l.* 1*s.*

A Latin translation of the above, by the same Editor. *Preparing.*

Eusebii Pamphili Eclogae Propheticae. E Cod. MS. nunc primum edidit T. Gaisford, S.T.P. 1842. 8vo. *cloth*, 10*s.* 6*d.*

Eusebii Pamphili Evangelicae Praeparationis Libri XV. Ad Codd. MSS. recensuit T. Gaisford, S.T.P. Tomi IV. 1843. 8vo. *cloth*, 1*l.* 10*s.*

Eusebii Pamphili Evangelicae Demonstrationis Libri X. Recensuit T. Gaisford, S.T.P. Tomi II. 1852. 8vo. *cloth*, 15*s.*

Eusebii Pamphili contra Hieroclem et Marcellum Libri. Recensuit T. Gaisford, S.T.P. 1852. 8vo. *cloth*, 7*s.*

Eusebii Pamphili Historia Ecclesiastica. Edidit E. Burton, S.T.P.R. 1856. 8vo. *cloth*, 8*s.* 6*d.*

Eusebii Pamphili Historia Ecclesiastica: Annotationes Variorum. Tomi II. 1842. 8vo. *cloth*, 17*s.*

Evagrii Historia Ecclesiastica, ex recensione H. Valesii. 1844. 8vo. *cloth*, 4*s.*

Origenis Philosophumena; sive omnium Haeresium Refutatio. E Codice Parisino nunc primum edidit Emmanuel Miller. 1851. 8vo. *cloth*, 10*s.*

Patrum Apostolicorum, S. Clementis Romani, S. Ignatii, S.
Polycarpi, quae supersunt. Edidit Guil. Jacobson, S.T.P.R. Tomi II.
Fourth Edition, 1863. 8vo. *cloth*, 1*l.* 1*s.*

Reliquiae Sacrae secundi tertiique saeculi. Recensuit M. J.
Routh, S.T.P. Tomi V. *Second Edition*, 1846-1848. 8vo. *cloth*
Price reduced from 2*l.* 11*s.* *to* 1*l.* 5*s.*

Scriptorum Ecclesiasticorum Opuscula. Recensuit M. J.
Routh, S.T.P. Tomi II. *Third Edition*, 1858. 8vo. *cloth*. *Price re-*
duced from 1*l.* *to* 10*s.*

Socratis Scholastici Historia Ecclesiastica. Gr. et Lat. Edidit
R. Hussey, S.T.B. Tomi III. 1853. 8vo. *cloth*. *Price reduced from*
1*l.* 11*s.* 6*d.* *to* 1*l.* 1*s.*

Sozomeni Historia Ecclesiastica. Edidit R. Hussey, S.T.B.
Tomi III. 1859. 8vo. *cloth*. *Price reduced from* 1*l.* 6*s.* 6*d.* *to* 1*l.* 1*s.*

Theodoreti Ecclesiasticae Historiae Libri V. Recensuit T.
Gaisford, S.T.P. 1854. 8vo. *cloth*, 7*s.* 6*d.*

Theodoreti Graecarum Affectionum Curatio. Ad Codices MSS.
recensuit T. Gaisford, S.T.P. 1839. 8vo. *cloth*, 7*s.* 6*d.*

Dowling (J. G.) Notitia Scriptorum SS. Patrum aliorumque vet.
Eccles. Mon. quae in Collectionibus Anecdotorum post annum Christi
MDCC. in lucem editis continentur. 1839. 8vo. *cloth*, 4*s.* 6*d.*

ECCLESIASTICAL HISTORY, BIOGRAPHY, &c.

Baedae Historia Ecclesiastica. Edited, with English Notes,
by George H. Moberly, M.A., Fellow of C.C.C., Oxford. 1869.
crown 8vo. *cloth*, 10*s.* 6*d.*

Bingham's Antiquities of the Christian Church, and other
Works. 10 vols. 1855. 8vo. *cloth*. *Price reduced from* 5*l.* 5*s.* *to* 3*l.* 3*s.*

Burnet's History of the Reformation of the Church of England. *A new Edition.* Carefully revised, and the Records collated
with the originals, by N. Pocock, M.A. With a Preface by the Editor,
7 vols. 1865. 8vo. 4*l.* 4*s.*

Burnet's Life of Sir M. Hale, and Fell's Life of Dr. Hammond.
1856. small 8vo. *cloth*. *Price reduced from* 5*s.* *to* 2*s.* 6*d.*

Cardwell's Two Books of Common Prayer, set forth by
authority in the Reign of King Edward VI, compared with each other.
Third Edition, 1852. 8vo. *cloth*, 7*s.*

Cardwell's Documentary Annals of the Reformed Church of
England; being a Collection of Injunctions, Declarations, Orders, Articles of Inquiry, &c. from 1546 to 1716. 2 vols. 1843. 8vo. *cloth*, 18*s.*

Cardwell's History of Conferences on the Book of Common Prayer from 1551 to 1690. *Third Edition*, 1849. 8vo. *cloth*, 7s. 6d.

Cardwell's Synodalia. A Collection of Articles of Religion, Canons, and Proceedings of Convocations in the Province of Canterbury, from 1547 to 1717. 2 vols. 1842. 8vo. *cloth*, 19s.

Councils and Ecclesiastical Documents relating to Great Britain and Ireland. Edited, after Spelman and Wilkins, by A. W. Haddan, B.D., and William Stubbs, M.A., Regius Professor of Modern History, Oxford. Vol. I. 1869. Medium 8vo. *cloth*, 1l. 1s.

Vol. II. *in the Press.*

Vol. III. Medium 8vo. *cloth*, 1l. 1s. *Just Published.*

Formularies of Faith set forth by the King's Authority during the Reign of Henry VIII. 1856. 8vo. *cloth*, 7s.

Fuller's Church History of Britain. Edited by J. S. Brewer, M.A. 6 vols. 1845. 8vo. *cloth*, 1l. 19s.

Gibson's Synodus Anglicana. Edited by E. Cardwell, D.D. 1854. 8vo. *cloth*, 6s.

Hussey's Rise of the Papal Power traced in three Lectures. *Second Edition*, 1853. fcap. 8vo. *cloth*, 4s. 6d.

Inett's Origines Anglicanae (in continuation of Stillingfleet). Edited by J. Griffiths, M.A. 3 vols. 1855. 8vo. *cloth*. *Price reduced from 1l. 11s. 6d. to 15s.*

John, Bishop of Ephesus. The Third Part of his Ecclesiastical History. [In Syriac.] Now first edited by William Cureton, M.A. 1853. 4to. *cloth*, 1l. 12s.

The same, translated by R. Payne Smith, M.A. 1860. 8vo. *cloth*, 10s.

Knight's Life of Dean Colet. 1823. 8vo. *cloth*, 7s. 6d.

Le Neve's Fasti Ecclesiae Anglicanae. *Corrected and continued from 1715 to 1853 by T. Duffus Hardy.* 3 vols. 1854. 8vo. *cloth*. *Price reduced from 1l. 17s. 6d. to 1l. 1s.*

Noelli (A.) Catechismus sive prima institutio disciplinaque Pietatis Christianae Latine explicata. Editio nova cura Guil. Jacobson, A.M. 1844. 8vo. *cloth*, 5s. 6d.

Prideaux's Connection of Sacred and Profane History. 2 vols. 1851. 8vo. *cloth*, 10s.

Primers put forth in the Reign of Henry VIII. 1848. 8vo. *cloth*, 5s.

Records of the Reformation. The Divorce. 1527—1533. Mostly now for the first time printed from MSS. in the British Museum and other Libraries. Collected and arranged by N. Pocock, M.A. 2 vols. 8vo. *cloth*, 36s.

Reformatio Legum Ecclesiasticarum. The Reformation of Ecclesiastical Laws, as attempted in the reigns of Henry VIII, Edward VI, and Elizabeth. Edited by E. Cardwell, D.D. 1850. 8vo. *cloth*, 6s. 6d.

Shirley's (W. W.) Some Account of the Church in the Apostolic Age. 1867. fcap. 8vo. *cloth*, 3s. 6d.

Shuckford's Sacred and Profane History connected (in continuation of Prideaux). 2 vols. 1848. 8vo. *cloth*, 10s.

Stillingfleet's Origines Britannicae, with Lloyd's Historical Account of Church Government. Edited by T. P. Pantin, M.A. 2 vols. 1842. 8vo. *cloth*. *Price reduced from* 13s. *to* 10s.

Strype's Works Complete, with a General Index. 27 vols. 1821–1843. 8vo. *cloth*, 7l. 13s. 6d. Sold separately as follows:—

Memorials of Cranmer. 2 vols. 1840. 8vo. *cloth*, 11s.

Life of Parker. 3 vols. 1828. 8vo. *cloth*, 16s. 6d.

Life of Grindal. 1821. 8vo. *cloth*, 5s. 6d.

Life of Whitgift. 3 vols. 1822. 8vo. *cloth*, 16s. 6d.

Life of Aylmer. 1820. 8vo. *cloth*, 5s. 6d.

Life of Cheke. 1821. 8vo. *cloth*, 5s. 6d.

Life of Smith. 1820. 8vo. *cloth*, 5s. 6d.

Ecclesiastical Memorials. 6 vols. 1822. 8vo. *cloth*, 1l. 13s.

Annals of the Reformation. 7 vols. 1824. 8vo. *cloth*, 2l. 3s. 6d.

General Index. 2 vols. 1828. 8vo. *cloth*, 11s.

Stubbs's (W.) Registrum Sacrum Anglicanum. An attempt to exhibit the course of Episcopal Succession in England. 1858. small 4to. *cloth*, 8s. 6d.

Sylloge Confessionum sub tempus Reformandae Ecclesiae editarum. Subjiciuntur Catechismus Heidelbergensis et Canones Synodi Dordrechtanae. 1827. 8vo. *cloth*, 8s.

Walton's Lives of Donne, Wotton, Hooker, &c. 1824. 8vo. *cloth*, 6s. 6d.

ENGLISH THEOLOGY.

Beveridge's Discourse upon the XXXIX Articles. *The third complete Edition*, 1847. 8vo. *cloth*, 8s.

Bilson on the Perpetual Government of Christ's Church, with a Biographical Notice by R. Eden, M.A. 1842. 8vo. *cloth*, 4s.

Biscoe's Boyle Lectures on the Acts of the Apostles. 1840. 8vo. *cloth*, 9s. 6d.

Bull's Works, with Nelson's Life. By E. Burton, D.D. *A new Edition,* 1846. 8 vols. 8vo. *cloth,* 2l. 9s.

Burnet's Exposition of the XXXIX Articles. 1846. 8vo. *cloth,* 7s.

Burton's (Edward) Testimonies of the Ante-Nicene Fathers to the Divinity of Christ. *Second Edition,* 1829. 8vo. *cloth,* 7s.

Burton's (Edward) Testimonies of the Ante-Nicene Fathers to the Doctrine of the Trinity and of the Divinity of the Holy Ghost. 1831. 8vo. *cloth,* 3s. 6d.

Butler's Works, with an Index to the Analogy. 2 vols. 1849. 8vo. *cloth,* 11s.

Butler's Analogy of Religion. 1833. 12mo. *cloth,* 2s. 6d.

Chandler's Critical History of the Life of David. 1853. 8vo. *cloth,* 8s. 6d.

Chillingworth's Works. 3 vols. 1838. 8vo. *cloth,* 1l. 1s. 6d.

Clergyman's Instructor. *Sixth Edition,* 1855. 8vo. *cloth,* 6s. 6d.

Comber's Companion to the Temple ; or a Help to Devotion in the use of the Common Prayer. 7 vols. 1841. 8vo. *cloth,* 1l. 11s. 6d.

Cranmer's Works. Collected and arranged by H. Jenkyns, M.A., Fellow of Oriel College. 4 vols. 1834. 8vo. *cloth,* 1l. 10s.

Enchiridion Theologicum Anti-Romanum.

> Vol. I.   Jeremy Taylor's Dissuasive from Popery, and Treatise on the Real Presence. 1852. 8vo. *cloth,* 8s.
>
> Vol. II.   Barrow on the Supremacy of the Pope, with his Discourse on the Unity of the Church. 1852. 8vo. *cloth,* 7s. 6d.
>
> Vol. III. Tracts selected from Wake, Patrick, Stillingfleet, Clagett. and others. 1837. 8vo. *cloth,* 11s.

[Fell's] Paraphrase and Annotations on the Epistles of St. Paul. 1852. 8vo. *cloth,* 7s. .

Greswell's Harmonia Evangelica. *Fifth Edition,* 1856. 8vo. *cloth,* 9s. 6d.

Greswell's Prolegomena ad Harmoniam Evangelicam. 1840. 8vo. *cloth,* 9s. 6d.

Greswell's Dissertations on the Principles and Arrangement of a Harmony of the Gospels. 5 vols. 1837. 8vo. *cloth,* 3l. 3s.

Hall's (Bp.) Works. *A new Edition*, by Philip Wynter, D.D.
10 vols. 1863. 8vo. *cloth. Price reduced from 5l. 5s. to 3l. 3s.*

Hammond's Paraphrase and Annotations on the New Testament. 4 vols. 1845. 8vo. *cloth. Price reduced from 1l. 10s. to 1l.*

Hammond's Paraphrase on the Book of Psalms. 2 vols. 1850.
8vo. *cloth. Price reduced from 1l. 1s. to 10s.*

Heurtley's Collection of Creeds. 1858. 8vo. *cloth, 6s. 6d.*

Homilies appointed to be read in Churches. Edited by J.
Griffiths, M.A. 1859. 8vo. *cloth. Price reduced from 10s. 6d to 7s. 6d.*

Hooker's Works, with his Life by Walton, arranged by John
Keble, M.A. *Fifth Edition*, 1865. 3 vols. 8vo. *cloth, 1l. 11s. 6d.*

Hooker's Works; the text as arranged by John Keble, M.A.
2 vols. 1865. 8vo. *cloth, 11s.*

Hooper's (Bp. George) Works. 2 vols. 1855. 8vo. *cloth, 8s.*

Jackson's (Dr. Thomas) Works. 12 vols. 1844. 8vo. *cloth,*
3l. 6s.

Jewel's Works. Edited by R. W. Jelf, D.D. 8 vols. 1847.
8vo. *cloth. Price reduced from 2l. 10s. to 1l. 10s.*

Patrick's Theological Works. 9 vols. 1859. 8vo. *cloth.*
Price reduced from 3l. 14s. 6d. to 1l. 1s.

Pearson's Exposition of the Creed. Revised and corrected by
E. Burton, D D. *Fifth Edition*, 1864. 8vo. *cloth, 10s. 6d.*

Pearson's Minor Theological Works. Now first collected, with
a Memoir of the Author, Notes, and Index, by Edward Churton, M.A.
2 vols. 1844. 8vo. *cloth. Price reduced from 14s. to 10s.*

Sanderson's Works. Edited by W. Jacobson, D.D. 6 vols.
1854. 8vo. *cloth. Price reduced from 1l. 19s. to 1l. 10s.*

South's Sermons. 5 vols. 1842. 8vo. *cloth. Price reduced from*
2l. 10s. 6d. to 1l. 10s.

Stanhope's Paraphrase and Comment upon the Epistles and
Gospels. *A new Edition.* 2 vols. 1851. 8vo. *cloth. Price reduced*
from 18s. to 10s.

Stillingfleet's Origines Sacrae. 2 vols. 1837. 8vo. *cloth, 9s.*

Stillingfleet's Rational Account of the Grounds of Protestant
Religion; being a vindication of Abp. Laud's Relation of a Conference,
&c. 2 vols. 1844. 8vo. *cloth, 10s.*

Wall's History of Infant Baptism, with Gale's Reflections, and Wall's Defence. *A new Edition*, by Henry Cotton, D.C.L. 2 vols. 1862. 8vo. *cloth*, 1*l*. 1*s*.

Waterland's Works, with Life, by Bp. Van Mildert. *A new Edition*, with copious Indexes. 6 vols. 1857. 8vo. *cloth*, 2*l*. 11*s*.

Waterland's Review of the Doctrine of the Eucharist, with a Preface by the present Bishop of London. 1868. crown 8vo. *cloth*, 6*s*. 6*d*.

Wheatly's Illustration of the Book of Common Prayer. *A new Edition*, 1846. 8vo. *cloth*, 5*s*.

Wyclif. A Catalogue of the Original Works of John Wyclif, by W. W. Shirley, D.D. 1865. 8vo. *cloth*, 3*s*. 6*d*.

Wyclif. Select English Works. By T. Arnold, M.A. 3 vols. 1871. 8vo. *cloth*, 2*l*. 2*s*.

Wyclif. Trialogus. *With the Supplement now first edited.* By Gotthardus Lechler. 1869. 8vo. *cloth*, 14*s*.

ENGLISH HISTORICAL AND DOCUMENTARY WORKS.

Two of the Saxon Chronicles parallel, with Supplementary Extracts from the Others. Edited, with Introduction, Notes, and a Glossarial Index, by J. Earle, M.A. 1865. 8vo. *cloth*, 16*s*.

Magna Carta, a careful Reprint. Edited by W. Stubbs, M.A., Regius Professor of Modern History. 1868. 4to. *stitched*, 1*s*.

Britton, a Treatise upon the Common Law of England, composed by order of King Edward I. The French Text carefully revised, with an English Translation, Introduction, and Notes, by F. M. Nichols, M.A. 2 vols. 1865. royal 8vo. *cloth*, 1*l*. 16*s*.

Burnet's History of His Own Time, with the suppressed Passages and Notes. 6 vols. 1833. 8vo. *cloth*, 2*l*. 10*s*.

Burnet's History of James II, with additional Notes. 1852. 8vo. *cloth*, 9*s*. 6*d*.

Burnet's Lives of James and William Dukes of Hamilton. 1852. 8vo. *cloth*, 7*s*. 6*d*.

Carte's Life of James Duke of Ormond. *A new Edition,* carefully compared with the original MSS. 6 vols. 1851. 8vo. *cloth. Price reduced from 2l. 6s. to 1l. 5s.*

Casauboni Ephemerides, cum praefatione et notis J. Russell, S.T.P. Tomi II. 1850. 8vo. *cloth,* 15s.

Clarendon's (Edw. Earl of) History of the Rebellion and Civil Wars in England. To which are subjoined the Notes of Bishop Warburton. 7 vols. 1849. medium 8vo. *cloth,* 2l. 10s.

Clarendon's (Edw. Earl of) History of the Rebellion and Civil Wars in England. 7 vols. 1839. 18mo. *cloth,* 1l. 1s.

Clarendon's (Edw. Earl of) History of the Rebellion and Civil Wars in England. Also His Life, written by Himself, in which is included a Continuation of his History of the Grand Rebellion. With copious Indexes. In one volume, royal 8vo. 1842. *cloth,* 1l. 2s.

Clarendon's (Edw. Earl of) Life, including a Continuation of his History. 2 vols. 1857. medium 8vo. *cloth,* 1l. 2s.

Clarendon's (Edw. Earl of) Life, and Continuation of his History. 3 vols. 1827. 8vo. *cloth,* 16s. 6d.

Calendar of the Clarendon State Papers, preserved in the Bodleian Library. Vol. II. From the death of Charles I, 1649, to the end of the year 1654. Edited by W. D. Macray, M.A. 1869. 8vo. *cloth,* 16s.

Freeman's (E. A.) History of the Norman Conquest of England: its Causes and Results. Vols. I. and II. *A new Edition,* with Index. 8vo. *cloth,* 1l. 16s.

> Vol. III. The Reign of Harold and the Interregnum. 1869. 8vo. *cloth,* 1l. 1s.
>
> Vol. IV. *Nearly Ready.*

Kennett's Parochial Antiquities. 2 vols. 1818. 4to. *cloth. Price reduced from 1l. 14s. to 1l.*

Lloyd's Prices of Corn in Oxford, 1583–1830. 8vo. *sewed,* 1s.

Luttrell's (Narcissus) Diary. A Brief Historical Relation of State Affairs, 1678–1714. 6 vols. 1857. 8vo. *cloth. Price reduced from 3l. 3s. to 1l. 4s.*

May's History of the Long Parliament. 1854. 8vo. *cloth,* 6s. 6d.

Rogers's History of Agriculture and Prices in England, A.D. 1259–1400. 2 vols. 1866. 8vo. *cloth,* 2l. 2s.

Sprigg's England's Recovery; being the History of the Army under Sir Thomas Fairfax. *A new edition.* 1854. 8vo. *cloth,* 6s.

Whitelock's Memorials of English Affairs from 1625 to 1660. 4 vols. 1853. 8vo. *cloth*, 1*l*. 10*s*.

Enactments in Parliament, specially concerning the Universities of Oxford and Cambridge. Collected and arranged by J. Griffiths, M.A. 1869. 8vo. *cloth*, 12*s*.

Ordinances and Statutes [for Colleges and Halls] framed or approved by the Oxford University Commissioners. 1863. 8vo. *cloth*, 12*s*.

Sold separately (except for Exeter, All Souls, Brasenose, Corpus, and Magdalen Hall) at 1*s*. each.

Statuta Universitatis Oxoniensis. 1870. 8vo. *cloth*, 5*s*.

Index to Wills proved in the Court of the Chancellor of the University of Oxford, &c. Compiled by J. Griffiths, M.A. 1862. royal 8vo. *cloth*, 3*s*. 6*d*.

Catalogue of Oxford Graduates from 1659 to 1850. 1851. 8vo. *cloth*. *Price reduced from* 12*s*. 6*d*. *to* 7*s*. 6*d*.

CHRONOLOGY, GEOGRAPHY, &c.

Clinton's Fasti Hellenici. The Civil and Literary Chronology of Greece, from the LVIth to the CXXIIIrd Olympiad. *Third edition*, 1841. 4to. *cloth*, 1*l*. 14*s*. 6*d*.

Clinton's Fasti Hellenici. The Civil and Literary Chronology of Greece, from the CXXIVth Olympiad to the Death of Augustus. *Second edition*, 1851. 4to. *cloth*, 1*l*. 12*s*.

Clinton's Epitome of the Fasti Hellenici. 1851. 8vo. *cloth*, 6*s*. 6*d*.

Clinton's Fasti Romani. The Civil and Literary Chronology of Rome and Constantinople, from the Death of Augustus to the Death of Heraclius. 2 vols. 1845, 1850. 4to. *cloth*, 3*l*. 9*s*.

Clinton's Epitome of the Fasti Romani. 1854. 8vo. *cloth*, 7*s*.

Cramer's Geographical and Historical Description of Asia Minor. 2 vols. 1832. 8vo. *cloth*, 11*s*.

Cramer's Map of Asia Minor, 15*s*.

Cramer's Map of Ancient and Modern Italy, on two sheets, 15*s*.

Cramer's Description of Ancient Greece. 3 vols. 1828. 8vo. *cloth*, 16*s*. 6*d*.

Cramer's Map of Ancient and Modern Greece, on two sheets, 15*s*.

Greswell's Fasti Temporis Catholici. 4 vols. 1852. 8vo. *cloth,* 2*l.* 1*cs.*

Greswell's Tables to Fasti, 4to., and Introduction to Tables, 8vo. *cloth,* 15*s.*

Greswell's Origines Kalendariæ Italicæ. 4 vols. 1854. 8vo. *cloth,* 2*l.* 2*s.*

Greswell's Origines Kalendariæ Hellenicæ. The History of the Primitive Calendar among the Greeks, before and after the Legislation of Solon. 6 vols. 1862. 8vo. *cloth,* 4*l.* 4*s.*

PHILOSOPHICAL WORKS, AND GENERAL LITERATURE.

A Course of Lectures on Art, delivered before the University of Oxford in Hilary Term, 1870. By John Ruskin, M.A., Slade Professor of Fine Art. 8vo. *cloth,* 6*s.*

A Critical Account of the Drawings by Michel Angelo and Raffaello in the University Galleries, Oxford. By J. C. Robinson, F S.A. Crown 8vo. *cloth,* 4*s.*

Bacon's Novum Organum, edited, with English notes, by G. W. Kitchin, M.A. 1855. 8vo. *cloth,* 9*s.* 6*d.*

Bacon's Novum Organum, translated by G. W. Kitchin, M.A. 1855. 8vo. *cloth,* 9*s.* 6*d.*

The Works of George Berkeley, D.D., formerly Bishop of Cloyne; including many of his writings hitherto unpublished. With Prefaces, Annotations, and an Account of his Life and Philosophy, by Alexander Campbell Fraser, M.A., Professor of Logic and Metaphysics in the University of Edinburgh. 4 vols. 1871. 8vo. *cloth,* 2*l.* 18*s.*

Also separately,
The Works. 3 vols. *cloth,* 2*l.* 2*s.*
The Life, Letters, &c. 1 vol. *cloth,* 16*s.*

Smith's Wealth of Nations. A new Edition, with Notes, by J. E. Thorold Rogers, M.A. 2 vols. 1870. *cloth,* 21*s.*

MATHEMATICS, PHYSICAL SCIENCE, &c.

Vesuvius. By John Phillips, M.A., F.R.S., Professor of Geology, Oxford. 1869. Crown 8vo. *cloth,* 10*s.* 6*d.*

Geology of Oxford and the Valley of the Thames. By the same Author. 8vo. *cloth,* 21*s.* *Just Published.*

Synopsis of the Pathological Series in the Oxford Museum. By H. W. Acland, M.D., F.R.S., Regius Professor of Medicine, Oxford. 1867. 8vo. *cloth*, 2s. 6d.

Archimedis quae supersunt omnia cum Eutocii commentariis ex recensione Josephi Torelli, cum novâ versione Latinâ. 1792. folio. *cloth*, 1l. 5s.

Bradley's Miscellaneous Works and Correspondence. With an Account of Harriot's Astronomical Papers. 1832. 4to. *cloth*, 17s.

    Reduction of Bradley's Observations by Dr. Busch. 1838. 4to. *cloth*, 3s.

Daubeny's Introduction to the Atomic Theory. *Second Edition*, greatly enlarged. 1850. 16mo. *cloth*, 6s.

Thesaurus Entomologicus Hopeianus, or a Description, with Plates, of the rarest Insects in the Collection given to the University by the Rev. William Hope. By J. O. Westwood, M.A., Hope Professor of Zoology. *Preparing*.

Treatise on Infinitesimal Calculus. By Bartholomew Price, M.A., F.R.S., Professor of Natural Philosophy, Oxford.

    Vol. I. Differential Calculus. *Second Edition*, 1858. 8vo. *cloth*, 14s. 6d.

    Vol. II. Integral Calculus, Calculus of Variations, and Differential Equations. *Second Edition*, 1865. 8vo. *cloth*, 18s.

    Vol. III. Statics, including Attractions; Dynamics of a Material Particle. *Second Edition*, 1868. 8vo. *cloth*, 16s.

    Vol. IV. Dynamics of Material Systems; together with a Chapter on Theoretical Dynamics, by W. F. Donkin, M.A., F.R.S. 1862. 8vo. *cloth*, 16s.

Rigaud's Correspondence of Scientific Men of the 17th Century, with Index by A. de Morgan. 2 vols. 1841-1862. 8vo. *cloth*, 18s. 6d.

BIBLIOGRAPHY.

Ebert's Bibliographical Dictionary, translated from the German. 4 vols. 1837. 8vo. *cloth*, 1l. 10s.

Cotton's List of Editions of the Bible in English. *Second Edition*, corrected and enlarged. 1852. 8vo. *cloth*, 8s. 6d.

Cotton's Typographical Gazetteer. *Second Edition*. 1831. 8vo. *cloth*, 12s. 6d.

Cotton's Typographical Gazetteer, Second Series. 1866. 8vo. *cloth*, 12s. 6d.

Cotton's Rhemes and Doway. An attempt to shew what has been done by Roman Catholics for the diffusion of the Holy Scriptures in English. 1855. 8vo. *cloth*, 9s.

BODLEIAN LIBRARY CATALOGUES, &c.

Catalogus Codd. MSS. Orientalium Bibliothecae Bodleianae :

> Pars I, a J. Uri. 1788. fol. 10s.
>
> Partis II Vol. I, ab A Nicoll, A.M. 1821. fol. 10s.
>
> Partis II Vol. II, Arabicos complectens, ab E. B. Pusey, S.T.B. 1835. fol. 1l.

Catalogus MSS. qui ab E. D. Clarke comparati in Bibl. Bodl. adservantur :

> Pars prior. Inseruntur Scholia inedita in Platonem et in Carmina Gregorii Naz. 1812. 4to. 5s.
>
> Pars posterior, Orientales complectens, ab A. Nicoll, A.M. 1814. 4to. 2s. 6d.

Catalogus Codd. MSS. et Impressorum cum notis MSS. olim D'Orvillianorum, qui in Bibl. Bodl. adservantur. 1806. 4to. 2s. 6d.

Catalogus MSS. Borealium praecipue Islandicae Originis, a Finno Magno Islando. 1832. 4to. 4s.

Catalogus Codd. MSS. Bibliothecae Bodleianae :—

> Pars I. Codices Graeci, ab H. O. Coxe, A.M. 1853. 4to. 1l.
>
> Partis II. Fasc. I. Codices Laudiani, ab H. O. Coxe, A.M. 1858. 4to. 1l.
>
> Pars III. Codices Graeci et Latini Canoniciani, ab H. O. Coxe, A.M. 1854. 4to. 1l.
>
> Pars IV. Codices T. Tanneri, ab A. Hackman, A.M. 1860. 4to. 12s.
>
> Pars V. Codicum R. Rawlinson classes duae priores, a Guil. D. Macray, A.M. 1862. 4to. 12s.
>
> Pars VI. Codices Syriaci, a R. P. Smith, A.M. 1864. 4to. 1l.
>
> Pars VII. Codices Aethiopici, ab A. Dillmann, Ph. Doct. 1848. 4to. 6s. 6d.
>
> Pars VIII. Codices Sanscritici, a Th. Aufrecht, A.M. 1859-1864. 4to. 1l. 10s.

Catalogo di Codici MSS. Canoniciani Italici, compilato dal Conte A. Mortara. 1864. 4to. 10s. 6d.

Catalogus Librorum Impressorum Bibliothecae Bodleianae. Tomi IV. 1843 to 1850. fol. 4l.

Catalogus Dissertationum Academicarum quibus nuper aucta est Bibliotheca Bodleiana. 1834. fol. 7s.

Catalogue of Books bequeathed to the Bodleian Library by R. Gough, Esq. 1814. 4to. 15s.

Catalogue of Early English Poetry and other Works illustrating the British Drama, collected by Edmond Malone, Esq. 1835. fol. 4s.

Catalogue of the Printed Books and Manuscripts bequeathed to the Bodleian Library by Francis Douce, Esq. 1840. fol. 15s.

Catalogue of the Manuscripts bequeathed to the University of Oxford by Elias Ashmole. By W. H. Black. 1845. 4to. 1l. 10s.

> Index to the above, by W. D. Macray, M.A. 1867. 4to. 10s.

Catalogue of a Collection of Early Newspapers and Essayists presented to the Bodleian Library by the late Rev. F. W. Hope. 1865. 8vo. 7s. 6d.

Catalogus Codd. MSS. qui in Collegiis Aulisque Oxoniensibus hodie adservantur. Confecit H. O. Coxe, A.M. Tomi II. 1852. 4to. 2l.

Catalogus Codd. MSS. in Bibl. Aed. Christi ap. Oxon. Curavit G. W. Kitchin, A.M. 1867. 4to. 6s. 6d.

Clarendon Press Series.

The Delegates of the Clarendon Press having undertaken the publication of a series of works, chiefly educational, and entitled the Clarendon Press Series, have published, or have in preparation, the following.

Those to which prices are attached are already published; the others are in preparation.

I. GREEK AND LATIN CLASSICS, &c.

A Greek Primer in English for the use of beginners. By the Right Rev. Charles Wordsworth, D.C.L., Bishop of St. Andrews. *Second Edition.* Extra fcap. 8vo. *cloth*, 1s. 6d.

Greek Verbs, Irregular and Defective; their forms, meaning, and quantity; embracing all the Tenses used by Greek writers, with reference to the passages in which they are found. By W. Veitch. *New Edition.* Crown 8vo. *cloth*, 10s. 6d. *Just Published.*

The Elements of Greek Accentuation (for Schools): abridged from his larger work by H. W. Chandler, M.A., Waynflete Professor of Moral and Metaphysical Philosophy, Oxford. Ext. fcap. 8vo. *cloth*, 2s. 6d.

Aeschines in Ctesiphontem and Demosthenes de Corona. With Introduction and Notes. By G. A. Simcox, M.A., and W. H. Simcox, M.A., Fellows of Queen's College, Oxford. *In the Press.*

Aristotle's Politics. By W. L. Newman, M.A., Fellow and Lecturer of Balliol College, and Reader in Ancient History, Oxford.

The Golden Treasury of Ancient Greek Poetry; being a Collection of the finest passages in the Greek Classic Poets, with Introductory Notices and Notes. By R. S. Wright, M.A., Fellow of Oriel College, Oxford. Ext. fcap. 8vo. *cloth*, 8s. 6d.

A Golden Treasury of Greek Prose, being a collection of the finest passages in the principal Greek Prose Writers, with Introductory Notices and Notes. By R. S. Wright, M.A., Fellow of Oriel College, Oxford; and J. E. L. Shadwell, M.A., Senior Student of Christ Church. Ext. fcap. 8vo. *cloth*, 4s. 6d.

Homer. Odyssey, Books I—XII (for Schools). By W. W. Merry, M.A., Fellow and Lecturer of Lincoln College, Oxford. Extra fcap. 8vo. *cloth*, 4s. 6d.

Homer. Odyssey, Books I–XII. By W. W. Merry, M.A., Fellow and Lecturer of Lincoln College, Oxford; and the late James Riddell, M.A., Fellow of Balliol College, Oxford.

Homer. Odyssey, Books XIII–XXIV. By Robinson Ellis, M.A., Fellow of Trinity College, Oxford.

Homer. Iliad. By D. B. Monro, M.A., Fellow and Tutor of Oriel College, Oxford.

Plato. Selections (for Schools). With Notes, by B. Jowett, M.A., Regius Professor of Greek; and J. Purves, M.A., Fellow and Lecturer of Balliol College, Oxford.

Sophocles. Oedipus Rex: Dindorf's Text, with Notes by the Ven. Archdeacon Basil Jones, M.A., formerly Fellow of University College, Oxford. *Second edition.* Ext. fcap. 8vo. *limp cloth,* 1s. 6d.

Sophocles. By Lewis Campbell, M.A., Professor of Greek, St. Andrews. formerly Fellow of Queen's College, Oxford. *In the Press.*

Theocritus (for Schools). With Notes, by H. Snow, M.A., Assistant Master at Eton College. formerly Fellow of St. John's College, Cambridge. Extra fcap. 8vo. *cloth,* 4s. 6d.

Xenophon. Selections (for Schools). With Notes and Maps, by J. S. Phillpotts, B.C.L., Assistant Master in Rugby School, formerly Fellow of New College, Oxford. Ext. fcap. 8vo. *cloth,* 3s. 6d.

Caesar. The Commentaries (for Schools). Part I. The Gallic War. With Notes, and Maps, by Charles E. Moberly, M.A., Assistant Master in Rugby School; formerly Scholar of Balliol College, Oxford. Ext. fcap. 8vo. *cloth,* 4s. 6d.
   Also, to follow: Part II. The Civil War. By the same Editor.

Cicero's Philippic Orations. With Notes, by J. R. King, M.A., formerly Fellow and Tutor of Merton College, Oxford. Demy 8vo. *cloth,* 10s. 6d.

Cicero pro Cluentio. With Introduction and Notes. By W. Ramsay, M.A. Edited by G. G. Ramsay, M.A., Professor of Humanity, Glasgow. Extra fcap. 8vo. *cloth,* 3s. 6d.

Cicero. Selection of interesting and descriptive passages. With Notes. By Henry Walford, M.A., Wadham College, Oxford, Assistant Master at Haileybury College. In three Parts. *Second Edition.* Extra fcap. 8vo. *cloth,* 4s. 6d.
   Each Part separately. limp, 1s. 6d.
   Part I.   Anecdotes from Grecian and Roman History.
   Part II.   Omens and Dreams: Beauties of Nature.
   Part III. Rome's Rule of her Provinces.

Cicero. Select Letters. With English Introductions, Notes, and Appendices. By Albert Watson, M.A., Fellow and Tutor of Brasenose College, Oxford. Demy 8vo. *cloth,* 18s.

Cicero de Oratore. With Introduction and Notes. By A. S. Wilkins, M.A., Professor of Latin, Owens College, Manchester.

Cicero and Pliny. Select Epistles (for Schools). With Notes by E. R. Bernard, M.A., Fellow of Magdalen College, Oxford, and the late C. E. Prichard, M.A., formerly Fellow of Balliol College, Oxford. *In the Press.*

Cornelius Nepos. With Notes, by Oscar Browning, M.A., Fellow of King's College, Cambridge, and Assistant Master at Eton College. Extra fcap. 8vo. *cloth,* 2s. 6d.

Horace. With Introduction and Notes. By Edward C. Wickham, M.A., Fellow and Tutor of New College, Oxford.

Also a small edition for Schools.

Livy, Books I-X. By J. R. Seeley, M.A., Fellow of Christ's College, and Regius Professor of Modern History, Cambridge. Book I. 8vo. *cloth,* 6s. *Just Published.*

Also a small edition for Schools.

Ovid. Selections for the use of Schools. With Introductions and Notes, and an Appendix on the Roman Calendar. By W. Ramsay, M.A. Edited by G. G. Ramsay, M.A., Professor of Humanity, Glasgow. *Second Edition.* Ext. fcap. 8vo. *cloth,* 4s. 6d.

Fragments and Specimens of Early Latin. With Introduction, Notes, and Illustrations. By John Wordsworth, M.A., Fellow of Brasenose College, Oxford.

Selections from the less known Latin Poets. By North Pinder, M.A., formerly Fellow of Trinity College, Oxford. Demy 8vo. *cloth,* 15s.

Passages for Translation into Latin. For the use of Passmen and others. Selected by J. Y. Sargent, M.A., Tutor, formerly Fellow, of Magdalen College, Oxford. *Second Edition.* Ext. fcap. 8vo. *cloth,* 2s. 6d.

II. MENTAL AND MORAL PHILOSOPHY.

The Elements of Deductive Logic, designed mainly for the use of Junior Students in the Universities. By T. Fowler, M.A., Fellow and Tutor of Lincoln College, Oxford. *Fourth Edition,* with a Collection of Examples. Extra fcap. 8vo. *cloth,* 3s. 6d.

The Elements of Inductive Logic, designed mainly for the use of Students in the Universities. By the same Author. Extra fcap. 8vo. *cloth,* 6s.

A Manual of Political Economy, for the use of Schools. By J. E. Thorold Rogers, M.A., formerly Professor of Political Economy, Oxford. *Second Edition.* Extra fcap. 8vo. *cloth,* 4s. 6d.

III. MATHEMATICS, &c.

Acoustics. By W. F. Donkin, M.A., F.R.S.. Savilian Professor of Astronomy, Oxford. Crown 8vo. *cloth*, 7s. 6d.

An Elementary Treatise on Quaternions. By P. G. Tait, M.A.. Professor of Natural Philosophy in the University of Edinburgh ; formerly Fellow of St. Peter's College, Cambridge. Demy 8vo. *cloth*, 12s. 6d.

Book-keeping. By R. G. C. Hamilton, Accountant to the Board of Trade, and John Ball (of the Firm of Messrs. Quilter, Ball, & Co.), Examiners in Book-keeping for the Society of Arts' Examination. *Second edition.* Extra fcap. 8vo. *limp cloth*, 1s. 6d.

A Course of Lectures on Pure Geometry. By Henry J. Stephen Smith, M.A.. F.R.S., Fellow of Balliol College, and Savilian Professor of Geometry in the University of Oxford.

A Treatise on Electricity and Magnetism. By J. Clerk Maxwell, M.A.. F.R.S., formerly Professor of Natural Philosophy, King's College, London. *In the Press.*

A Series of Elementary Works is being arranged, and will shortly be announced.

IV. HISTORY.

Select Charters and other Illustrations of English Constitutional History, from the Earliest Times to the Reign of Edward I. Arranged and Edited by W. Stubbs, M.A., Regius Professor of Modern History in the University of Oxford. Crown 8vo. *cloth*, 8s. 6d.

A Constitutional History of England. By W. Stubbs, M.A.. Regius Professor of Modern History in the University of Oxford.

A Manual of Ancient History. By George Rawlinson, M.A., Camden Professor of Ancient History, formerly Fellow of Exeter College, Oxford. Demy 8vo. *cloth*, 14s.

A History of Germany and of the Empire, down to the close of the Middle Ages. By J. Bryce, B.C.L., Fellow of Oriel College. Oxford.

A History of Germany, from the Reformation. By Adolphus W. Ward. M.A., Fellow of St. Peter's College, Cambridge, Professor of History. Owens College, Manchester.

A History of British India. By S. J. Owen, M.A., Lee's Reader in Law and History. Christ Church, and Teacher of Indian Law and History in the University of Oxford.

A History of Greece. By E. A. Freeman, M.A., formerly Fellow of Trinity College, Oxford.

A History of France. By G. W. Kitchin, M.A., formerly Censor of Christ Church.

V. LAW.

Elements of Law considered with reference to Principles of General Jurisprudence. By William Markby, M.A., Judge of the High Court of Judicature, Calcutta. Crown 8vo. *cloth*, 6s. 6d. *Just Published.*

Gaii Institutionum Juris Civilis Commentarii Quatuor; or, Elements of Roman Law by Gaius. With a Translation and Commentary by Edward Poste, M.A., Barrister-at-Law, and Fellow of Oriel College, Oxford. 8vo. *cloth*, 16s. *Just Published.*

Commentaries on Roman Law; from the original and the best modern sources. By H. J. Roby, M.A., formerly Fellow of St. John's College, Cambridge; Professor of Law at University College, London.

VI. PHYSICAL SCIENCE.

Natural Philosophy. In four volumes. By Sir W. Thomson, LL.D., D.C.L., F.R.S., Professor of Natural Philosophy, Glasgow; and P. G. Tait, M.A., Professor of Natural Philosophy, Edinburgh; formerly Fellows of St. Peter's College, Cambridge. Vol. I. 8vo. *cloth*, 1l. 5s.

By the same Authors, a smaller Work on the same subject, forming a complete Introduction to it, so far as it can be carried out with Elementary Geometry and Algebra. *In the Press.*

Descriptive Astronomy. A Handbook for the General Reader, and also for practical Observatory work. With 224 illustrations and numerous tables. By G. F. Chambers, F.R.A.S., Barrister-at-Law. Demy 8vo. 856 pp., *cloth*, 1l. 1s.

Chemistry for Students. By A. W. Williamson, Phil. Doc., F.R.S., Professor of Chemistry, University College, London. *A new Edition, with Solutions.* Extra fcap. 8vo. *cloth*, 8s. 6d.

A Treatise on Heat, with numerous Woodcuts and Diagrams. By Balfour Stewart, LL.D., F.R.S., Director of the Observatory at Kew. *Second Edition.* Extra fcap. 8vo. *cloth*, 7s. 6d.

Forms of Animal Life. By G. Rolleston, M.D., F.R.S., Linacre Professor of Physiology, Oxford. Illustrated by Descriptions and Drawings of Dissections. Demy 8vo. *cloth.* 16s.

Exercises in Practical Chemistry (Laboratory Practice). By A. G. Vernon Harcourt, M A , F.R.S., Senior Student of Christ Church, and Lee's Reader in Chemistry; and H. G. Madan, M.A., Fellow of Queen's College, Oxford.

Series I. Qualitative Exercises. Crown 8vo. *cloth*, 7s. 6d.
Series II. Quantitative Exercises.

Geology of Oxford and the Valley of the Thames. By John Philips, M.A., F.R.S., Professor of Geology, Oxford. 8vo. *cloth*, 21s. *Just Published.*

Geology. By J. Phillips, M.A., F.R.S., Professor of Geology, Oxford.

Mechanics. By Bartholomew Price, M.A., F.R.S., Sedleian Professor of Natural Philosophy, Oxford.

Optics. By R. B. Clifton, M.A., F.R.S., Professor of Experimental Philosophy, Oxford; formerly Fellow of St. John's College, Cambridge.

Electricity. By W. Esson, M.A., F.R.S., Fellow and Mathematical Lecturer of Merton College, Oxford.

Crystallography. By M. H. N. Story-Maskelyne, M.A., Professor of Mineralogy, Oxford; and Deputy Keeper in the Department of Minerals, British Museum.

Mineralogy. By the same Author.

Physiological Physics. By G. Griffith, M.A., Jesus College, Oxford, Assistant Secretary to the British Association, and Natural Science Master at Harrow School.

Magnetism.

VII. ENGLISH LANGUAGE AND LITERATURE.

A First Reading Book. By Marie Eichens of Berlin; and edited by Anne J. Clough. Extra fcap. 8vo. *stiff covers*, 4d.

Oxford Reading Book, Part I. For Little Children. Extra fcap. 8vo. *stiff covers*, 6d.

Oxford Reading Book, Part II. For Junior Classes. Extra fcap. 8vo. *stiff covers*, 6d.

On the Principles of Grammar. By E. Thring, M.A., Head Master of Uppingham School. Extra fcap. 8vo. *cloth*, 4s. 6d.

Grammatical Analysis, designed to serve as an Exercise and Composition Book in the English Language. By E. Thring, M.A., Head Master of Uppingham School. Extra fcap. 8vo. *cloth*, 3s. 6d.

The Philology of the English Tongue. By J. Earle, M.A., formerly Fellow of Oriel College, and Professor of Anglo-Saxon, Oxford. Extra fcap. 8vo. *cloth*, 6s. 6d. *Just Published.*

Specimens of Early English; being a Series of Extracts from the most important English Authors, from A.D. 1250 to A.D. 1400. With Grammatical Introduction, Notes, and Glossary. By R. Morris. Extra fcap. 8vo. *cloth*, 7s. 6d.

Specimens of English Literature, A.D. 1394 to A.D. 1579. With Introduction, Notes, and Glossarial Index, by W. W. Skeat, M.A., formerly Fellow of Christ's College, Cambridge. Extra fcap. 8vo. *cloth*, 7s. 6d. *Just Published.*

The Vision of William concerning Piers the Plowman,
by William Langland. Edited, with Notes, by W. W. Skeat, M.A., formerly Fellow of Christ's College, Cambridge. Extra fcap. 8vo. *cloth*, 4s. 6d.

Typical Selections from the best English Authors from the Sixteenth to the Nineteenth Century, (to serve as a higher Reading Book,) with Introductory Notices and Notes, being a Contribution towards a History of English Literature. Extra fcap. 8vo. *cloth*, 4s. 6d.

Specimens of the Scottish Language; being a Series of Annotated Extracts illustrative of the Literature and Philology of the Lowland Tongue from the Fourteenth to the Nineteenth Century. With Introduction and Glossary. By A. H. Burgess, M.A.

See also XII. below for other English Classics.

VIII. FRENCH LANGUAGE AND LITERATURE.

An Etymological Dictionary of the French Language, with a Preface on the Principles of French Etymology. By A. Brachet. Translated by G. W. Kitchin, M.A., formerly Censor of Christ Church. *In the Press.*

Brachet's Historical Grammar of the French Language. Translated into English by G. W. Kitchin, M.A., formerly Censor of Christ Church. Extra fcap. 8vo. *cloth*, 3s. 6d.

Corneille's Cinna, and **Molière's** Les Femmes Savantes. Edited, with Introduction and Notes, by Gustave Masson. Extra fcap. 8vo. *cloth*, 2s. 6d.

Racine's Andromaque, and **Corneille's** Le Menteur. With Louis Racine's Life of his Father. By the same Editor. Extra fcap. 8vo. *cloth*. 2s. 6d.

Molière's Les Fourberies de Scapin, and **Racine's** Athalie. With Voltaire's Life of Molière. By the same Editor. Extra fcap. 8vo. *cloth*. 2s. 6d.

Selections from the Correspondence of **Madame de Sévigné** and her chief Contemporaries. Intended more especially for Girls' Schools. By the same Editor. Extra fcap. 8vo. *cloth*, 3s.

Voyage autour de ma Chambre, by **Xavier de Maistre** ; Ourika, by Madame de Duras ; La Dot de Suzette, by **Fievée** ; Les Jumeaux de l'Hôtel Corneille, by **Edmond About** ; Mésaventures d'un Écolier, by **Rodolphe Töpffer**. By the same Editor. Extra fcap. 8vo. *cloth*, 2s. 6d.

A French Grammar. A Complete Theory of the French Language, with the rules in French and English, and numerous Examples to serve as first Exercises in the Language. By Jules Bué, Honorary M.A. of Oxford ; Taylorian Teacher of French, Oxford ; Examiner in the Oxford Local Examinations from 1858.

A French Grammar Test. A Book of Exercises on French Grammar; each Exercise being preceded by Grammatical Questions. By the same Author.

Exercises in Translation No. 1, from French into English, with general rules on Translation; and containing Notes, Hints, and Cautions, founded on a comparison of the Grammar and Genius of the two Languages. By the same Author.

Exercises in Translation No. 2, from English into French, on the same plan as the preceding book. By the same Author.

IX. GERMAN LANGUAGE AND LITERATURE.

Goethe's Egmont. With a Life of Goethe, &c. By Dr. Buchheim, Professor of the German Language and Literature in King's College, London; and Examiner in German to the University of London. Extra fcap. 8vo. *cloth*, 3s.

Schiller's Wilhelm Tell. With a Life of Schiller; an historical and critical Introduction, Arguments, and a complete Commentary. By the same Editor. Ext. fcap. 8vo. *cloth*, 3s. 6d.

Lessing's Minna von Barnhelm. A Comedy. With a Life of Lessing, Critical Commentary, &c. By the same Editor.

X. ART, &c.

A Handbook of Pictorial Art. By R. St. J. Tyrwhitt, M.A., formerly Student and Tutor of Christ Church, Oxford. With coloured Illustrations, Photographs, and a chapter on Perspective by A. Macdonald. 8vo. *half morocco*, 18s.

A Treatise on Harmony. By Sir F. A. Gore Ouseley, Bart., M.A., Mus. Doc., Professor of Music in the University of Oxford. 4to. *cloth*, 10s.

A Treatise on Counterpoint, Canon, and Fugue, based upon that of Cherubini. By the same Author. 4to. *cloth*, 16s.

The Cultivation of the Speaking Voice. By John Hullah. Crown 8vo. *cloth*, 3s. 6d.

XI. MISCELLANEOUS.

A System of Physical Education: Theoretical and Practical. By Archibald Maclaren, The Gymnasium, Oxford. Extra fcap. 8vo. *cloth*, 7s. 6d.

The Modern Greek Language in its relation to Ancient Greek. By E. M. Geldart, B.A., formerly Scholar of Balliol College, Oxford. Extra fcap. 8vo. *cloth*, 4s. 6d.

XII. A SERIES OF ENGLISH CLASSICS.

Designed to meet the wants of Students in English Literature: under the superintendence of the Rev. J. S. BREWER, M.A., *of Queen's College, Oxford, and Professor of English Literature at King's College, London.*

THERE are two dangers to which the student of English literature is exposed at the outset of his task;—his reading is apt to be too narrow or too diffuse.

Out of the vast number of authors set before him in books professing to deal with this subject he knows not which to select: he thinks he must read a little of all; he soon abandons so hopeless an attempt; he ends by contenting himself with second-hand information; and professing to study English literature, he fails to master a single English author. On the other hand, by confining his attention to one or two writers, or to one special period of English literature, the student narrows his view of it; he fails to grasp the subject as a whole; and in so doing misses one of the chief objects of his study.

How may these errors be avoided? How may minute reading be combined with comprehensiveness of view?

In the hope of furnishing an answer to these questions the Delegates of the Press, acting upon the advice and experience of Professor Brewer, have determined to issue a series of small volumes, which shall embrace, in a convenient form and at a low price, the general extent of English Literature, as represented in its masterpieces at successive epochs. It is thought that the student, by confining himself, in the first instance, to those authors who are most worthy of his attention, will be saved from the dangers of hasty and indiscriminate reading. By adopting the course thus marked out for him he will become familiar with the productions of the greatest minds in English Literature; and should he never be able to pursue the subject beyond the limits here prescribed, he will have laid the foundation of accurate habits of thought and judgment, which cannot fail of being serviceable to him hereafter.

The authors and works selected are such as will best serve to illustrate English literature in its *historical* aspect. As "the eye of history," without which history cannot be understood, the literature of a nation is the clearest and most intelligible record of its life. Its thoughts and its emotions, its graver and its less serious modes, its progress, or its degeneracy, are told by its best authors in their best words. This view of the subject will suggest the safest rules for the study of it.

With one exception all writers before the Reformation are excluded from the Series. However great may be the value of literature before that epoch, it is not completely national. For it had no common organ of language; it addressed itself to special classes; it dealt mainly with special subjects. Again; of writers who flourished after the Reformation, who were popular in their day, and reflected the manners and sentiments of their age, the larger part by far must be excluded from our list. Common sense tells us that if young persons, who have but a limited time at their disposal, read Marlowe or Greene, Burton, Hakewill or Du Bartas, Shakespeare, Bacon, and Milton will be comparatively neglected.

Keeping, then, to the best-authors in each epoch—and here popular estimation is a safe guide—the student will find the following list of writers amply sufficient for his purpose: Chaucer, Spenser, Hooker, Shakespeare, Bacon, Milton, Dryden, Bunyan, Pope, Johnson, Burke, and Cowper. In other words, Chaucer is the exponent of the Middle Ages in England; Spenser of the Reformation and the Tudors; Hooker of the latter years of Elizabeth; Shakespeare and Bacon of the transition from Tudor to Stuart; Milton of Charles I and the Commonwealth; Dryden and Bunyan of the Restoration; Pope of Anne and the House of Hanover; Johnson, Burke, and Cowper of the reign of George III to the close of the last century.

The list could be easily enlarged; the names of Jeremy Taylor, Clarendon, Hobbes, Locke, Swift, Addison, Goldsmith, and others are omitted. But in so wide a field, the difficulty is to keep the series from becoming unwieldy, without diminishing its comprehensiveness. Hereafter, should the plan prove to be useful, some of the masterpieces of the authors just mentioned may be added to the list.

The task of selection is not yet finished. For purposes of education, it would neither be possible, nor, if possible, desirable, to place in the hands of students the whole of the works of the authors we have chosen. We must set before them only the masterpieces of literature, and their studies must be directed, not only to the greatest minds, but to their choicest productions. These are to be read again and again, separately and in combination. Their purport, form, language, bearing on the times, must be minutely studied, till the student begins to recognise the full value of each work both in itself and in its relations to those that go before and those that follow it.

It is especially hoped that this Series may prove useful to Ladies' Schools and Middle Class Schools; in which English Literature must always be a leading subject of instruction.

A General Introduction to the Series. By Professor Brewer, M.A.

1. **Chaucer.** The Prologue to the Canterbury Tales; The Knightes Tale; The Nonne Prestes Tale. Edited by R. Morris, Editor of Specimens of Early English, &c., &c. *Second Edition.* Extra fcap. 8vo. *cloth,* 2s. 6d.

2. **Spenser's Faery Queene.** Books I and II. Designed chiefly for the use of Schools. With Introduction, Notes, and Glossary. By G. W. Kitchin, M.A., formerly Censor of Christ Church. Extra fcap. 8vo. *cloth,* 2s. 6d. each.

3. **Hooker.** Ecclesiastical Polity, Book I. Edited by R. W. Church, M.A., Rector of Whatley; formerly Fellow of Oriel College, Oxford. Extra fcap. 8vo. *cloth,* 2s.

4. **Shakespeare.** Select Plays. Edited by W. G. Clark, M.A., Fellow of Trinity College, Cambridge; and W. Aldis Wright, M.A., Trinity College, Cambridge.

 I. The Merchant of Venice. Extra fcap. 8vo. *stiff covers,* 1s.

 II. Richard the Second. Extra fcap. 8vo. *stiff covers,* 1s. 6d.

 III. Macbeth. Extra fcap. 8vo. *stiff covers,* 1s. 6d.

5. **Bacon.** Advancement of Learning. Edited by W. Aldis Wright, M.A.   Extra fcap. 8vo, *cloth*, 4s. 6d.

6. **Milton.** Poems. In Two Volumes. Edited by R. C. Browne, M.A., and Associate of King's College, London.   2 vols.   Extra fcap. 8vo. *cloth*, 6s. 6d.

   Sold separately, Vol. I. 4s., Vol. II. 3s.

7. **Dryden.** Select Poems. Stanzas on the Death of Oliver Cromwell; Astraea Redux; Annus Mirabilis; Absalom and Achitophel; Religio Laici; The Hind and the Panther. Edited by W. D. Christie, M.A., Trinity College, Cambridge.   Ext. fcap. 8vo. *cloth*, 3s. 6d.

8. **Bunyan.** Grace Abounding; The Pilgrim's Progress. Edited by E. Venables, M.A., Canon of Lincoln.

9. **Pope.** With Introduction and Notes. By Mark Pattison, B.D., Rector of Lincoln College, Oxford.

   I. Essay on Man.   Extra fcap. 8vo. *stiff covers*, 1s. 6d.

   II. Epistles and Satires.   *Nearly Ready.*

10. **Johnson.** Rasselas; Lives of Pope and Dryden. Edited by C. H. O. Daniel, M.A., Fellow and Tutor of Worcester College, Oxford.

11. **Burke.** Thoughts on the Present Discontents; the two Speeches on America; Reflections on the French Revolution.   By Mark Pattison, B.D., Rector of Lincoln College, Oxford.

12. **Cowper.** The Task, and some of his minor Poems. Edited by J. C. Shairp, M.A., Principal of the United College, St. Andrews.

Published for the University by

MACMILLAN AND CO., LONDON.

The DELEGATES OF THE PRESS *invite suggestions and advice from all persons interested in education; and will be thankful for hints, &c. addressed to either the Rev.* G. W. KITCHIN, *St. Giles's Road East, Oxford, or the* SECRETARY TO THE DELEGATES, *Clarendon Press, Oxford.*

www.ingramcontent.com/pod-product-compliance
Lightning Source LLC
Chambersburg PA
CBHW021215270326
41929CB00010B/1138